Growing a Forest Schc from the roots up!

Edited by Nic Harding

FOREST SCHOOL
ASSOCIATION

First Published in 2021

By the Forest School Association

C/O Institute for Outdoor Learning,
Warwick Mill Business Centre,
Warwick Bridge,
Carlisle,
Cumbria, CA4 8RR
United Kingdom

ISBN (paperback) 978-1-3999-0529-9

Printed in the UK by Swallowtail Print Limited

Cover Design by Stoo Elvin

Cover Photo by Corin Jones, CoCo Jones Photography

Contents

Acknowledgements

A book like this cannot be just thrown together, and when we think of books we immediately think of authors, editors and researchers. Often, we forget about the hordes of people that go above and beyond in the background to get a book into print. We love you all!

We must first and foremost thank the Ashden Trust for making this long-standing dream a reality.

We would also like to thank Sara Knight for her wisdom, assistance and gentle steering; Andrew Lowe from Sandler Merseyside for some wonderful sales advice. Jackie Rowe (of Little Grubs Kindergarten), Corin Jones (of CoCo Jones Photography) and Sarah Lawfull (director of Where The Fruit Is) are offered thanks for donating some wonderful photographs which, when combined with many other image donations from our FSA members, brighten these pages immeasurably. We need to thank our FSA Recognised Providers whose case studies bring the real-life drama to our pages. We must thank Fabienne and Twigg, for making sure we stayed on track and for their support when the going got tough.

A huge thank you must go to our fabulous proof reader Bridget Barr, who pulled nothing short of a miracle getting this tome licked into shape and ready for publication. We also need to thank a small army of test rest readers including Luschka Van Onselen who jumped in to help with the exceptionally tricky index.

And finally, we must also acknowledge our wonderful members, without whom we would not be here.

About Our Authors

Louise Ambrose

Louise wants to live in a world where everyone is connected to nature; where people of all ages have muddy knees, twigs in their hair, woodsmoke-infused clothes, a sparkle in their eyes and warmth in their hearts. Since discovering the groovy world of Forest School in 2003, she has worked as a Forest School leader with mainstream groups and more vulnerable young people. She has coordinated Forest School development for a local authority and been a Forest School trainer since 2007.

Currently she is enjoying being a mama and having a small human attached to her 24/7, which has enabled her to confront her Luddite ways and create a YouTube channel – 'Forest School Lou' – to share all things Forest School-y. www.youtube.com/c/forestschoollou

Charlotte Atkinson

Charlotte first developed a love of nature through her childhood explorations of the fields, hedgerows and woodland near to her home. She studied ecology and geography for her first degree, and botanical illustration whilst working as an ecologist in Sheffield. Charlotte went on to train as a teacher and worked for 15 years in primary education as a class teacher, LA Consultant and headteacher. She completed her MA in 2001 and later taught Research Methodology to postgraduate students on MA courses at Huddersfield University.

Charlotte completed her Forest School Leadership training in 2011; with her passion for environmental education re-ignited, she decided to leave her headship to concentrate on building her understanding of Forest School and spreading the word on the benefits of getting children out into nature. She became a Forest School trainer in 2014 and one of the first FSA Endorsed Trainers in 2017. Charlotte currently lives in Suffolk where she runs a variety of training, events and sessions from 'Charlotte's Wood'.

Jon Cree

Jon Cree is a long-time ecological educator and trainer, currently self-employed and the proud guardian of a small ash wood in the West Midlands. He was the Training Coordinator at the well-known Bishops Wood Centre in Worcestershire for 20 years. Jon, a qualified Forest School leader and trainer, coordinated the centre's alternative curriculum provision, and ran a whole suite of environmental education training courses for educators.

He is a director of the Forest School Association, being the founding chair up until 2016, and has run Forest School training at Bishops Wood and other parts of the UK and the world for the last 13 years! He has also been an international trainer for the Institute for Earth Education for 25 years, and a passionate advocate for earth education for more years than he can remember.

He has just co-written, with Marina Robb, the acclaimed *The Essential Guide to Forest School and Nature Pedagogy*, published by Routledge in May 2021. Jon loves canoe paddling at weekends and singing in the week, along with growing oddly shaped veg and sharing the odd story with his daughters and now grandson!

Gareth Davies

Gareth is an experienced not-for-profit sector manager, having worked for charities, local government, social enterprises, international NGOs and higher education organisations for 20+ years.

His early childhood was 'free range' as a result of growing up on an island in the Pacific. After qualifying as a science teacher, he realised that mainstream education in the UK was not for him. Three years of teaching in Botswana confirmed that education was good yet there was something lacking with the mainstream approach.

Gareth developed a love for the varied natural environments that southern Africa has to offer. He would later learn that these feelings were called 'nature connection'. He assumed that they were only to be found in the most exotic and pristine parts of the world. Gareth spent the next ten years seeking them out, only to discover that they could be found much closer to home.

Gareth joined the FSA when it started in 2012 and has supported the FSA Board of Directors in his capacity as CEO since 2014.

Nic Harding

Nic trained in Forest School in 2004 and began running Forest School as part of the practical assessment section of the course, and from that point he was hooked. He worked as a countryside ranger for 23 years and with a couple of awesome friends ran an Experiential Education Company delivering bespoke educational packages to schools. Of course, Forest School was a large part of that process. In 2013 Nic and his team successfully ran Forest School in seven public parks for thousands of children. Nic became the Projects Officer for the FSA in 2018 and has since learned a great deal more about Forest School from other leaders, FSA webinars and Endorsed Trainers, and through helping with the Recognised Provider Scheme.

Lily Horseman

Lily loves to play in nature and nerd-out about the nature of play. She has been following the juice in the ideas and understandings that underpin the Forest School approach since the late '90s, with increasing involvement in Forest School directly since 2004. Her work has included working as a Forest School leader in a school and an Early Years Foundation Unit, working with one of the Wildlife Trusts to develop the WildPlay Project, managing self-build adventure playgrounds, play rangers and playpods in Bradford, and a whole range of creative and playful projects from 17ft dinosaur themed fire sculptures to land art and craft projects.

Lily has been involved in networking at a local and national level. She delivers Forest School training and projects through her business Kindling Play and Training (www.kindlingplayandtraining.co.uk). She also delivers community building creative projects across Cumbria and North Lancashire through Stomping Ground CIC. https://stompingground.org.uk/

Carol Middleton

Carol lives on the East Coast of the UK – a great place for seabirds and small boats. She is a qualified teacher, Early Years professional and Forest School leader, with over thirty years of experience working with people of all ages.

Carol co-founded *huathe* in 2011 and now works as an Endorsed Forest School trainer and nature connection facilitator. Training has taken her across the globe and has included incredible journeys in China and the USA, and most recently as part of the NI peace project. Her passion is to get people back outside to appreciate and care for the world they live in.

Dawn Preston

Dawn trained with Bridgwater College and qualified as a Forest School leader in 2007. She has worked for Hampshire & Isle of Wight Wildlife Trust for over 11 years, managing play and teaching spaces sustainably with wildlife in mind, in her role as Education Officer.

Dawn has been actively involved with the FSA, including setting up and standing as Chair of the FSA Hampshire Local Group, and became an FSA Endorsed Trainer in February 2020.

'I find myself stating "I love my job!" at least once a day – I feel very passionate about the opportunities I have to inspire children and adults alike to connect with and care for the natural world around them.'

Nell Seal

An ecologist and secondary geography teacher by training, Nell has worked in the education sector for 22 years, including heading up Wells Field Study Centre and as an Advisory Teacher for Norfolk County Council.

She originally became involved in Forest School in 2006 whilst working for Norfolk County Council's Environmental and Outdoor Learning Team, who worked closely with FSA Director Louise Ambrose to embed the Forest School approach across the county. Nell is now a freelance consultant juggling many professional interests! She specialises in facilitating CPD training in the areas of learning for sustainability, curriculum-led outdoor learning, and primary Geography. She is also a consultant to the Geographical Association and facilitates much of their primary phase CPD.

Nell is a Level 3 Forest School leader herself and facilitates sessions to EYFS/Key Stage 1 children from her local school in woodland opposite her home. Nell began working for the FSA in 2016 when she worked in partnership to develop their Endorsed Forest School Trainer Scheme, and went on to redevelop their Recognised Forest School Provider Scheme too.

Francesca 'Froo' Signore

Froo spent many years puddle-jumping in education, working in various settings including teaching RE in a secondary school, French in an international school, English in a Ugandan school, and being a support tutor to undergraduates with dyslexia. She hit upon Forest School in 2013 and knew very quickly that she had found her tribe.

She lives and works in Liverpool delivering Forest School predominantly to children with special needs. Froo is a little bit addicted to CPD and wishes she had more time for reading for her work.

Elizabeth Swift

Elizabeth is a nature connection facilitator, Forest School trainer, natural voice leader and Early Years specialist. In 2011, she co-founded *huathe* to reconnect adults and children to nature, to each other and to themselves.

Inspired equally by a love of nature, the child-led parenting ethos of various indigenous cultures, research about Development Movement, and the writing of Jay Griffiths; she is excited by children's holistic development through play and the positive effects of nature connection. Elizabeth's MA and subsequent research projects explore traditional and innovative attitudes to children's learning and their instinctive play and development. She also loves to sing.

Introduction

Nic Harding

Creating a book to support such a vast and diverse industry is no easy task. Like everything, this wonderful guidebook began life as an idea, born of need – the need to help Forest School leaders overcome some of the common issues they face on a day to day basis. However, as we began researching and writing, the book took on a life of its own, informed by new questions and problems from our community and it evolved into something much greater – a way of supporting the creation of sustainable and successful Forest School practice.

It is impossible to explain why I chose to take on this mammoth task without indulging in an explanation of why I got into Forest School in the first place. I entered into the Forest School world, like so many others, wanting to make a difference in the lives around me. During my childhood in the bad old days, I struggled with undiagnosed dyslexia and faced many challenges in the classroom. My teachers decided that I was *intelligent enough* that my difficulties could be 'encouraged' away by providing me with extra work or dragging me about by my hair. Thankfully this kind of physical intervention doesn't happen anymore, yet children still struggle with similar difficulties; and whilst diagnosis and support are better than they were, these children are still pushed through a system ill-suited to their optimal methods of learning. It became clear to me as I entered secondary education that I simply didn't think the same way as other people, and although I struggled to remember dates or facts, I often solved complex problems more quickly than my peers. Many years later, as an adult working in conservation, I learned about Forest School, and instantly saw a way to help other people who struggled in the academic, curriculum-based teaching environment of school. I wanted them to have the opportunity to discover, as I had, that not thinking like others is not a weakness but a strength.

My friends and I started our first company with purely social goals in mind. If we could change just one life, we felt, our efforts would all be worthwhile; and if we made a bit of extra money in the process, so much the better. We soon saw the impact Forest School had on our participants and celebrated our success. But it wasn't long before we were struggling with cash flow, staffing, land use agreements, logistics and marketing. It is clear from social media and FSA correspondence that others are struggling too.

As you have chosen to read this guide I will assume at least one of the following is true for you:

- You are curious about what Forest School can do for you or your school.
- You are looking for information on how to create a successful Forest School.
- You have picked up this illuminating text as a way to start your journey and want to ensure that your money is spent in the best possible way.
- You want to improve the sustainability or success of your Forest School after running into a problem.
- You have received this book as a gift and have been challenged with the responsibility of changing the world.

Whatever the reason, this guide will help you to find *your* right path from the outset, and help you to identify and avoid the trips, traps and brambles along the way.

'I truly wish I had this book when I set up my Forest School business.'

Forest School's Four Big Questions

This in-depth guide will support you through the process of answering the four most important questions when it comes to developing a Forest School. It draws on the real-life experiences of our team of authors, experts and recognised providers. It is designed to help you to explore these four key questions:

- **What is Forest School?**
- **Is Forest School right for me, my setting, or my organisation?**
- **How can I get it? How can I be part of it?**
- **How do I make sure it is sustainable?**

With this book, we aim to allow readers to make some educated guesses about what you want or need from Forest School, and perhaps also decide whether Forest School is the right kind of outdoor provision for you.

Forest School can seem like a leap of faith into the unknown. It will take self-discovery, courage, time, and reflection to succeed.

The FSA

The Forest School Association (or FSA to its friends) is the professional body for Forest School in the UK. We promote and protect the principles and ethos of Forest School while providing a unified voice for our community. We protect the wider interests of the community and provide advice and support to our members.

Members of the FSA invest their working lives to create the opportunity for quality Forest School for everyone; to change the world for our children and their friends, parents, and grandparents. We offer this book to you, so that you may go and change a life, a world or an existence. As Forest School leaders we are often approached by past participants asking if we remember them. They talk with such fondness of their time with us and our Forest School teams. They talk of how it gave them hope, encouraged them to find their voices, or simply let them break free and just *be*. We hope that you may one day be the recipient of this feedback; and be the leafy, soggy and often muddy voice of encouragement; the name spoken by future parents with awe and love as they say: '*I remember Forest School – it changed my life.*'

About this Book

This comprehensive and illustrative guide has been compiled by an amazingly knowledgeable group of 11 authors. All have extensive experience of the Forest School world and running Forest School businesses or projects in myriad different settings. Each author has entered Forest School on their *own* path and provides insight from their unique perspective. In this thought-provoking book, we hope to give you all the relevant and reflective insight you will need in Growing a Forest School from the roots up!

Language in this book

There are several key choices the authors make in the language we use in this book. Whilst our choices are clear to us, they are not universally accepted within our community and are often debated (over a beverage or a fire) when two or more Forest Schoolers get together. Often, the words we use seem interchangeable, but as we started to put words into print, we became aware of their nuances and hidden meanings. We have therefore included a very brief explanation of the words we chose and why:

- **Forest School leader** – We chose to use the word *leader*, rather than *practitioner*, because we felt that *leader* better fitted the extra, often unseen, tasks and business management aspects of the role.
- **Participant** – We use the word *participant* because Forest School is for all, not just for Early Years settings (as it is so often misconstrued). There are Forest Schools which deliver solely to adults, elderly people, prison inmates, or teenagers; and so *participant* covers a multitude of users.
- **Client** – In Forest School the *client* is often the person paying for the Forest School experience, and not necessarily the one attending the sessions.
- **Setting** – A business or organisation that delivers Forest School. We use the word *setting* to prevent confusion when we are talking about *sites*.
- **Site** – The physical location at which Forest School takes place.

Conventions used in this book

Online resource page

In order to save space and keep the cost of this book to a minimum, we have an online resource page containing useful examples and resources which can be reached by visiting https://forestschoolassociation.org/book-resources/ [1]

Links

As a dyslexic I find it particularly difficult to negotiate hyperlinks in print, and so in the interests of inclusivity, all hyperlink addresses used in this book also appear in our online resource. Each link in the text will be given a consecutive number in square brackets as shown in the link for the online resource page above [1]. Links within the text will appear in blue and will be underlined, as is the standard practice in online materials, and there will be live links in the eventual e-book version of this book.

Where links are shown to cross over two lines of text, no additional hyphens have been added, so if a hyphen appears in a link it is supposed to be there.

Reflective exercises

Reflection is a key part of Forest School, and is how participants and leaders evaluate where they are now and how they feel about it, as well as allowing them to learn how to work out what their next steps are. Throughout this book we offer a range of **Reflective Exercises** to support you through the process of creating a Forest School. Many of these exercises will help break tasks down into smaller, more palatable and achievable pieces. Having completed them, you will hopefully find that your business planning or management **(Chapters 6** and **7)** is much less daunting, as you will already have made some significant choices that will assist you with the ultimate question: **Is Forest School right for me?**

Reflective exercises are highlighted in light green boxes with a border, as in the example below.

Let's get started with our first Reflective Exercise.

Reflective Exercise 1 – Why do you want to set up or access a Forest School?

For this exercise, divide a piece of paper into four equal parts. In each quarter, reflect on one of the following questions:

1. What are my personal needs and wants? (e.g. I want to work outdoors more; I want a fun job.)
2. What are my setting's/organisation's/clients' needs and wants?
3. What are the problems and issues we face, which Forest School may help us to manage?
4. What do I/we want to achieve by introducing Forest School provision?

You may want to do this exercise as a collective with your colleagues or face it alone. Either way, keep hold of your responses – they will play a part later in the book as you begin to plan your project or business. It is also useful to revisit these answers at a later date, to see if your provision is indeed meeting your needs.

If you work towards a common goal as an organisation or through a business/client relationship, you may find these requirements change. It is thus worth revisiting this exercise regularly.

The following chapter will give you a fast and dirty overview of Forest School.

Chapter 1 – What is 'Forest School?'

Nic Harding

The first task that we must tackle in this book is to find out whether Forest School is what you are looking for. There are a lot of things to consider before you can make an informed choice. So, before we dive deep into the processes and choices, let us deal with the first of the Four Big Questions raised in the introduction: **What is Forest School?**

The definition of a Forest School

Forest School is a form of outdoor education, which has an inspirational and participant-centred learning process at its core. This offers opportunities for holistic growth through regular sessions. It is a long-term programme that supports play, development, exploration, and risk-taking. It increases confidence and self-esteem through participant-centred, hands-on experiences in a natural setting. The process is underpinned by **the six core principles**, that define Forest School. You must have *all six* principles in place, to be delivering Forest School. There is a short 5-minute video called *What is Forest School?* on the FSA website.

https://forestschoolassociation.org/what-is-forest-school/ **[2]**

Introducing the **Six Core Principles** and their **Criteria**

The six core principles create the ethos of Forest School. It is commonplace for the principles to carry numbers 1 – 6; though there is no hierarchy in the principles we found each leader or trainer numbered them differently. In this book we therefore choose to refer to them by their subject matter: nature, risk, leadership, community, holistic learning and long-term. The following section looks at each principle's definition. When the principles were created by the Forest School Community in 2012, a series of qualifying *criteria* were also produced. These criteria help to illustrate good practice and quality provision, and refine the boundaries and aims of our ethos.

The Long-Term Principle: Forest School is a long-term process of regular sessions, rather than one-off or infrequent visits; the cycle of planning, observation, adaptation and review links each session.

- Forest School takes place regularly, ideally at least every other week, with the same group of participants over an extended period of time, and encompassing the seasons if practicable.
- A Forest School programme has a structure based on the observations and collaborative work between participants and leaders. This structure should clearly demonstrate progression of learning.
- The initial sessions of any programme establish physical and behavioural boundaries as well as making initial observations on which to base future programme development.

One of the most common questions we are asked is: how long does something have to be to be long-term? Well, ideally programmes should run all year round, but programmes should be at least 24 weeks long and each session is at least two hours in duration. This will mean that the programme will cover at least two seasons. You can find out why this is so important in **Chapters 2, 3** and **4**.

The Nature Principle: Forest School takes place in a woodland or natural environment to support the development of a lifelong relationship between the learner and the natural world.

- Whilst woodland is the ideal environment for Forest School, many other sites (some with only a few trees) are able to support good Forest School practice.
- The woodland is ideally suited to match the needs of the programme and the leaders, providing them with the space and environment in which to explore and discover.
- A Forest School programme constantly monitors its ecological impact and works within a sustainable site management plan agreed between the landowner or manager, the Forest School leader, and the participants.
- Forest School aims to foster a relationship with nature through regular personal experiences in order to develop long-term, environmentally sustainable attitudes and practices in staff, participants, and the wider community.
- Forest School uses natural resources for inspiration, to enable ideas and to encourage intrinsic motivation.

The Community Principle: Forest School uses a range of participant-centred processes to create a community for being, development, and learning.

- Forest School employs a participant-centred pedagogical approach that is responsive to the needs and interests of participants.
- The Forest School leader models the pedagogy, which they promote during their programmes through careful planning, appropriate dialogue, and relationship building.
- Play and choice are an integral part of the Forest School learning process, and play is recognised as vital to learning and development at Forest School.
- Forest School provides a stimulus for all learning preferences and dispositions.
- Reflective practice is a feature of each session to ensure participants and leaders can understand their achievements, develop emotional intelligence, and plan for the future.
- Leader observation is an important element of Forest School pedagogy. Observations feed into 'scaffolding' and tailoring experiences to learning and development at Forest School.

Forest School does not follow a prescribed path or curriculum and is participant-centred – which means the participants choose what they learn at Forest School and when they need to learn it. *Wait a minute,* I hear you cry, *that sounds like anarchy*! Don't panic – it's not, I promise. Forest School does have structure, aims, and objectives that can be observed and measured. It just has different aims compared to other educational processes. This is because it is based in the developmental education arena. It helps and facilitates more than just knowledge-gathering and relies on a participant's natural curiosity, interests, and motivations to create links and connections on multiple levels you can find out more about that in **Chapter 2**. But what do we mean by participant-centred?

A participant-centred process is very strongly guided by the participant's goals and aims, and follows their interests and motivations (their wants) while also taking into account their needs. The leader acts as facilitator, observing, reflecting upon and facilitating learning opportunities for each individual. The participant expands their soft skills – communication, collaboration, problem solving – and is offered support as and when it is required. The leader may role model skills, like risk/benefit analysis and critical questioning, and reinforces the non-judgemental growth mindset created as part of the learning process. Leaders are therefore collaborators in the students' learning. They may simply intervene by asking questions – *'Why do you think that happened?' 'What other options have we got?' 'That's interesting, I wonder why that didn't work?'* – or offer help in the form of skills: *'This knot might work better.'* These skills may not be immediately grounded in what the participant wants to do but rather informed by the participant's journey. This is especially apparent when participants desire *change* but they don't know how to achieve it, such as when they want to engage with someone but lack the skills to communicate this. In short, a participant-centred process may nudge an outcome towards the best interests of the participants.

A participant-centred process also works in tandem with the participant's current stage in their development. It is a holistic process, helping participants to develop socially, emotionally, spiritually, physically and intellectually whilst simultaneously building self-esteem, confidence and communication skills. It gives them the power over their own journey while helping them to see which options are available along the way.

A participant-led process is where a learner initiates all the activity. It is subtly different to a participant-centred approach, and is often seen in advanced sessions of long-term programmes. In participant-led systems, participants need a set of skills to assess their own learning and progress, as well as a degree of resilience. Critical thinking, problem solving, and reflective reasoning are key. The leader will become involved when the participants *ask* for support, and will often restrict their interventions to reducing imminent threats or hazards.

It is typical to develop a large amount of participant-led activity within a participant-centred process over time.

The Holistic Learning Principle: Forest School aims to promote the holistic development of all involved, fostering resilient, confident, independent and creative participants.

- Where appropriate, the Forest School leader will aim to link experiences at Forest School to home life and to work or school education.
- Forest School programmes aim to develop, where appropriate, the physical, social, cognitive, linguistic, emotional, and spiritual aspects of the learner.

The word *holistic* means to encompass the whole of something, not just a part of it. In Forest School, when we use the term in conjunction with development, we mean that *all* aspects of the participant develop, not just their intellectual knowledge. We deal with this in more depth in the next chapter.

The Risk Principle: Forest School offers participants the opportunity to take supported risks appropriate to the environment and to themselves.

- Forest School opportunities are designed to build on an individual's innate motivation, positive attitudes, or interests.
- Forest School uses tools and fires only where this is deemed appropriate for the participants, and dependent on completion of a baseline risk assessment.
- Any Forest School experience follows a Risk–Benefit process, managed jointly by the leader and learner, that is tailored to the developmental stage of the learner.
- Often risks are seen as purely physical things. At Forest School we understand risk as a holistic thing – life is risky stuff! There are physical risks, like falling from a tree; emotional risks like falling in love; social risks such as answering a question in class; spiritual risk, like feeling connected to something or dealing with loss; there are risks in saying the wrong thing (or the right thing at the wrong time); and intellectual risks when attempting to solve something new. Risk-taking is healthy and a key part of creating a healthy world view.

The Leadership Principle: Forest School is run by qualified Forest School leaders, who continuously maintain and develop their professional practice.

- Forest School is led by qualified Forest School leaders, who are required to hold an accredited Level 3 Forest School qualification at the minimum.
- There is a high ratio of leaders (and supporting adults) to participants.
- Leaders and adults regularly helping at Forest School are subject to relevant checks into their suitability to have prolonged contact with children, young people, and vulnerable people.
- Leaders need to hold an up to date First Aid qualification; this is usually a 16-hour Level 3 qualification incorporating paediatric (if appropriate) and outdoor elements.
- Forest School is backed by relevant working documents, which contain all the policies and procedures required for running Forest School and which establish the roles and responsibilities of staff and volunteers.
- The Forest School leader is a reflective practitioner and therefore sees themselves as a learner too.

What do we mean by qualified, reflective leaders?

It will come as no surprise that trained leaders are better placed to deliver Forest School.

- To run a Forest School a leader must be qualified to **Level 3 Forest School leader status**.
- They must also hold a relevant **First Aid Certificate**.

Leaders must adapt for each group of participants. They are trained to assess risks and benefits, and to write and implement policy and procedure. They are trained to plan and develop learning opportunities, and must be aware of whose need is driving the sessions. To ensure leaders do this effectively, they must be reflective about their practice, understand their current limitations, and continue to expand their skills and understanding around their participants, site, sessions, and clients. To find out more about a leader's role at Forest School, visit **Chapter 4**. To find out more about Forest School qualifications and the skills needed for assistants and helpers, take a look at **Chapter 5**.

Myth-busting: Forest School is not...

- A way to teach the curriculum outdoors (no matter how you sneak it in)
- A badge or award
- A one-off activity, like a children's party
- A short-term fix
- A replacement for therapy (although it may have therapeutic outcomes)
- A cheap alternative to therapy (although an early intervention may reduce the need for and cost of support)
- *Just* playing in the woods!

The five most commonly asked questions about Forest School and their answers

- Where does it take place?
- When does it happen?
- How does it work?
- Who is it for?
- What happens in a typical session?

Where does Forest School take place?

The principles state that Forest School takes place in a natural space with some trees. There are hundreds of different models of Forest School in operation in the UK and around the world. Some take place on the edge of playgrounds, some on modified areas on playing fields, some in parks and others deep in the woods far away from civilisation. They all have their place, and their pros and cons. You can find out more about this in **Chapter 2** and **Chapters 10** and **11**. The more natural a site is, the more variation in experience your participants will have; the less like a classroom it is, the more freedom your participants will find and the greater the biophilia or *biophilic connection* will be.

> ## What on earth is biophilia?
>
> The Cambridge dictionary states biophilia is 'the inborn affinity human beings have for other forms of life'. The term biophilia is derived from the Ancient Greek terms *bio* (life) and *philia* (love) – literally translating to life-love or love of life. Biophilic connection is therefore connection through love of life.

When does it happen?

Forest School often takes place in school time, as an afterschool club, at weekends, and throughout the holidays. However, as it is not delivered solely to children, it may take place at any time. Forest School is a process that promotes development and is most effective when it happens regularly and over a long period of time. The longer it goes on (and the more regular the sessions) the better. It takes place in all weathers (except strong winds, thunder, and extreme weather) and all seasons. To find out more, see **Chapters 2** and **3**.

How does it work?

Forest School utilises the physiological changes the exposure to nature catalyses in participants, to develop a safe, nurturing community which supports opportunities for overcoming risks and challenges. The leader facilitates the creation of an emotionally safe space in which leaders and participants co-create a community of learning and exploration. The participant-centred nature of Forest School empowers participants to explore their worlds (both internal and external) and expand their curiosity and reflection, whilst the long-term aspect allows them to revisit and explore concepts, skills, and ideas. The non-judgemental community facilitated by the leaders at Forest School creates a spirit of curiosity and changes attitudes to learning, whilst nature provides an ever-changing window of opportunity. This enables participants to develop life skills and life experiences, which are then transferred back into the rest of the participants' lives, in the form of attitude to learning, self-esteem, confidence, communication, and spirituality. To find out more, see **Chapters 2** and **3**.

Who is Forest School for?

There is a popular misconception that Forest School is just for Early Years or primary aged children, yet this is simply not the case. The FSA's mantra is *'quality Forest School for all!'* for a reason and, as it suggests, Forest School is for everyone. The ethos is as relevant for the elderly as it is for the young. Because it values the learning and experience on a holistic level, it can be tailored to meet the needs of anyone. Below is a list of examples of participant groups you may want to consider working with:

- Babes-in-arms and their care givers
- Toddlers and pre-schoolers
- Primary or secondary age children and young people
- Young offenders
- Looked-after children (children in care)
- People struggling with communication, or with emotional or behavioural difficulties
- Parents alongside their children
- Home educated children and young people
- Isolated adults and adults requiring support
- Older people
- People with autism, or neurodiverse groups
- Refugees
- People with multiple and complex needs.

Forest School does not need to be limited to one group, and often works well with mixed groups, or groups of different ages. Cross-generational groups can be particularly effective, and groups that allow inclusion on multiple levels are also very rewarding. Here are some case studies in which Forest School is used in subtly diverse situations.

Case Study – Children of the Forest – FSA Recognised Provider

Forest School Leaders – Lewis Ames and Gemma Southerden

Home-Ed Group

Our home education group is facilitated for a mixed age range of children from 6 to 16 years. The sessions are run on a rolling programme and we haven't had anyone leave in three years, so we must be doing *something* right! Originally, we felt our role might be one of instructing in bushcraft, nature and skills, but we have found that this is rarely the case and now see our role as quite simply meeting needs wherever we see them. As a community we create a comfortable environment which is safe and secure, and participants feel understood and accepted.

The mixed age group gives us the opportunity to revisit things each year, and the participants access the opportunities in different ways each time. This means younger children get to learn from the older ones, and the older ones can break peer expectation, strip away the teenage façade, and do what they want (or need) to do – '*I am doing this for the younger kids*.' It gives children the opportunity to switch groups as their energy levels change. It challenges our expectations and allows children to surprise us (and themselves) with their capabilities. In other groups with narrower age ranges it can sometimes be a challenge to break the feel of hierarchy in the sessions, especially when the children are five years old and the leader is thirty, hairy, and covered in tattoos. The mixed age range also challenges assumed barriers, allowing children to see that, for example, the biggest person is not always in control, and the oldest is not always the leader or the best at a task.

Case Study – Bishops Wood Alternative Curriculum Team

Forest School Leader, Trainer and Alternative Curriculum Coordinator – Jon Cree

Bishops Wood has run a number of interventions for specific groups with their alternative curriculum team in the last 21 years, particularly when the centre was part of Worcestershire County Council Children's Service. This team has had several qualified Forest School leaders.

Intervention for Gifted and Talented Group

The gifted-and-talented group were a selection of young people who were academically gifted but struggling with emotional or behavioural difficulties. Each participant was challenged by the high pressure to perform at school. The participants were 14–18 years old and their difficulties impacted their mental health and triggered episodes of anxiety and self-harm.

This programme gave the participants time outdoors, which helped reduce stress whilst providing a safe and non-judgemental space to build resilience, talk about problems, and work with their hands without the pressure of evaluation or grading. The therapeutic aims of these sessions allowed the students to rest and refocus, and the amount of self-harm decreased significantly. The sessions revolved around the interests and motivations of each student, giving them control over their learning.

One such group, of young women studying for A-levels, found solace and new skills in making bentwood chairs. While working with their hands they were able to talk about the pressures of life and their own self-harming episodes.

One of the most important aspects of providing this programme was ensuring that the individuals were linked to additional support available to them at school and in the local area when the programme was still running, so that the participants knew there was a place for them before the sessions finished.

Pupil Referral Service

This programme was created in partnership with a number of pupil referral units, special needs schools, and several schools offering secondary level education. The pupils were referred because they were challenged by 'mainstream' school environments. The participants were often labelled as disruptive or challenging. This long-term programme ran one day a week for a full year, mainly for 12–16-year-old students. Through self-reflection and journaling (written, spoken, drawn) and the observations of leaders, the participants engaging in practical and social skills were able to evidence that they had met enough criteria for vocational qualifications. A few wanted to link their achievements to opportunities like the John Muir Trust award. The participants were often quite distressed, but the sessions allowed them to explore and develop holistically. The self-reflection journals became a major part of this process but they also gained life skills and communication skills and spent time working with their hands outdoors. The participants were encouraged to self-motivate and explored their environments in their own way. As well as a form of alternative provision, the sessions offered a therapeutic environment with opportunities for socialisation with small groups. Some of the participants were young offenders, and the space and the Forest School ethos allowed them to let off steam whilst trying new experiences in a community of non-judgement and acceptance. Play was an essential part of the programme – anything from creating the highest swings through to large wide games.

They had freedom and space to pursue their interests and dig into their passions, be it handcrafts, building, gardening, conservation, painting, poetry or even golf!

The wood was next to a golf course and a favourite activity was collecting golf balls. Several students went on to make their own golf clubs, linking their motivations with the environment and problem solving. The process of coppicing, carving and creating helped them to connect their external and internal worlds, giving them a feeling of belonging.

Participants were part of the self-evaluation of the programme and gained skills in reflection. They weren't aware these new skills could result in a vocational qualification and so, unhampered by the usual classroom judgment, creativity flowed.

Case study – Wood Learn Forest School – Recognised Forest School Provider

Forest School Leader – Geoff Mason

One-to-one supporting teenagers with Special Educational Needs

We run four one-to-one sessions each week for young people 11–16 years of age and many of our sessions have been running for several years. The places are financed by direct funding from the Local Authority and the parents are able to select where the funds are spent to allow the best possible fit for the young person.

The participants all require different things from Forest School, so it is easiest to give a specific example. I have been working with one young person for the last 5 years; he was referred to me as being autistic and presenting obsessive compulsive disorder traits. Over the years I have encouraged play-based activities and we have explored many topics and skills that my participant became interested in or motivated by – from axes to whittling, chisels to metal detecting. Most sessions revolve around making something. During lockdown we have been a lifeline for our clients (as well as their parents and carers – giving them a much-needed break) and we have been lucky to see an increase in the number of programmes we run.

It can be daunting at times working on a one-to-one basis with our participants, but if you take it steady, be honest and open and give a little of yourself, it can also be very rewarding. After five years working with one participant, you have the privilege of feeling like you are part of the family.

SEND Primary School Provision

I am lucky enough to work with the local SEND primary school where the headteacher has fully embraced the Forest School ethos and is entirely committed to the benefits for the children. Every single child in the school has a two-hour session of Forest School every week throughout their entire school life.

The students may be autistic, paraplegic or quadriplegic, have Down's Syndrome or be suffering from locked in syndrome. Because of this we have built a fully accessible Forest School site in association with the local Mencap charity. The site has ramps in the trees and other adaptations to give as much diversity of experience as possible. The site is fully fenced for children who are at risk of running off, so they can be out of sight yet still safe and experiencing the freedom of being in our wonderful wood. When I was first asked to work with the school, I was terrified – I had a plan but really didn't know what to expect. If you are looking to work with a group like this forget the Special Educational Needs and remember that these are a group of kids, just like any others, and they want to play!

My biggest tips for new leaders are keep your overheads to a minimum and don't be afraid to diversify.

If I could give advice to Senior Leadership Teams from schools I would say don't expect immediate results. Give it time: by its nature, Forest School is a long-term process. Benefits will come. Trust in the six principles and ethos of Forest School. The soft skills your students will develop whilst taking part in Forest School will reap dividends in the classroom – if you let them.

Reflective Exercise 2 – Clients

One of the biggest choices that you will need to make as a Forest School leader is which participant groups (sometimes referred to as client groups) you are happy delivering to.

Why do you feel you are suited to this particular client group?

Do you need any extra knowledge, skills, or qualifications to work with this group?

What happens in a typical Forest School session?

As Forest School is a participant-centred process, it is really difficult to outline a typical session – no two programmes are alike and they change and follow participants' needs or interests. However, there are some similarities in every programme:

- **Structured beginning and end** – To help participants deal with the transition from school or home to the new environment at Forest School and return to class or home after the session. The length of this structured section of your delivery will need to be adapted to the group.
- **Free play** – Play is the most natural way to learn, explore and try things out. Forest School is a play-based ethos. If you don't want 'free play' in your sessions then Forest School is *not* what you are after.
- **Tool use and other higher risk experiences** – Forest School is a long-term programme and can introduce tools, fire, tree climbing and foraging gradually and appropriately as part of that programme. Participants build a progression of skills which leaders support and scaffold with health, safety and risk awareness and with body-based games to build coordination, stamina, and muscle memory before the tools are introduced.
- **Exploration and curiosity** – Participants and leaders are encouraged to be curious about the world (both internal and external) and explore it with questions and reflection. If you don't want exploration, curiosity or reflection Forest School is probably not what you are looking for.
- **Forest School takes place in most weathers** – Except for during high winds, extreme weather and thunderstorms, Forest School carries on. If you don't like being outside in different weathers, Forest School is *definitely* not for you. However, if you have never worked outdoors in all weathers you may be pleasantly surprised by how enjoyable it can be.
- **Forest School uses natural materials to construct and make things** – Sticks and stones may well break bones but they also create universal play queues. A plastic car will always be a plastic car (even if it occasionally flies) but a pine cone can be anything – a rocket, a hedgehog, a car, a head for a puppet, or a spinning top. A plastic bottle can make an adequate bird feeder but there is little skill progression in making it; very little natural connection is gained from sourcing the materials and the activity lacks the holistic value of more naturally foraged alternatives.
- **Fun** – Forest School is often fun, and we learn best when we are having fun. Fun can be risky, exciting or quietly focused; not all fun is the same.
- **Intrinsic motivation** – It would be lovely to think that all our participants have fun all the time, but this would not be realistic. Motivation may feel fun but this is not always the case. Forest School can challenge and motivate. At the start of programmes participants can be scared, or they may become upset when getting wet or muddy, and the overcoming of these vulnerabilities helps us to grow and develop.
- **Risk** – Participants are encouraged to take supported risks at Forest School (learn more about this in **Chapter 2**). If you don't want participants to explore risk and develop confidence in their abilities and skills, then Forest School is not for you. However, the idea of letting others take risks is in itself a risk for you, and so risk assessment, risk-benefit analysis, and health and safety are all key components of the Level 3 training course.

- **Nature connection and grounding** – Connecting with nature runs through all the experiences at Forest School. Participants learn about sustainability and patience as they harvest or wait to harvest raw materials from their environments through foraging. They connect to the weather, trees, bugs, mud, and so much more. This enriches their life experience and can help to ground them.
- **Nature care** – Caring for the plants and animals in a Forest School site is an important aspect of what we do as leaders. We role model this choice to our participants, who combine their connection with care and so learn to love the outdoors. If you can love what is outside you, you may be able to love what is on the inside too!

Where next?

The next chapter will take a much deeper dive into the Forest School ethos and principles. Before we embark on that exploration, let's take a few minutes to reflect on what we have read so far, how it fits with our goals and aims, and our feelings about it. Below are some questions that might help you.

Reflective Exercise 3 – Six Principles

Do the six principles fit with what you thought Forest School was?

From what you have read in this chapter, do you think Forest School will deliver what you need?

Can you and your organisation commit to a long-term programme of sessions? To the continued training and development of staff?

After reading this chapter does the idea of Forest School still excite you?

Chapter 2 – A deeper dive into the Forest School Principles

Carol Middleton and Elizabeth Swift

This chapter delves more deeply into this ethos and explores each of the Forest School principles. We explain the holistic nature of Forest School and how the principles interact with each other. We hope it also helps you decide if this is the outdoor education or intervention that fits your needs as we introduce and illustrate some of the underlying pedagogy of Forest School.

The roots of Forest School

Forest School is a relatively new ethos or intervention. But it is also strikingly similar to the oldest pedagogy in the world; one in which children reach adulthood through playing in nature. As such, it is one that even our most ancient ancestors would recognise. Additionally, the findings and theories of great minds in education's history help us to interpret what is going on, giving us some sense of what Forest School is and the role that a Forest School leader plays. Of course, this book only skims the surface and this subject is covered in more depth on Forest School leadership training. Before we dive more deeply into the six core principles, it will be helpful to understand a little of the ancestry of Forest School.

Over the last few centuries, there have been consistent, progressive attempts to understand and explain how children learn. Some of these theories are part of the Forest School ethos.

Amongst these is the work of **Friedrich Fröbel (1782 - 1852),** whose contribution includes a deep love of nature and the strong belief that the appropriate place for children is in nature. He designed special gardens within which children could develop holistically, and coined the term *kindergarten* – a garden for children. He recognised the role that mothers play in children's education and saw the home as the primary seat of learning.

'Play is the highest expression of human development, for it alone is the free expression of what is in a child's soul.' – Friedrich Fröbel

---

Rudolf Steiner (1861 - 1925), whose theories also contributed to the Forest School ethos, outlined a holistic view of children and their development. Steiner believed children learn through their heads, hearts and hands and ought to spend much of their learning time outdoors. His influence is also apparent when we look at the geographical seat of Forest School – Scandinavia and Germany – where Steiner education has long had a stronger hold on local pedagogy.

'Our highest endeavour must be to develop free human beings who are able to impart purpose and direction to their lives. The need for imagination, a sense of truth and a feeling of responsibility – these three forces are the very nerve of education.' – Rudolf Steiner

---

Forest School has homegrown British theory at its heart too. In 1911, sisters **Margaret MacMillan (1860 - 1931)** and **Rachel MacMillan (1859 - 1917)** opened the first Open Air Nursery School and Training Centre in the slums of Blackheath. The school was attended by 30 children between 18 months and seven years old.

Its play-oriented, open-air environment was a response to the health problems the sisters witnessed in poor communities. It was designed as a model for other schools, as well as a training centre for future and current teachers. These social reformer sisters recognised that many poorer children were lacking both care and education, and thus their programme, which they called a *nursery school*, was as equally concerned with the health and nurture of the children as with their learning. Education at nursery school was focused on the child's sense of wonder. They believed that effective teaching stemmed from knowing what attracted the children's attention.

At a similar time, the extraordinary **Susan Isaacs (1885 - 1948)** was head of the experimental Malting House School. She advocated for freedom of exploration rather than conformity and punishment, and developed rich learning environments both indoors and out. She placed huge importance on play as the driving force of children's learning.

'Play is the breath of life to the child since it is through play activities that he finds mental ease, and can work upon his wishes, fears and fantasies so as to integrate them into a living personality.' – Susan Sutherland Isaacs

The need for children to renew and reinforce their connections with nature was already high on some societal influencers' agendas. Baden Powell's Boy Scout Movement and Leslie Paul's Woodcraft Folk, for example, are also found amongst the roots of the Forest School ethos.

This summary of the influences on Forest School cannot pass without reference to the constructivist theorists of the twentieth century (though we have no space here for more than a cursory glance at their work). The ideas of both **Jean Piaget (1896 - 1980)** and **Lev Vygotsky (1896 - 1934)** were popularised in the 1960s and had significant impact on the shape of education throughout Europe.

Swiss-based Piaget argued that a child needs to interact with the world to construct their own view and understanding of it. New information causes children to reconstruct their understanding of the world around them, and so each child – and indeed, each adult – has their own *unique* view of the world. This world must be interacted with to build the construction: giving us an image of the child, or the participant, as scientist.

Vygotsky, working around the same time in Russia, put the 'social' into Social Constructivism. He saw learning as very much a social process, in which children learn from someone with more information about a subject than they have themselves. Armed with a More Knowledgeable Other (an MKO), children gradually build up their skills and knowledge.

'We become ourselves through everyone else.' – Lev Vygotsky

By frequently revisiting a subject or skill, a learner expands their knowledge safely. Vygotsky called this gradual expansion of a skill or area of knowledge the Zone of Proximal Development (ZPD). Another way to look at it is 'the child as an apprentice'. This is summed up in Vygotsky's view as the child building gradually, supported by a master.

Such is the rich meadow of pedagogy in which Forest School sits! And still, as we said at the start, children learning through play in nature is the oldest pedagogy of them all.

Scandinavian roots

The Scandinavian roots of Forest School share this pedagogical base. In 1993, a group of lecturers from Bridgewater College in Somerset visited a Forest School in Denmark. The enthusiasm generated by this visit led to the initial spread of a range of Forest Schools in the UK. These proliferated through the 1990s and each differed slightly from its peers. In 2002, a group of leaders, at the first Forest School conference, came up with a definition – 'An inspirational process that offers children, young people and adults regular opportunities to achieve, develop confidence and self-esteem through hands-on learning experiences in a local woodland environment' – and an early version of the Forest School principles was born. The Forest School ethos has six principles, which were agreed by the UK Forest School community in 2011. These principles have been a game-changer for anyone interested in the assured success of the ethos and manage to draw a (somewhat wiggly) line between what is and what isn't Forest School. We know from three decades of practice that the level of success in delivering our holistic outcomes depends on working within these six core principles. Recent research from Cambridgeshire County Council (Knight and Arnold, 2019) has shown that Forest School's impact on life and learning is at its most effective when it meets this quality framework. Think of it like soup: on a cold day any soup is good, but to be a delicious minestrone, you need all the ingredients: olive oil, tomato paste, pasta, carrots, onion, water and seasonal vegetables.

So, Forest School is a good fix, but it's not a quick fix; not many good fixes are. It changes participants' lives by connecting them to themselves and to nature. It grows strong, resilient learners who are well equipped to manage the challenges of life. Forest School is also play-based, and participant-centred, and this combination of nature and intrinsically motivated learning are key, symbiotic components of Forest School. There are many reasons that this combination is so powerful, as our exploration of the Forest School principles will show us.

The next section explores each of the Forest School principles in turn, contextualising each one in the whole picture of Forest School. We also look at the importance of adhering to each principle for the best results at your Forest School setting.

A deeper dive into The Six Principles

The Long-Term Principle

Forest School is a long-term process with frequent and regular sessions. Planning, adaptation and observation are integral elements of Forest School.

First, let's establish what long-term means and what we mean by regular and frequent. The life-changing, confidence-raising, resilience-building impact of Forest School comes about when sessions are delivered across the seasons (e.g. from early autumn to mid-winter), and this impact is magnified when the programme runs over two terms or two season changes. For participants to gain the benefits of Forest School sessions they must be able to depend on attending their sessions regularly and frequently. The FSA Recognised Forest School Provider Scheme defines the minimum benchmark for long-term as running for either:

- A minimum of two hours per session, for 24 consecutive weeks (or the equivalent of two full school terms) in one year, covering two seasons with the same core group of participants; *OR*

- A minimum of two hours per session, for 12 consecutive weeks in each year over two years, covering two seasons with the same core group of participants.

Whilst these are the agreed minimum benchmarks for quality provision, many leaders are running year-long programmes to maximise the positive outcomes.

Long-term and the change in seasons

There is something powerful about seeing nature change yet simultaneously stay the same. The use of a consistent site gives participants a sense of place, a base of operations that is comforting and familiar. The move through the seasons helps build experiences, excitement and a feeling of inevitable change whilst expanding an experience-based vocabulary. Be in a woodland space for January (frost, snow, wet gloves and frozen feet); February (mud so deep it pulls your wellies off); and then sweet March (filling the world with colour and song once more), and you begin to see how the long-term aspect of Forest School plays such an important role. Some aspects of a site stay constant – the trees which retain their structure; the thickets and brambles defining the shape of the space; and the slopes and hills and flat areas of the land – and it is this constancy amid change that can help children manage inevitable changes in their own lives. With regular and frequent visits, participants can return to the land, activities, games and more week after week, and this builds a good strong sense of place, self and community.

Long-term and settling in

Unfortunately, being in nature is not a common experience for some participants. This means that not all participants feel comfortable in the woodland at first. It takes time for participants to adapt to the rules, boundaries and relationships created during the sessions, and participants will take different amounts of time to settle in. Each participant will build new relationships as part of Forest School, with the leaders, the teachers, their peers and the environment. The relationship with the environment is often the first to be explored.

During a recent training session, we spoke to one Forest School trainee who had two different children ask *'why can't someone just clean up all the leaves and mud so it was nicer to play in?'* If you are a child who hasn't experienced much nature, or who is anxious around mud and irregularity, then the early weeks of Forest School are about adapting to become comfortable in the space, learning about the weather, the natural materials and sometimes even about endurance! Participants on a short-term programme often leave the woodland before they have a chance to progress past this and may be left with an 'it's not for me' attitude towards nature. This means they not only miss out on perhaps a lifetime of connection to nature but also on the opportunities that other, more environmentally-confident participants have gained. Conversely, when the children become accustomed to weekly visits to the Forest School site over a long period, they can find and develop their own connections. They have time to test their boundaries and reach outside their comfort zones. By the end of a long-term programme, the community of participants has bonded with the place in a whole range of different ways and developed new relationships with nature.

Excitement, safety and encouraging risk-taking – the long-term factor

Another benefit of the long-term aspect is that it enables us to work safely with the participants. In the early weeks (typically weeks one through six), participants (and especially children) often arrive at Forest School with a kind of 'fizzy' excitement. This is highly appropriate: Forest School is often very exciting! As we observe new groups of participants, they approach the sessions with high energy, a reluctance to focus for long periods, lots of physical movement, or a desire to get involved in lots of things. This can be a very exciting time for a participant and the leader but for a completely different set of reasons!

Forest School's long-term programme allows participants to become relatively calmer, to focus for longer periods, and to regulate their levels of energy in line with the activities on offer. This allows for the introduction of new experiences like fire and tool use. After the initial weeks, the participants become familiar with the site and the boundaries. Once this happens, they often arrive knowing where they want to be and what they want to do. They begin to feel comfortable within this new environment and it is then and only then that they will risk trying something new.

We find that if the number of sessions is known, limited, and small, the anticipation of Forest School ending is in the participant's minds from the start and this adds a sense of urgency. Children tend to find it harder to wait for a turn, or perhaps attempt things too soon, if they think it will be the only chance they have. This immediacy works against the Forest School ethos, and children are often pushed to engage before they are ready, or feel that they have missed out. Because Forest School is not pressured by a curriculum or plan, participants are happy to stop when they reach their limits, knowing that they can revisit this activity in later sessions and stretch their comfort zone a little wider with the support of either the leader or their peers. We see children make their biggest and sturdiest changes to confidence and resilience when they are into the main body of sessions and are not anxious about the programme finishing.

The effects of long-term provision on play

> **Eliza was part of a pre-school group I took to Forest School. Over the first ten weeks of this particular programme, she repeated the same intention in the opening circle: 'I want to play in the mud'. By the tenth week, her play had changed hugely. At the start, she played on her own with a small trowel and investigated the properties of mud. By week four she was jumping and splashing in the mud with a group of friends and by the end of the programme, a rescue game had emerged.**

Eliza's case is typical of participants at Forest School. The long-term connection with and exploration of 'the mud' opened opportunities for her holistic development and learning. The first tentative steps playing alone with a trowel build her understanding and confidence around mud and her feelings about it through free play. This is supported by Ginsburg et al. (2007) who suggest that 'free play aids the physical, emotional and cognitive and social development of a child'. The nature connection forged by concentrated and repeated visits into the mud not only builds confidence but may also help to develop concentration and self-disciplined study (Taylor, Frances, & Sullivan, 2002). The freedom offered by unstructured play in nature can create a source of independence and inner strength that may be drawn upon in stressful times

(Wells & Evans, 2003; Milligan & Bingley, 2007). As Eliza progresses through the sessions she begins to interact with the mud with more confidence: jumping, splashing and playing with ropes, she is developing muscles, stamina, balance and core strength. Fjørtoft (2001) says 'For children, outdoor play in a natural setting can improve motor strength, balance and coordination' and Cleland et al. (2008) suggest that 'Each additional hour a child spends outdoors is associated with an extra 27 minutes per week of moderate and vigorous physical activity.' Bell et al. (2008), who want to promote outdoor experiences, go further, noting that getting children outside and engaged in healthy behaviours can tackle childhood obesity. For Eliza, playing in the mud is an important experience but it is also great fun, and we know children who enjoy time outdoors in nature are more likely to include it in their lifestyles in the future (Petty, et al., 2009). Finally, after week four, we begin to see a social progression and extended play cues as other children join in Eliza's play, creating a community of learning and important lessons in empathy, cooperation and communication.

Long-term and the positive cycle of observation

Another aspect of the 'Long-Term Principle' relates to the Forest School leader as a facilitator rather than a teacher. One of the primary roles of the Forest School leader is to actively observe what is happening during the session, to reflect on those observations and to plan the next session based on these reflections. This is covered in detail in **Chapter 4.** This active observation is critical in any participant-centred ethos. The observation informs the unique feel of each programme as it is created by the community of participants and leaders together at that time and in that space. Within each programme of sessions a new, varied, rich dynamic recipe is created by the unique group dynamics, the drives and goals of the participants and the skills of the leaders, and this process takes time. We talk about this much more in **The Community Principle**. We have talked about how the long-term process allows connection to nature, and so it makes sense to look at the Nature Principle next.

The Nature Principle

Forest School takes place in woodland, or a natural wooded environment, to support the development of a relationship between nature and the participant.

It will come as no surprise that trees and the woodland space are both important elements of Forest School. They can be a source of constant inspiration. Loris Malaguzzi, the founder of the inspirational Reggio Emilia approach to learning, saw the environment as the 'third teacher' but the role of nature in Forest School is much more than this.

'This takes place between an active, or very active, organism, the very active child, and its environment, but also through the way this child-environment interaction is conditioned by interconnections.' – Loris Malaguzzi

Natural space provides a constantly changing but stable world; a unique place to learn and an ever-increasing source of inspiration. This is where participants learn about their world by being a regular part of it. The growth of a mushroom, the death of a squirrel, or the life under a log can all tap into a participant's natural curiosity. Through the use of natural materials for props in play or as materials in craft activities, participants gain a working intimacy with their site and an understanding of the sustainable use of resources. If curiosity is the seat on which all learning sits then nature is the room in which that seat sits most comfortably. We have talked about nature being a source of inspiration but it also helps condition our participants for learning.

Nature and a sense of place

The natural world offers us a sense of place. Many indigenous cultures are nomadic and tied to the cycles of the seasons (putting down temporary roots for particular purposes). There are similarities between the way these camps are set up and the layout of a Forest School space: a central feature such as a fire pit and other areas for reflection, crafting, cooking, etc. This provides the community with a sense of place in a vast space and creates a welcoming and stable environment for opportunities that link with the holistic needs of our participants.

Nature, philosophy and spirituality

Nature is amazing. The magnitude and diversity of the natural world can create a sense of awe: a feeling of being very big yet very small at the same time. Some of the ways we understand the world are through repeated time in nature. Participants often develop strong views and gain emotional understanding as they witness birth, growth, maturation, flowering, setting seed, dying back and death through the natural turn of the year.

Nature and risk

Nature provides opportunities to play in areas that contain learning risks. Getting stung by nettles means you very quickly learn what a nettle looks like and how it feels. Climbing a tree can be more of a challenge than climbing in a play park. Fire can be terrifying but when used sensibly can be an important tool.

At Forest School we learn to identify and assess risks as we discover them. This is all part of connecting with nature. It also makes us less likely to take uncalculated or dangerous risks later in life. We will talk about this in greater depth in **The Risk Principle**.

Connection to nature

In *Connection to nature: children's affective attitude towards nature* (Cheng, 2010) a child's attitude to nature is described as having four key aspects of nature connection:

- Enjoyment of nature

- Empathy for creatures

- Sense of oneness

- Sense of responsibility

To illustrate this, let's take a look at this snapshot of a Forest School session and consider where Cheng and Monroe's four aspects of nature connection fit.

It is week eight of a Forest School programme; the children are well settled in, and showing typical development outcomes. The leader has created these observational notes for the session as part of their observation, planning and facilitation.

'The children now arrive and sink into their playful learning with ease. Saiqa has the idea of adding to their fairy house by building an adventure playground. At once, the children scatter to places they know, gathering sticks, acorn cups, bracken and the thorns of hawthorn that was cut back earlier in the year. The Forest School leader has already shown them how to use the thorns to pin leaves together. Once there, Pete sees a new kind of fungus growing under the hawthorn branches and calls the others over to see it. They decide to call it Purple Wonder and remind each other not to touch it. Sascha collects the plentiful broad leaves of the sycamore to make the track of the roller coaster. "Not over there," calls George, "the wren was there last week."'

Re-read the observation again using these four questions to help you reflect on Cheng and Monroe's four aspects of nature connection.

- Can you find examples of enjoyment of nature, and the appropriate use of natural resources?

- Can you see when the children have empathy for creatures, real and imagined?

- Do you read a sense of oneness, as the children settle in to play and are at one with the natural space?

- Are the children demonstrating a sense of responsibility, as they check in with each other and the safety of the species they notice?

Hopefully, you can see how these connections naturally occur at Forest School!

It is well worth visiting a provider offering Forest School in line with all six principles to see what they observe during a session. This is an important skill for a leader and may help you to decide if Forest School is for you. All our FSA Recognised Forest School Providers deliver Forest School in line with the six principles of the ethos. **You can find one near you by using the FSA Recognised Providers map:** https://forestschoolassociation.org/find-a-forest-school-provider/ **[3]**

'This is not about some luxury, a hobby, a bit of playtime in the garden. This is about the longest, deepest necessity of the human spirit to know itself in nature.' – Jay Griffiths

---

Case Study – Little Grubs Kindergarten – FSA Recognised Forest School Provider

Forest School Leader – Jacqui Rowe

Little Grubs Kindergarten opened its doors to the community in September 2019. Based in the grounds of Oakly Park Estate in Shropshire, the children and staff have access to a variety of natural environments, from lone ancient oaks, beech copse and rhododendrons to grassy meadows, fields of crops and the River Teme. We have our dedicated woodland on the estate, with fencing and natural boundaries, a cabin for shelter, a fire circle and a tool area.

Our daily programme, aimed at children aged from two and a half to five years old, is led by qualified teachers who are also Level 3 Forest School practitioners. Our morning Forest School session is embedded within the kindergarten's ethos and philosophy: we believe that natural environments are conducive to wonder, beauty, mystery and peacefulness, something we respect and aim to protect for every child. From its inception, the vision and ethos for Little Grubs Kindergarten has embraced the beauty of nature, sparking the flame of wonder in both the children and the adults. In designing our programme, our Forest School offer naturally embeds itself, uncompromisingly, within the FSA's six guiding principles.

At Little Grubs, we encourage our children to lead the way and to be active in their learning, nurturing attention and joy through first-hand experiences in real-life contexts. Children attend three days per week, where they tune in to the familiar, repetitive daily rhythm. Arriving togged up in seasonally appropriate clothing, we begin our day with a welcome circle before heading off to either our dedicated woodland site, or another natural space on the estate, where we spend three hours each morning engaging, playing, and learning in nature.

The journey to our chosen site is an important part of our time outside, attuning us to the seasons and changes that nature brings as we pass familiar sites. A popular stop on our journey is a large clump of nettles where we have watched the mysterious metamorphosis of the ladybird and the decay of the plants through the winter. Children articulate their observations with increasing sophistication, hypothesising, reflecting, and imagining what is happening or has happened, and *why*. We will answer some of the children's questions or investigate answers with the children but in many cases, we suggest 'Let's wait and see!' sparking curiosity and patience. Speech and language development is also encouraged as the daily discussions allow children to communicate changes they see and the ideas they have.

Our child-centred approach continues throughout the morning, where children play freely and explore the environment. We are responsive to the children and their play, observing, reflecting and being receptive to the needs of each child and their development. We often plan 'in the moment' with the children, developing knowledge and skills through discussion, modelling and demonstrating, but always being careful to intervene only if it will enhance the play. When we observe a child to be ready for his or her next step in learning and development but do not want to interrupt their moment, we plan for opportunities in the following session. This will take into consideration the child's interests and aim to build on the play observed. An example of this in practice occurred when a child was interested in hammering a stick into the ground using another stick. His pride and satisfaction in getting the sticks to stay upright was evident as it took some perseverance. To support the child with this skill, the following day we asked him if he'd like to use a mallet. Over a few sessions, we saw his coordination and strength increase and later in the term we progressed to the short-handled hammer and nails.

At Little Grubs we embrace our natural environment, and we strive to learn in, from and with nature. We feel passionate about keeping our woodland site as natural as possible, not only for ecological reasons but also because we believe cluttering a natural environment with toys is unnecessary. We play with what we find, such as sticks, moss, acorns, stones and so on, transforming these in our play and imagination. As leaders, we carefully select items that will enhance play, such as twine for binding birch twigs to make a broom or a magnifying glass to look at minibeasts in more detail. We find that our children are resourceful, creative, and natural problem-solvers, persevering because there is time and space to think, ask questions, and try many times over. When we compare our children playing and learning in the natural environment, compared to the playroom in the afternoon, we notice that they tend to be far less distracted outside. They spend longer on an activity, persevering and problem-solving, and are more patient, independent and confident.

Throughout our morning we incorporate moments of stillness and tune in to nature or ourselves. When children first join us, they find being still and quiet quite a challenge, but with daily opportunities, we find even the youngest children enjoying moments of stillness and connecting with nature. A three-year-old lying face down on a log recently said to an adult who was checking in on him, 'I'm relaxing, just relaxing.' There he stayed for 20 minutes or so, peaceful in his own space and mind, joining the group when he was ready. These moments are encouraged and respected by children and staff at Little Grubs. 'I think I'll just sit here and watch the leaves and the birds.' 'I like watching the clouds, do you want to watch with me?' Ripple effects have also been observed, with more parents asking to leave their cars to go for a walk once they have dropped off their child at kindergarten.

As with all Forest School principles, there is a continuum of provision: with wild untrodden forest at one end (think Forest School meets Bambi) and a school playground surrounded by tower blocks on all sides at the other. We urge you to push, pull, cajole, barter and work your way as far to the first side as you can. If the playground is the only way that you have of getting outside, make it as natural as you can. If you can bargain your way onto a field, a meadow, a woodland, to a wilder woodland, then do it. Don't settle for the easiest space. Settle for the best space with the words, 'I haven't got any eggs, so how shall I make the omelette?' ringing in your ears. You will need eggs! But you may need to think outside the box (eggs come in many shades and sizes).

The Holistic Learning Principle

Forest School fosters the holistic development of all those involved so learners grow in confidence, resilience, independence and creativity.

What is holistic development?

In the introduction, we define holistic development as a positive change of the whole person. This means we develop in multiple ways at the same time. It includes knowledge-gathering and literacy, maths and science but is not limited to these areas. Holistic development is a challenging concept to explain because it is a difficult process to break apart. Each part affects another and they often take place simultaneously and without us consciously knowing about it. However, we can separate the development into six discrete categories or aspects, and isolate some examples within each. These include:

- **Physical**
  - o Building muscles
  - o Stamina
  - o Muscle memory
  - o Coordination and balance
  - o Fine and gross motor skills
  - o Practical skills e.g. climbing or tool use

- **Emotional**
  - o Understanding our feelings
  - o Building an emotional vocabulary
  - o Developing empathy and sympathy for others

- **Communication**
  - o Ways to communicate wants and needs
  - o Verbal and non-verbal communication
  - o Communicating our feelings
  - o Listening to others
  - o Following and giving instructions

- **Intellectual**
  - o Knowledge
  - o Problem-solving
  - o New skills
  - o Self-awareness

- **Social**
  - o Relationships
  - o Community-building
  - o Understanding the needs of others

- **Spiritual**
  - o Connection to something bigger (the world)
  - o A sense of awe
  - o A relaxed focus or being (calmness)
  - o A balance
  - o Death, loss and regrowth

As we start to dig deeper into holistic learning, we become aware of just how much is being learned and at what levels. We are all born with the capacity to learn. Not only that, but we are born with a fierce curiosity and genetic blueprint that directs our holistic development. At Forest School, we aim to enable intrinsically-motivated learning. This is because we are delivering a participant centred ethos. Forest School leaders are not teachers and imparting knowledge is only a tiny part of what we do. We simply facilitate learning and provide opportunities and inspiration for self-guided exploration. Often the learning is surprising and it is always multifaceted and effective. 'Unconditional' learning like this means that the participants are held with active positive regard and given power over and recognition of their learning needs.

A Forest School leader exercises 'active observation' and is always on the lookout for what learning is taking place and reflecting on whose needs it fulfils. The leader therefore often becomes an advocate for the participants' learning needs. This is critical in Forest School because the holistic learning needs of the participant don't always match the learning our society wants for them; sometimes the tools they need to reach their learning goals are deeply hidden or obscured by expectations, learned patterns, behaviours or habits. Nevertheless, we believe that children are as equipped for learning as they are for breathing, and that they have the tools they need to do it. We inherit this ability from our primate ancestors. Long before curricula and schools, children learned by watching others and then making sense of what they saw through play. This is evident in all primates (and many other animals too) and this is how holistic learning takes place at Forest School. So, we could just call holistic development, natural development (or does that lead to educational anarchy?).

'Children do not need to be motivated. From the beginning, they are hungry to make sense of their world.' – Alfie Kohn

---

How does Forest School promote confidence and resilience?

The terms confidence and resilience are often used interchangeably in conversation. They are subtly different, although they appear to mean similar things. This means you can be confident but not resilient or resilient yet lacking confidence. Forest School provides learners with the opportunity to try a massive array of new skills and experiences. Some will be unusual to the participants, which may leave them feeling vulnerable or challenged (though this is also a very levelling experience). By overcoming these challenges in a supported system (as a community together), in bite-size chunks, participants develop confidence. At first, this confidence may be in one particular activity, such as tying a knot, talking to peers, jumping in the mud, sliding down a muddy bank, using a saw or exploring. Later, as participants get more successes under their belts, they develop a sense of confidence in one or more of our holistic aspects. As confidence grows, they are more willing to try new things. Here's an example: I am confident in sliding down a muddy bank on my bottom, so I will now have a go standing up. That is all great until I lose my balance, and this is where the difference between confidence and resilience begins to show!

Resilience can be seen as a capacity to bend rather than break under duress. In Forest School, resilience is a holistic construct and grows with our development. A person who has survived and adapted to failure often enough is rewarded with a change in mindset, to one of resilience. The determination and mindset to problem-solve difficulties are encouraged and modelled by the leader. We explore the promotion of resilience in the next section as we look at **The Risk Principle**, and again in **The Leader Principle** later in the chapter.

How does Forest School promote creativity?

In 1995 Westby and Dawson published their research on teacher attitudes to creativity. They found that whilst the teachers in their study supported the *idea* of creativity in the classroom, students with personality traits associated with creativity were less appealing than those without. Characteristics of the creative child included: making up the rules as they go along; being impulsive; non-conformist behaviour; taking chances; and trying to do what others think is impossible. In the classroom, reliable children who were responsible, logical and good-natured were favoured. This may be due to the pressures on teachers who are expected to get the best results from every child, with limited time and a very full curriculum. Sometimes the curriculum does pop up in Forest School (Celts escaping Romans, levers and balances, learning about the natural world, etc). I have a powerful memory of two four-year-old children engaged in a complicated role-play game, delightedly discovering equality of number as they matched the number of sticks each needed for their game! It is clear that this rich and complex play leads to rich and complex children who are confident, resilient, independent and creative. When they are back in the classroom, walking home from school or looking for the answer to a complicated problem, they intuitively employ all the skills they have honed at Forest School. The skills are part of them now.

Creativity is a risky thing to exercise, in a world where you are judged on your successes and failures. At Forest School, we see both as part of the same journey. Participants can try logical and illogical solutions to problems, and often enjoy the journey of learning that this experimentation takes them on. It is by learning like this that they develop their creativity and change their attitude to learning. At Forest School, participants are encouraged to climb, explore and discover in their *own* ways, for their *own* reasons and in their *own* time. This gives participants the freedom to be as creative as they want, whilst the support and skills of the leader give them the safety net they need. Unlike curriculum-based learning, Forest School leaders are not interested in judging the end products of a participant's experiments. This means that participants are free to set their own goals, aspirations and success criteria, giving them the space to adapt and learn from mistakes as well as granting them power over their learning experience. Of course, it doesn't look like conventional learning. It may look muddled, playful, messy or even purposeless to an untrained eye – which is why the learning theories that are taught during training are so important. It often looks as though the children are 'just playing' and our culture has been misled to distrust play as a learning tool. At Forest School, the children are encouraged to play and the leaders can trust in the learning taking place. Play is a chaotic beast. It roams and rolls and rollicks about and the learning is irritatingly holistic! It is difficult to put in boxes, making it tricky for adults to quantify (which is doubtless one of the reasons it has been eroded in school), but it is joyous and rich to unpack. The other reason is that we as adults do not remember the holistic journey we took as children or the lessons we had to learn. We simply remember the end product of that learning. We began this paragraph identifying the inherent risks of creativity, and so it feels logical to explore the Risk Principle next.

The Risk Principle

Forest School offers opportunities to take supported risks appropriate to the learner and the environment.

Risk-taking is such an important part of children's development that it has its own dedicated Forest School principle. Think about that: it's that important! It's that important because, in our current society and culture, taking risks is so seriously misunderstood.

'But I wouldn't let my kids do that!'

When training Forest School leaders, it is common to be brought to the edge of our seats by exciting stories of the trainee's adventures in risk-taking during their childhood, only to be dumped anticlimactically in the mud by the utterance of the phrase *'but I wouldn't let my kids do that!'* This suggests that our current societal ethos seeks more to protect children from danger than to equip them with the experience needed to deal with difficulty. This need to wrap our children in cotton wool and protect them from harm is a systemic change in the way we view risk-taking in childhood.

Not having the experience of overcoming risk is having a huge impact on our children, and increasingly on our young adults, in all sorts of ways. We explore these a little here and you will spend much more time on these on your good quality Forest School training. Overall, Forest School seeks to restore healthy, considered risk-taking; to this end, Forest School leaders and assistants are trained to assess risk-taking as well as risk management.

A Forest School leader will embrace risk as a learning tool. How will you ensure that your setting understands that this is a part of the ethos?

Why is risk-taking so important?

As we have said, risk is critical to holistic development and is gradually accommodated over a long-term Forest School programme. Risks are everywhere and in everything we do, so we cannot avoid risk: our only real choice is which risks we take and which we don't. Thankfully, our ability to manage risk is hard-wired into our DNA. We are designed to seek out vulnerabilities, motivated to challenge them through practising risky behaviours, and then we assimilate it, so it no longer feels risky.

Take learning to walk as an example: nobody manages to become proficient at walking without taking a few tumbles and unexpected landings on the backside! Yet children don't give up at the first injury, and it's a calculated risk that pays off as the child becomes more skilled in movement until they can run, jump, skip, dance and balance along a wall or kerb: each increment is a risk they perceive, practise, explore, and assimilate, and they do this instinctively.

Carrying out our *own* Risk Assessments

Let's face it, our ancestors needed to be good at managing risk – the ones who were bad at it are far less likely to *be* our ancestors! Taking risks has always been part of a child's development and our ancestors learned to manage these risks through play, meaning by the time they reached adulthood, they were skilled risk-takers and got to create the next generation of risk-takers. There are two parts to the process: knowing which risks to take and building up your skills bit by bit until you are competent enough to move on. We see children instinctively risk assess each activity in every session and push themselves, or hold back and change their plans, as their self-preservation or vulnerability kicks in.

Kieran was a confident mover and, on this occasion, kept visiting a part of the woodland where there was a fallen tree close to a large mud patch. Another child played here alone and each time Kieran approached he said, 'When you've finished, can I have a go?' This caught my attention: the area was easily big enough for both children to play together. After a while, the second child moved away and Kieran took his chance. He climbed to a good point on the fallen tree and then leapt off into the mud! It splashed in all directions and he fell slightly forward. Coming out, grinning, he repeated the move again and again until he had accomplished it. He had planned this *and* he had risk-assessed it *for himself*! Kieran realised that he couldn't try out his manoeuvre with anyone else in the vicinity and so waited for a good moment before starting. This is the completely ordinary and completely amazing natural risk assessment that children instinctively do. It doesn't mean that the Forest School leader hands responsibility over to the children; it means that the children instinctively take responsibility for themselves.

Kieran illustrates that we can make risk-benefit analyses from a very early age and it is critical we explore this capacity as we develop. To be clear, we are not saying we adults should not remove hazards (like broken glass in the soil) or restrict some risks until later (such as climbing higher in that tree), but we must recognise what is a hazard and what is a risk and see the benefits of the child overcoming the risk themselves. At Forest School, we do just that.

But there's more about this risk-taking aspect of Forest School: it's also good for us!

Taking risks makes us happier, healthier and more fulfilled

Participants who have practised appropriate risk-taking are healthier and happier than those who are more risk-averse. Appropriate risk-taking, self-esteem, confidence and resilience are inextricably interlinked. When children can seek out their own risky situations they practise having and managing the feelings around risk, of vulnerability, of challenging their concerns or fears, and the thrill of success. Mostly they succeed, but they can also practise good mistake-making.

'Children frequently seek and engage in challenging and risky forms of physical play, even though, and to some degree because, it is related to fear and thrills and involves the real possibility of getting hurt.' – Ellen B. H. Sandseter

By allowing supported risk-taking, Forest School promotes the development of resilience. Guy Claxton claims that resilience is at the root of all learning (Claxton, 2002). A resilient child will try, try, and try again but will also be confident to stop trying if they decide that it isn't for them after all. A resilient child will raise their hand to answer a question or seek clarification on a task. They will try out new ways of doing things and come up with their *own* ideas. Sometimes they work and sometimes they don't and that's okay. Learning to manage mistakes appropriately is also a key component of risk-taking: the child who can set themselves a task just outside their comfort zone (so they can effectively risk-assess) and then try out the activity, making changes and perhaps deciding that the log is too slippery today, is a resilient learner.

Risky play, nature and community

> I regularly visited a group of eight- and nine-year-olds at Forest School and they delighted in telling me about their experiences and the games and activities that thrilled and excited them. Unsurprisingly, many of those activities contained an element of risk. Most of the children were involved in a high-energy socially-interactive game on the rope swings, while some children were invested in creating a series of dens in a thicket on a steep slope. There was a great deal of 'risky' tree climbing and a hiding game in the long grass and nettles. I was immediately struck by the energy, knowledge and connection the children had with one another throughout this risky play.

Risk and play go hand in hand with the children playing in groups and overcoming social risks as they try out new communication strategies, words and actions, and we know that 'Time spent in places with natural landscaping can encourage social interactions and integrations' (Kweon, Sullivan, & Wiley, 1998). Dealing with risk and overcoming vulnerability when climbing trees or engaging in risky play can help build resilience (Gull et al, 2017). The children had built a series of groups within a fluid community and almost instinctively worked together; we know that natural features and open spaces play an important role in a sense of community (Kim & Kaplan, 2004). We also know that, per Hine, Peacock & Pretty (2007), being in nature, and especially exercising in nature, has positive effects on our mental health. It can have beneficial effects on anxiety, depression and attention deficit hyperactivity disorder (Sugiyama et al, 2008), and it can also have profound effects on our physical health too (O'Brien & Murray, 2006). There were a lot of things being explored and it was obviously great fun to learn.

Transferable skills

We noted previously that being a successful risk-taker is a transferable skill and that this is another key benefit of appropriate risk-taking at Forest School.

When adults interfere with children's natural risk-taking, they are often well-meaning and looking out for the well-being of those children. However, they are operating in the short term, whereas being a child and becoming an adult is a long-term process. The skills and attributes that children instinctively develop through their playful risk-taking (e.g. balancing, learning to climb trees, developing negotiating skills, carrying sticks and logs, being safe around fire and tools, or hiding and being found) carry an appropriate amount of risk. The likely injuries are small, such as cuts, grazes, bruises, or possibly a minor break. These are the ordinary injuries of childhood from which we all recover easily (indeed we can be quite proud of them!). When we prevent these ordinary injuries from taking place – or when we respond inappropriately to them – we expose children to a greater long-term risk: that of creating the risk-averse child who is frightened to try. This leads to teenagers and adults who are very poor at assessing risk and are either risk-averse or inappropriately thrill-seeking. On the one hand, excessive risk aversion can lead to anxiety and the mental health repercussions of an unfulfilled life; on the other, think about the kinds of risks teenagers and adults are likely to take when they haven't had the opportunity to learn 'common sense' through their childhood. Children who become good at risk-taking in the woodland are also good at taking risk in the classroom, or as Catherine Prisk put it when she was Director of Play England, 'if you can risk climbing a tree, you might risk reading aloud in the classroom'.

'If you can risk climbing a tree, you might risk reading aloud in the classroom.' –
Catherine Prisk

> ### Reflective Exercise 4 – Risk
>
> As we have seen, in the explanation above, risk-taking is pivotal in the delivery of Forest School. How do you feel about risk-taking? How do you feel about participants' ability to assess the risks around them? Where is *your* risk comfort zone? Is Forest School an acceptable risk for you or your organisation to take on?

The Leadership Principle

Forest School is run by qualified Forest School leaders who continuously maintain and develop their professional skills.

The Leadership Principle is where we address the quality and competence of people who run Forest School projects or programmes. Forest School has the power to be transformative for its participants. It is leadership training, observation skills, reflection and flexibility that advances this transformation down a positive path. The role of a Forest School leader is complicated and is explored in much more detail in **Chapter 4: What does a Forest School leader have to do?**

Quality counts

Quality training helps to ensure that every Forest School leader understands and can apply all the Forest School principles, maintaining professional standards and consistency of practice across the country. It is the application of *all* the principles that makes Forest School what it is. Being a qualified Forest School leader ensures participants at Forest School experience the learning opportunities which make a difference to the holistic development of their whole person: well-being; resilience; risk-taking and creativity. The Leadership Principle requires those who run Forest Schools to be qualified, in recognition of the varied and ongoing skill set needed to run successful programmes. For some, the training will augment knowledge they already have; for others, there will be a whole new set of skills to learn.

Being a Forest School leader is not the same as being a teacher indoors, and it takes a different set of skills (or at least a different way of looking at them). The immersion in a practical, outdoor experience during your training helps to reset your thinking and develops a range of new skills.

Research indicates that Forest School has a positive impact on children's confidence, independence, resilience, creativity, and nature connection (Knight & Arnold, 2019) and, of course, high standards of training will lead to Forest School leaders delivering more effective Forest School programmes (which in turn makes a difference to the participants attending). Whilst the Forest School ethos is set up to work at its optimum level, this hinges on the leader's ability to create the right environment, provide the right level of support, and advocate for the participants' learning needs.

Interpreting baseline assessments, observation and planning

Given that under the holistic development model children learn in all holistic aspects at once, you might think that planning and organising this kind of learning is an impossible task for the Forest School leader. How do you plan for a single child to learn in every domain? How do you plan for a group? What if you are running more than one Forest School a week? All that planning! Luckily, we have a magic trick to help us: we let the participants do it themselves. A Forest School leader can begin planning sessions as soon as they get some background information, which may take the form of a baseline assessment, or by meeting the participants or talking to their teachers, school, carers or parents. The leader will then observe the participants in the natural environment and see if there are any immediate changes in behaviour and whether any new learning goals, motivations or behaviours are communicated. Thus begins the observation, planning, delivery, reflection and reporting cycle. This is explored in more detail in **Chapter 4.**

Embedding skills, knowledge and attributes

Forest School training supports Forest School leaders in several ways which are intrinsically linked to the principles. It also embeds new skills for observing and supporting all Forest School participants and for managing safe, well-maintained and sustainable outdoor environments. There is a clear grounding in best pedagogy and how it relates to the learning that is happening in sessions. This includes educational theory alongside the psychology of self-esteem and confidence-building.

How does the Forest School leader support the six principles?

A Forest School leader facilitates the holistic development of participants through the six principles.

A Forest School leader is expected to understand the holistic development of each participant and support them in their development by providing opportunities to facilitate learning and growth. The leader observes, reflects and plans these opportunities in line with specific learning goals or motivations for each participant. They are constantly reflecting on balancing when to step in or step back from a participant's experience to maximise the potential growth, and the benefits and practicalities of this approach are explored in **Chapter 4**. The Forest School leader creates robust policies and procedures that support the delivery of this unique educational paradigm. Leaders must be aware of environmental processes and understand and manage their impact on their classroom (**see Chapter 11**) and be able to assess risks and benefits for participants both in the moment (dynamically) and as a planned process (risk assessment). Finally, they should support appropriate risk-taking in their sessions in line with each participant's needs and level and role model effective responses, feelings, and communication. If this sounds like a lot to do whilst you are lighting the fire, cooking, playing, joining in or skill sharing: it is! It is also hugely rewarding and your training and pilot sessions will mean that a lot of this becomes intuitive and feels very natural once you can embrace the process.

Additionally, the leadership of a Forest School requires a constantly expanding tool box of practical skills (safe use of hand tools; how to build, maintain and cook on a fire; how to build shelters and dens; how to tie a range of useful knots) and knowledge of how to identify and care for flora and fauna. Most of all, the Forest School training gives leaders the confidence to get outdoors, to deliver some great learning opportunities, and to advocate for this with parents, governors and other teachers or stakeholders.

The life-long learning model and Forest School leaders

You may want to think of a Forest School level 3 qualification like a driver's licence. Like driving, the real learning starts as you experience delivery after you qualify. Discussing your experiences with other leaders can be hugely beneficial. The FSA supports a number of local groups across the UK, and an annual national conference, that can support your development. The FSA Recognised Forest School Provider Scheme recognises continuing professional development (CPD) as critical in the sustainable delivery of Forest School. This CPD may be reached by way of courses, reading or skill-sharing, and ensures that Forest School leaders stay in touch with the latest developments and thinking in the field. This helps them maintain their skills levels and to continue to ensure best practice is in place. This is also space for leaders to delve into the parts of Forest School that they are passionate about. It could be anything from primitive tool use to bird watching, from foraging to storytelling.

Forest School training

Forest School training is typically delivered by qualified (level 4) tutors. A vast array of trainers and courses are on offer, comprising a great deal of variation in quality and value for money. FSA Endorsed Trainers have undergone an exhaustive quality assurance evaluation over several years. This evaluation ensures they are delivering the course content to an extremely high level, that they maintain their experience in the field, and that they keep up to date with new research, skills and opportunities. You can find out more about the FSA Endorsed Trainers in **Chapter 5** and find their contact details on our website by visiting: https://www.forestschoolassociation.org/find-a-forest-school-trainer/ **[4]**

The Community Principle

Forest School uses a range of participant-centred processes to create a community for being, development and learning.

The Oxford English Dictionary defines community as: *'the feeling of sharing things and belonging to a group in the place where you live'* (Lexico, 2021). Te Whāriki – New Zealand's Early Years Curriculum, a cultural co-creation of Māori and Western settlers to the islands – includes the importance of shared attitudes and dispositions that develop when a child is held and nurtured in a community. This understands and celebrates how a community actively shapes and grows its members for the benefit of that community.

'Children's learning and development is enhanced when culturally appropriate ways of communicating are used and when parents, whānau [family] and community are encouraged to participate in and contribute to the curriculum.' – from Te Whāriki (Ministry of Education, New Zealand Government, 2017)

Humans are innately social: our physiology is designed for us to live in groups. Being part of a community gives a sense of belonging, a sense of shared culture and a set of ethics; it is vital to our well-being. Our community encompasses support for each other and the knowledge that each member of that community matters. Each community works within specific boundaries to serve their own shared needs. In the case of Forest School, community helps to develop nature connection, competence, reliance (friendship and trust), independence and creativity – as well as building skills and knowledge.

Belonging to, or feeling part of, a community helps us to feel part of something bigger than ourselves. This nurtures our emotional and spiritual development, and is part of holistic learning: being an accepted part of a community allows you to ask for support, to support others, to be inspired and to develop your passions and interests. It grows empathy, for without empathy there is no community.

The creation of a Forest School community is part of the role of the Forest School leader – it doesn't just happen on its own. The social and emotional structures built by the Forest School leader (and supported by the other staff) establish the foundation of this community, enabling everyone to grow together, within all the principles. There are clear steps that will help this community grow.

This is modelled and explored in depth during quality Forest School training. Here we give a very brief overview of some of the techniques that are used.

Boundaries and expectations

These are the parameters of the group. These are initiated by the Forest School leader, but it takes the whole community to work with them and form them into the shape that suits *this* group in *this* woodland. They might include: how boundaries are established; the routine of the session; how the group will talk and listen respectfully to each other; and how they will look after the natural space. Building these into the routine of Forest School means they can be developed by the group as time goes on. Everybody involved needs to be comfortable with the agreement and this can take some working out! Take playing with sticks as an example: the age, ability and experience of the children and the possibilities presented by the sticks in that particular woodland, will all form the basis of this particular agreement.

Hive mind

Community is built by a whole range of shared experiences. This creates a kind of 'Hive Mind' for the programme. They learn a shared map of the space ('I found it over by the bear tree' suggests both the speaker and listener know the trees in this woodland well enough to name them) and develop a shared routine. These together help to create a community and a landscape that is bespoke for that group. A story or experience builds for each group, making it unique and special.

Helpful routines

The composite of Community is much studied by anthropologists. The rich ingredients include singing together, sharing food and fires, celebrating successes, negotiation and management of disagreements, playing games, and telling the stories that define a culture (e.g. sharing what you have learned or explored, reminding community members where the best play or food sources are and where the dangers lie). Together these inspire and influence the whole group's knowledge and collective learning and this grows into a mutual and appropriate care for oneself, each other and the woodland.

Once this is in place, the stage is set for those learner-centred processes.

Participant-centred processes: it's what we do and the way that we do it!

If you remember our discussion in **Chapter 1**, we identified that:

A participant-centred process is a 'doing' (rather than a 'done') around and including the participant. We are more focused on the process rather than the product. It is very strongly guided by the participant's goals and aims, following their interests and motivations (their wants), whilst also taking into account their needs.

We also stated that a participant-centred process works in tandem with each participant's position in their development. It is a holistic process, helping learners develop socially, emotionally, spiritually, physically, and intellectually whilst simultaneously building self-esteem, confidence and levels of communication, and giving them the power over their own journey whilst helping them to choose which options they have along the way.

The Forest School leader as a part of a learning community

This is inextricably linked to the skills and understanding of the Forest School leader. The Forest School leader's role is thus complex: simultaneously having an overall awareness of what is happening in various places in the woodland, monitoring activities and risks, and, as one of the learners, being involved in their *own* learning – modelling their preferred learning style and inspiring others by their *own* passion and enthusiasm.

It takes a change of perception to understand this kind of facilitation and the resultant learning is powerful and sticky (it stays with the learner)!

The words *Teacher* and *Leader* carry with them cultural expectations of what it is to *be* one of these; what it looks like, how one should act and so on. The current most prevalent pedagogical model is that the teacher has a set of expected outcomes and the knowledge to deliver them, and that the learner receives this with varying degrees of active engagement in the process. Embedding a participant-centred process shifts the emphasis of power and control in learning.

A Forest School leader does not arrive with a rigid plan of activities and outcomes, and does not deliver knowledge to a passive learner. Instead, the Forest School leader gets to know their participants as part of a learning community. Because of this, Forest School leaders get to know their participants very well, quite quickly. This enables them to focus on the *how* of learning. Once they accept that they too are learning alongside the participants, the Forest School leader no longer needs to know everything or to anticipate the learning outcomes of the participants and can take a more intuitive and curious role in the process, role-modelling a more natural learning process of exploration. This expands the possibilities of content and outcomes infinitely.

'The biggest mistake of past centuries in teaching has been to treat all students as if they were variants of the same individual and thus to feel justified in teaching them all the same subjects the same way.' – Howard Gardner

---

Everyone's a learner

To get back to the wording of this principle: the underlying assumption is that everyone in the Forest School community (participants, adults and children) is learning. This concept recognises that learning is not just academic but experiential, rich and varied. It includes small things (such as fetching a cup for someone who needs it), chaotic moments when the unexpected happens, moments of revelation (so *this* is an *oak* tree) and risky moments (when a participant is at the very edge of their ability level and trying something new). All are equally valid experiences and all contribute to a participant's life-long learning and create a transferable toolkit of skills.

Forest School creates a sense of empowered community and responsibility. It is a safe, non-judgmental, nurturing environment for learners (and leaders) to try things out, trust others and take risks. Forest School inspires a deep and meaningful connection to the world and an understanding of how a learner fits within it. It joins the participant's external environment to their internal world, to their feelings, motivations and interests.

Transition to a participant-centred process

Participant-centred processes are not usual in most classrooms and it can sometimes be an uncomfortable mind shift (with attendant feelings of vulnerability) to move from a familiar indoor classroom role to one of mentor, facilitator and learner in the outdoors. We are all part of a learning journey, and that learning will be embedded by our experiences whatever happens. It might be unexpected; it might be an enormous leap in understanding. Sometimes it is directly linked to developmental stages and other times far surpasses them.

'Children understand and remember concepts best when they learn from direct personal experience.' – Joseph Cornell

Most importantly, this type of learning offers each participant an opportunity to embed their *own* sophisticated learning skills (which are transferable back into the classroom or life) and it acknowledges that learning is different for each person whatever their age.

Examples of participant-centred processes include:

ACTIVE learning. Participants explore, ask questions, find answers, and solve problems. They are curious about what is happening around them: *'How do you know that's a rabbit hole?' 'Where are the best sticks for dens?' 'How can we cross the stream?'*

COOPERATIVE learning. Participants work together to solve problems, achieve something they cannot do alone, and learn from one another. This also includes opportunities for complex social learning to develop social skills and language, and to build an understanding of interpersonal dynamics. It also includes personal responsibility and positive interdependence.

INDUCTIVE learning. The Forest School leader might offer or model an opportunity and offer some instruction such as how to navigate their way around a field guide or how to use a tool in a real and relevant way. Instructions and invitations are embedded in the necessity to use them (e.g. participants want to know the names of plants they have found, or need to remove a spiky branch on their favourite climbing tree).

EMPATHIC learning. All shared learning includes an element of empathy. To build a bridge that takes us over the stream, we need to ensure that it doesn't break with only half of us on the other side. If a child sets up a throwing game that only they can manage, they soon learn loneliness in their game and adapt it to include others – and that often leads to the honing of their *own* throwing skills too. Standing back and letting children manage some of the difficult situations themselves – including the difficult feelings – helps them to learn empathy. And learning when to step back and when to step in is a good learning journey for the Forest School leader too!

CREATIVE learning. Some of the best learning experiences happen when we leave our comfort zones. The toy-less woodland environment, littered with potential (sticks, leaves, mud, trees, grass, etc), encourages a far greater range of games and activities than a built playground (Nicholson 1972).

EXPERIENTIAL learning. However it happens, all the learning at Forest School is experiential. This learning is enhanced by the environment it takes place in (we talk more about this under **The Nature Principle**). Nature offers holistic opportunities for learning in 3D, engaging all the senses all the time: colours and shapes to excite the eyes; smells of the air and earth for the nose; the sounds of birdsong and wind in the trees for the ears; different temperatures and weather for the skin; cooking and foraging for the mouth; and climbing, swinging, sliding and rolling for the proprioceptive and vestibular senses. This is FULL ON sensory experience!

All of these methods of learning wrapped up together are called Play. Everyone who learns like this is in a state of play.

All children and young people need to play. The impulse to play is innate. Play is a biological, psychological and social necessity and is fundamental to the healthy development and well-being of individuals and communities.

'Play is a process that is freely chosen, personally directed and intrinsically motivated. That is, children and young people determine and control the content and intent of their play, by following their own instincts, ideas and interests, in their own way for their own reasons.' – Playwork Principles Scrutiny Group

---

Forest School empowers participants to lead their *own* learning, in their *own* way, supported by both the affordance of the environment and the familiarity and trust of their Forest School community. And this is why it works!

Reflective Exercise 5 – Community of learning

What is my experience of Community?

How does this make me feel and affect the way I learn?

Do I already build and support community learning in my setting?

Reflective Exercise 6 – Do the Forest School principles fit my expectations and skills?

Can I accept and adopt all six principles in my delivery or am I looking at delivering another form of nature connection?

What skills and abilities make me the ideal candidate to run Forest School for my chosen client group?

What am I most looking forward to when I think about delivering Forest School?

References

Arnold, G. & Knight, S. (2019). An analysis of the impact of forest school provision on early years foundation stage outcomes using CASEY. In M. Shelley & S.A. Kiray (Ed.). Education Research Highlights in Mathematics, Science and Technology 2019 (211-221). ISRES Publishing, ISBN:978-605-698540- 9.

Bell, J. F., Wilson, J., & Liu, G. (2008). Neighborhood Greenness and 2-year Changes in Body Mass Index of Children and. *American Journal of Preventive Medicine, 35*, 547-53.

Chen-Hsuan Cheng, J., & Monroe, M. (2010). Connection to Nature:children's affective attitude towards nature. *Environment and behaviour, 44* (1), 31-49

Claxton, G. (2002). *Building Learning Power.* Bristol: TLO.

Cleland, V., Crawford, D., Baur, L., Hume, C., Timperio, A., & Salmon, J. (2008). A prospective examination of children's time spent outdoors, objectively measured physical activity and overweight. *Int J Obes (Lond)*, 1685-93. doi: 10.1038/ijo.2008.171

Cornell, J. (1979). *Sharing Nature with Children: The classic Parents' and Teachers' Nature Awareness Guidebook.* Navada City: Dawn Publications.

Fjørtoft, I. (2000). The natural environment as a playground for children: Landscape description and analyses of a natural playscape. *Landscape and Urban Planning, 48*, 83-97.

Forest School Association. (2021, 02 22). *Find a Forest School Trainer.* Retrieved from Forest school Association: https://www.forestschoolassociation.org/find-a-forest-school-trainer

Forestry Commission. (2009, March). *Physical Activity in Forest School.* Retrieved from Forestry commission Scotland: https://www.owlscotland.org/images/uploads/resources/files/Physical_Activity_at_Forest_School_Research.pdf

Fröbel, F. (1826). *The Education of Man.* New York: D.Appleton and Co.Harris W.T (eds)(1887)

Griffiths, J.(eds) (2013). *Kith: The Riddle of the Childscape.* London, Hamish Hamilton.

Gull, C., Levenson Goldstein, S., & Rosengarten, T. (2017). Benefits and risks of tree climbing on child development and resiliency. *International Journal of Early Childhood Environmental Education, 5*(2), 10-29.

Kim, J., & Kaplan, R. (2004). Physical and Psychological Factors in Sense of Community: New Urbanist Kentlands and Nearby Orchard Village. *Environmental Behaviour*, 313-340. doi:https://doi.org/10.1177/0013916503260236

Kweon, B., Sullivan, W., & Wiley, A. (1998). Green common spaces and the social integration of inner city older adults. *Environment and behaviour*, 30(6), 832-858. doi:https://doi.org/10.1177/001391659803000605

Malaguzzi, L., Caligari, P., Castagnetti, M., Guidici, C., Rinaldi, C., Vecchi, V., & Moss, P. (2016). *Loris Malaguzzi and the School of Reggio Emilia: A selection of his speeches.* Abingdon: Routledge.478

Milligan, C., & Bingley, A. (2007). Restorative places or Scary spaces? The impact of woodland on the mental wellbeing of young adults. *Health and place 13*, 799-811.

Ministry of Education, New Zealand Government. (2017). *Te whāriki: he whāriki mātauranga mō ngā mokopuna o Aotearoa.* Wellington: Ministry of Education.

Nicholson, S. (1972). *How not to cheat children: the theory of loose parts. Landscape Architecture* Harrisburg, PA: Lay, Hubbard & Wheelr. 62,30-34

O'Brien, L., & Murray, R. (2006). *A marvellous opportunity : A participatory evaluation of Forest School.* Farnham: Social and Economic Research Group. Retrieved from https://www.forestresearch.gov.uk/documents/805/fr0112forestschoolsreport.pdf

Petty, J., Angus, C., Bain, M., Barton, J., Gladwell, V., Pilgrim, S., . . . Sellens, M. (2009). Nature, Childhood, Health and Life Pathways. *Interdisciplinary Centre for Environment and Society Occasional Paper*. Retrieved from http://www.lotc.org.uk/wp-content/uploads/2011/04/Nature-Childhood-and-Health-iCES-Occ-Paper-2009-2-FINAL.-1-.pdf

Play Wales. (2005). *The Playwork Principles*. Retrieved from play wales: https://www.playwales.org.uk/eng/playworkprinciples

Robertson, J., & Shaughnessy, M. (1994, March). An Interview with Howard Gardner : Educating for Understanding. *Phi Delta Kapan v75 n7*, pp. 563-66.

Sandseter, E. (2010). *Scaryfunny: A qualitative study of risky play in Pre-School Children.* Trondheim: Norwegian University of Science and Technology. 126

Sugiyama et al. (2008). Associations of neighbourhood greenness with physical and mental health: do walking, social coherence and local social interaction explain the relationships? *Journal of Epidemiology & Community Health, 62*(9). 6.

Taylor, A., Frances, E., & Sullivan, W. (2002). VIEWS OF NATURE AND SELF-DISCIPLINE: EVIDENCE FROM INNER CITY CHILDREN. *Journal of Environmental Psychology, 22*(1-2), 49-63. doi:https://doi.org/10.1006/jevp.2001.0241

Vygotsky, L. S. (1987). The Genesis of higher mental functions. In R. R. (Ed.), *The history of higher mental functions vol 4* (pp. 97-120). New York: Plenum.

Wells, N., & Evans, G. (2003). Nearby Nature: A buffer to Life stress among Rural Children. *Environment and Behaviour*, 35(3), 311-330.

Westby, E., & Dawson, V. (1995). Creativity: Asset or burden in the classroom. *Creativity Research Journal Vol 5 (1)*. 1-10, DOI: 10.1207/s15326934crj0801_1

Chapter 3 – Benefits of Forest School

Lily Horseman and Francesca 'Froo' Signore

In **Chapter 1** we explored what Forest School is. Now we'll look at *why* we do Forest School. '*Why?*' is the question that children ask relentlessly when they are most curious about the world. It's a brilliant question. *Why* does Forest School do what it does? *Why* invest in it? *Why*? Forest School has myriad benefits not just for participants but also for their families, schools, settings and communities. Liz O' Brien says of the 'ripple effects beyond Forest School' (Jennison, 2019):

> 'The children brought their experience home and asked their parents to take them outdoors at the weekend or in the school holidays. Parents' interest and attitude towards Forest School changed as they saw the impacts on their children.'

We've seen countless examples of this too. Two cousins started mapping the route they took as they walked to Forest School so they could meet there with their families. We know a child in care who took staff to the woods at the weekend, and often observed families introduced to games that were favourites of their children during Forest School sessions. This, in turn, has benefits for the woodland. We come to love a place by being there frequently and regularly. People who love somewhere take care of it and become champions for it (Wikimedia Foundation, Inc., 2021).

It also shouldn't be forgotten that the leaders also feel the benefits. Many find being outdoors puts them in their 'best place' and Forest School brings out their best side – it is very much seen as a passionate vocation rather than a career.

> Thomas struggled with his behaviour in the classroom and at home. His frustration was palpable and disruptive, and he struggled to engage meaningfully with his peers, siblings, teachers or his parents. We were amazed to see a profound change in Tom after going to Forest School. It was nothing short of magical. It started small, [prior to FS] Tom delighted in sliding on or treading on the coats of other children, often damaging or dirtying them in the process. He was often rebuked for his behaviour by school staff, parents and peers. After only a few weeks at Forest School Tom was observed picking up other children's coats that had fallen to the floor and hanging them up. When asked about it he simply said 'clothes keep us warm and dry, not everyone has the right clothes and they can be sad and cold'. He started to develop friendships with other children and his brothers at home. Whilst he was still somewhat disruptive, his disruptions were often due to excitement rather than frustration and he asked every day if it was Forest School today.

Before we can dive into the details, we need to address something really important: the difficulty of measuring outcomes. Firstly, noting an improvement in social and emotional development ('*X managed the transition into Forest School more calmly this week.*') feels less assured or permanent than an intellectual or physical development ('*X solved the problem of how to throw a rope over a branch high enough for a swing.*'). Once an intellectual or physical benchmark has been reached, we can assume that, with a little effort and encouragement, it will be reached again. But there is less assurance with social or emotional developments. These are more complex and far less linear. Though physical bodies remain largely unchanged from week to week, participants' emotional capacities may vary significantly, depending on the week they've had. The week's emotional baggage is invisible to us as leaders, bar the behaviour that is in front of us. Forest School leaders are trained to see that *all* behaviour is communication, which brings us to our second difficulty.

We can describe behaviour with an observation ('*He sat in the fire circle, looking down into his lap with his arms folded. He did not join in the game.*'). But if we want to measure the impact of Forest School by depicting this behaviour as an improvement or deterioration, we need to *interpret* the behaviour ('*He was unhappy about losing control over the game.*'). Ultimately, these interpretations are guesses. They might be well-informed and empathetic guesses, but they are guesses nonetheless; and so we must be aware that our interpretations will be loaded with our own hopes and biases, however hard we try to set those aside. This does not make them redundant as pieces of evidence for the value of Forest School, however. Our interpretations are in good company when combined with anecdotal evidence, research and, perhaps most importantly, what the participants themselves share with us. This is a far cry from quantitative research that, quite literally, ticks boxes, yet it still has great value to us as Forest School leaders. As Sackville-Ford writes:

'Reflective *diaries and notes on the session [...] are a legitimate form of data that can be robust and informative. Through time, these notes can provide clear evidence of the progress that children and young people make during the project. [...] Rather than focus on things that are measurable, this approach gives a very holistic view of learning, able to notice the social, behavioural and practical learning.' – Mark Sackville-Ford*

We identified in the previous chapter that Forest School uses a holistic approach. It thus feels a bit counterintuitive to break the approach apart, but it's a good way in: it helps us examine each element of the Forest School process individually and also to recognise that no one of these elements exists in isolation.

As we explore the benefits, we will be thinking about why a Forest School approach creates particular conditions for growth and how each of the principles has its part to play.

Benefits to physical development and well-being

Being in nature affects us on a physiological level. Though we have spent the last two centuries or so adapting to a lifestyle that is more indoors, our bodies and brains are adapted to flourish in the natural world. A wealth of research has been published over the last 40 years demonstrating that our bodies and brains are affected by nature, and specifically by trees. Our bodies relax when we get to the woods; our cortisol levels, blood pressure and pulse rates drop, meaning our stress levels are lower (Selhub, 2014). This is why Forest School needs nature. That's not all though: the production of feel-good hormones like dopamine and serotonin is stimulated by Forest School. Actively engaging with the woods, putting hands in the soil, increases serotonin levels. Not only do we *feel* happier; the bacteria in the soil goes through the skin, changing our brain states, making us more receptive to **learning** and **improving our immune systems** (Natural England, 2016). Just being out there gives you a dose of the good stuff.

Forest School being participant-centred also has an impact on overall wellbeing – the state of being comfortable, healthy and happy. Anything that places value on play and choice will increase that sense of wellbeing over time, especially if the participant can adjust the difficulty of the task to match their skills. Psychologist Csikszentmihalyi calls this sweet spot 'flow state' and he links human happiness to the ability to find it, as it increases **dopamine production** in the brain (Gold, 2020). Flow states are connected to positive feelings and a sort of relaxed alertness which is very motivating. This **increase in self-motivation** allows people to stay on task for longer, enhancing any gains.

Having a trained, reflective and self-aware leader to support this is vital. Flow states can't be achieved if someone is constantly stepping in. We need to be in control to learn how to **control**. To achieve those **flow states** we must stretch ourselves, and this is where the support should be offered.

'Better a broken bone than a broken spirit.' – Lady Allen of Hurtwood

An element of challenge is also useful in reaching flow states. In the previous chapter we looked at the Forest School principle of risk-taking and the importance of supporting risk. This process of risk-benefit analysis is about weighing up the benefits to the individual against potential hurt or harm. Lady Allen of Hurtwood – a key figure in the growth of the adventure play movement in the 1940s – said 'Better a broken bone than a broken spirit.' (Hurtwood, 1968). This isn't to say that children should be encouraged into situations they can't cope with, but rather that when they are pushing their limits it is developing something more than just their physical skills. The Health and Safety Executive says, 'The goal is not to eliminate risk, but to weigh up the risks and benefits. No child will learn about risk if they are wrapped in cotton wool.' (HSE, 2012). A game of hide and seek in the woods allows the adrenaline to build and then, with safe boundaries in place, the breathing slows and the surge of cortisol ebbs as you hide behind a tree. Having these moments where you can feel scared and then safe in play allows the body to practice **up-regulating cortisol levels** and then returning to **resilience.**

'The goal is not to eliminate risk, but to weigh up the risks and benefits. No child will learn about risk if they are wrapped in cotton wool.' – Health and Safety Executive

As well as physiological benefits there are also wide-reaching physical benefits to Forest School. There is extensive scope for learners to integrate physical movement into their learning. It is known that developing a child's core control or strength also helps with their **fine motor skills**, including their ability to hold a pencil (SWFT NHS, 2012). The core will develop if a child can balance and wobble, pull themselves off the ground, kneel, squat or lean on their arms. Forest School provides a rich diet of stimuli to develop **Perceptual Motor Development** (the body's ability to receive, interpret and respond to sensory information) (Tarakci, 2016). Being able to move and use our bodies in unusual ways, such as hanging upside down from trees, improves **spatial awareness** by strengthening the vestibular system, which provides feedback on where our body is in space. The range of physical activity available at Forest School – pushing, pulling, squeezing, climbing, lifting, and stretching, to name but a few – stimulates the receptors of the proprioceptive system. This sense gives us feedback on where a certain body part is and how it is moving.

Having freedom of movement and choice allows participants to be in control of meeting their body's needs. This is especially true of children who struggle with sensory processing. The woods are a richly immersive, full body sensory experience. Linear movements like swinging or rolling down a hill can help regulate and calm. Spinning can help those seeking sensation. Nature can offer a stimulating environment without overloading or being stressful. After considering all the available evidence, Gill surmised that spending time in nature 'is part of a balanced diet' of childhood experiences that promote children's healthy development and well-being (Gill, 2014).

All these muscles and systems of the body need regular and frequent exercise. We know that increasingly sedentary lifestyles have had an impact on our physicality in terms of weight gain. Obesity affects approximately one quarter of people in the UK (NHS, 2019). The cost of this is high. In 2014-15, the NHS spent an estimated £6.1 billion treating overweight and obesity-related ill health (Tedstone, 2018). One particularly interesting study into children's physical exercise showed that they 'were found to be significantly more active during Forest School than on typical school days; the levels of activity during Forest School were 2.2 times greater than those on the active school days and 2.7 times greater than on the inactive school days.' (Lovell, 2009). This means that children tended to exceed the recommended daily hour of moderate to vigorous physical activity on Forest School days. When we consider that three quarters of UK children spend less time outside than prison inmates, the importance of the level of activity in Forest School becomes clear (The Guardian, 2016). Evidence shows that children who spend lots of time sitting still are more likely to develop depression by the age of 18. Researchers at University College London looked at the activity levels of 4,257 12- to 16-year-olds. Those who did an additional hour of light activity each day, such as walking or chores, had **fewer depressive symptoms** when they reached adulthood (Kandola, 2020). An **increase in stamina** is also especially noticeable when getting to the site involves a long walk.

As Forest School takes place through the seasons, it develops both our resilience to different types of weather and also our ability to physically cope with and adapt to different temperatures and conditions that we may find challenging. The development of Forest School participants' physical wellbeing, including their gross and fine motor development, is something we can measure. We have seen participants becoming more confident walking on uneven ground. In the woods and in nature no two footsteps are the same. We have to exercise muscles in different planes to compensate for sticks and stones in our path, boosting core strength and keeping joints healthy. On flat surfaces, by comparison, repetitive motions in our joints and muscles create wear and tear in one direction. When swinging and wobbling we move in unexpected ways, forcing the trunk muscles to work harder. We also notice increased dexterity in the way tools and ropes are manipulated. Even unconscious actions like twiddling blades of grass are developing skill, ease and precision in the way the hands and fingers work together. It's easy to underestimate the power of excitement in driving development: an Occupational Therapist described how tricky it was in indoor sessions to encourage one young man to work on his fingertip grasp. The activities simply did not interest him. In the woods, however, she witnessed him using the exact same skills over and over again as he picked up sticks to feed the fire. Not only was he working the muscles, he was doing it with a big smile on his face. Building up this 'muscle memory' over time changes the brain, creating links that are hard-wired and can be accessed again, even quite far into the future. It's not just the physical muscles and flexibility and strength that are developing, but the integration of the body and the brain.

Benefits to social and emotional development

The benefits in this section are numerous. As we saw above, the very fact of being in a natural space helps our bodies regulate. This impacts on our nervous system, feeding into our social and emotional output. Gill tells us that 'Spending time in nearby nature leads to improvements in mental health and emotional regulation.' (Gill, 2014). A systematic review found that compared with indoor activities, physical activity in natural environments is associated with greater feelings of **revitalisation** and positive engagement, **decreases in tension, confusion, anger and depression**, and with **increased energy** (Natural England, 2016). This is supported by Kerr and Schneider (2008):

> *'Children engaged in woodland settings are more likely to interact and socialise as part of a group [...] This is of particular value to children with varying emotional health since the forest setting can help stabilise anger.' – Kerr & Schneider*

The Forest School principle of participant-centred play and choice enables opportunities for growth and learning aplenty. Adapting to this aspect of Forest School may take more effort for new participants and leaders alike. Indeed, some may feel out of their comfort zone, but this conscious choice to deliberately hand over control to participants creates the conditions for growth.

If we're choosing the game and sorting out the teams, we're taking away a lot of opportunities for our participants: opportunities for improved **communication** (Tiplady, 2018) (*'What game shall we play?'*), **negotiation** (*'I don't want to play that game. Can we play something else?'*) and **collaboration** (Coates, 2018) (*'How about we play this game first, and then your game next...?'*). Our participants need the chance to stretch their emotional muscles, as well as their physical ones. If we never let our learners sit with disappointment or struggle with rejection, we cannot expect their **resilience** to grow (Coates, 2021). And if we insist everyone has to join in, what **creative solutions** might we have unwittingly stamped out? If we are fully in control, who is doing the learning?

However, the leader has a key role in holding all this together. One of the most finely-tuned aspects of being a leader is finding the right balance of skilfully 'holding the space' for our learners, providing a structure or scaffolding. Handing over control to people who are struggling with their social and emotional interactions needs even more careful reflection. People can't learn and develop when they are in crisis mode, so it is important to find the balance such that they have the freedom to choose whilst feeling – and being – safe.

Another principle of Forest School is sneaking in here too – the importance of our participants taking risks. As we discussed in **Chapters 1** and **2**, we more readily think of risk at Forest School as being physical. Just as growth is holistic, so too is risk taking. Risks can be emotional and social: asking to join in, or asking to stroke a passing walker's dog. All these interactions take courage and expose our vulnerability. Physical risks also create emotional growth, as facing something we perceive as dangerous tests and stretches the stress-and-relax response of the sympathetic nervous system. And of course, if we succeed, we feel great about ourselves for having achieved something. We set up internal measures by which we can assess future risks. Being able to internalise risk management reduces anxiety and related mental health issues such as phobias and fear responses to imagined or exaggerated threats and dangers (Sandseter, 2011).

Building a connection to nature, feeling safe enough to take risks, and developing social skills and communication all takes time. Being able to see progress in social and emotional development can only happen with long-term Forest School. Noticing something as nuanced as an improvement in the participants' reading of **social cues**, or witnessing them coping much better with transitions, or indeed spotting more dominant players having increased **empathy** for those who are classically on the periphery of the action – well, these all take time, and lots of it. That time is also needed for nurturing the web of relationships at Forest School. Forest School can foster connections between any and all of the following players, and in any combination: the leaders, the participants, accompanying staff, and the woodland space itself. Being in something as colossal and powerful as nature whilst being drawn in by the details, like the velvety feel and irregular appearance of a hazel leaf, can lead us to feel both very big and very small at the same time. That's the spiritual sense we're aiming for. Again, it needs *time*.

We'll be looking at the skills needed to hold this together in **Chapter 4**, but it's worth noting here that the importance of modelling emotional intelligence (self-connection and dealing with difficulty) is hard to overstate. We aren't just reflecting *about* our participants – we're reflecting *with* them.

Benefits to intellectual development

What do we mean by 'intellectual development?' It isn't just about gathering facts, although this is part of it. It is also an increase in our capacity to think and reason, otherwise known as 'cognitive development'. This is the way we make sense of the world; of our knowledge and understanding of it, our place in it, and our effect on it. An extra element of cognition is 'metacognition'. This is the process of thinking about thinking, learning about learning, and understanding how we learn.

Attention is critical in order to achieve higher states of cognition, but it is a limited resource in the brain. The directed part of attention could be thought of as the 'prime real estate'. Being in nature allows for what the Kaplans (cited in Ackerman, 2021; Kaplan, 1995) call **'attention restoration'**. No one is yet sure quite how it works or what other factors also feed into the effect, but our brains are hard-wired for being in nature and are less stressed by it than they are by other environments. Natural environments stimulate us in a way that is 'softly fascinating'. Our involuntary attention on a bird or moving branch allows our brain to remain in an **open and ready state for learning and discovery** without distracting us completely (Stenfors, 2019). Our brains become more **receptive.**

There's a really interesting theory about the brain having key 'executive functions', and one of these is cognitive or **mental flexibility** (Tremblay, 2013)**.** This flexibility helps us choose whether to stay focused or to shift our attention and also helps us to apply different rules in different settings. This requires creative thinking. Woodlands are like breeding grounds for **creative thinking**. There is something about the range of natural bits and bobs (like sticks, leaves and fallen trees) that encourages us to be creative and resourceful. Sticks and logs become percussion, autumn leaves become works of art and fallen trees are the stage for performances. (This can be one of the challenges for Forest School programmes that don't have a rich abundance of nature.) A participant's relationship with their surroundings becomes more complex as their confidence grows over time (Brown, 2003). For example, a group in Forest School started to view certain logs as precious because of the sounds they made when hit. They would hide them in the woods between sessions, understanding that some bits of wood are better and more valuable than others. In addition, the chance encounters afforded us by nature excite our **curiosity**. We ask questions and go off in directions that we can't plan for. The '*Whoa! What was that!?*' moments which come from discovering a weird-looking insect or hearing a peculiar noise set us off on a deeply motivated quest for answers that could be described as **sticky learning**: where the information is memorable and really sticks. Experiencing this deep level learning and mental flexibility is how a Forest School environment changes attitudes to learning and creates **transferable skills**.

The reflective leader can be an ally in this enquiry. Rather than just giving participants the answers, there are a number of ways in which a skilled leader can **extend learning**. These will be explored in **Chapter 4**. 'While learning from a teacher may help [participants] get to a specific answer more quickly, it also makes them less likely to discover new information about a problem and create new and unexpected solutions.' (Gopnik, 2011).

None of this can happen without self-motivation. The more choice and control we have, the more chance there is of accessing deeply motivated learning (Patall, 2008). This is why at Forest School the emphasis needs to be on the participants' interests and passions. We see so many examples of **problem solving** when the participants really want to do something. If a slackline is too high, then finding a stump to stand on is important, leading to the challenge of moving the stump into the right position, which then creates the question of which tree stump will roll and which won't. Learners discover how to **think outside the box** and **persevere** without even realising it. We just don't see this when the task is driven by someone else's agenda. The ethologist Eibl-Eibesfeldt talks about play as 'scientific experiments conducted by children.' This explains why young children, given space and time, will often repeat the same activity and revisit ideas. Children have their learning needs coded into their play (Hughes, 2012). Older children and adults often feel the need for more permission to be playful. If we can create playful, supportive communities of learning where we feel safe to try out different versions of ourselves, we can **discover capacities** we didn't know we had.

Taking risks, challenging ourselves, play and social interactions are all things that develop those executive functions of the brain. Risks may be varied: perhaps our participants are singing out loud for the first time, or making marks or manipulating materials in a way they have never tried before. Persevering through difficulty cultivates the **cognitive flexibility** and **self-control** that are essential for successful, adaptable learning.

Developing the brain's executive function requires supportive and reliable relationships, with peers and with facilitators. The emphasis in Forest School on process over product can allow for **experimentation without judgement**. Treating mistakes as positive experiences to learn from can have a huge impact on how people view themselves. The trained leader reflects on how to create the conditions which allow people to **think for themselves**, cultivating and exploring an environment in which participants discover *how* to think, not *what* to think.

Transfer of benefits

Forest School can unlock learning that was previously inaccessible. Classroom teachers have noticed improvements in the quality of written work when children can build on real-world tangible experiences in Forest School. Children who showed no interest in mathematical concepts became very involved with measuring, comparing and ordering sticks when building dens. An adult who had never spent time in nature discovered a passion for finding out the names and uses of plants. Children who have English as an additional language or are selectively mute in the classroom have found their voices in Forest School.

Over time, participants become more aware of their own learning preferences and strategies. As confidence and experience develop, they may revisit concepts and skills. On the surface this may seem like they are not stretching their learning muscles but the intellectual development that is taking place – indeed, that is driving this learning – is the honing and refinement of understanding coupled with increasing independence.

The social and emotional toolbox of skills is transferred, explored, and developed outside of the Forest School setting, enabling time for participants to experiment and gain experience with the skills in different situations. The better we can communicate our wants and needs, the less likely we are to demonstrate our unspoken messages through behavioural outbursts.

Advocating for Forest School

We began with that brilliant question: *why? Why* Forest School? To answer that, we separated the benefits into three areas (physical, emotional and social, and intellectual) and hung the benefits on the six principles. You will have seen how closely interlinked the outcomes are: it was almost impossible for us to mention a benefit in one area that was not also present elsewhere.

There is one benefit we haven't yet discussed, that always comes up when we chat with our participants and it's the one that matters most to many of them: **Forest School is fun.** Let's not diminish the importance of that. Looking forward to Forest School can be the thing that allows a child who isn't thriving in the classroom to cope with school for the rest of the week (Tiplady, 2018).

Hopefully you will now have a better understanding of the benefits of Forest School. If you are looking to set up on your own this will strengthen your business case or plans. If you are writing a funding bid or trying to persuade senior managers in your setting, think about the needs of those you are hoping to persuade. Give them the information about the benefits of Forest School that aligns most closely with their interests, and they will be much more likely to get on board and be as excited as you are.

> **Reflective Exercise 7 – Benefits**
>
> - Which benefits of Forest School am I most excited about explaining to others?
> - Can you see how these benefits could ripple out to society?
> - Now you know more about the Forest School ethos, do you feel it is something you want to invest in?

Many of the benefits discussed in this chapter contribute to participant-led development, but they would often not be possible without the Forest School leader and the community that emerges within the sessions. The next chapter will give a fantastic insight into what is expected of a Forest School leader and how they facilitate learning and development within a participant-led setting.

References

Ackerman, C.E. (2021, August 01). *What is Kaplan's Attention Restoration Theory (ART)?* Retrieved August 17, 2021, from Positive Psychology: https://positivepsychology.com/attention-restoration-theory/

BBC. (2020, February 12). *Children who sit too much 'more likely to get depressed*. Retrieved from BBC News: https://www.bbc.com/news/education-51475399

Brown, F. (2008). *Playwork Theory and Practice.* Maidenhead: Open University Press. 228.

Coates, J., & Pilmott-Wilson, H. (2018, February). Learning while Playing: Children's Forest School experiences in the United Kingdom. *British Educational Research Journal, 45*(1), 21-40.

Coates, J., & Pilmott-Wilson, H. (2021). *Forest schools: how climbing trees and making dens can help children develop resilience*. Retrieved from Loughborough University News and Events.

Gill, T. (2014). The Benefits of Children's Engagement with Nature:. *Children, Youth and environments, 24*(2), 10-34.

Gold, J., & Ciorciari, J. (2020). A review on the Role of the Nueroscience of Flow States in the Modern World. *Behavioural Sciences*, 10(9), 9-137. Retrieved from https://www.mdpi.com/2076-328X/10/9/137

Gopnik, A. (2011, August 9). The Theory Theory 2.0: Probabilistic Models and Cognitive Development. *Child Development perspectives, 5*(3), 161-163. doi: https://doi.org/10.1111/j.1750-8606.2011.00179.x

Hughes, B. (2012). *Evolutionary Play work.* Routledge. 424

Hurtwood, M. A. (1968). *Planning for play.* United Kingdom: Thames and Hudson. 140.

Jennison, Jane. (2021). Does Facilitating Forest School Increase Resilience in Adults. 10.13140/RG.2.2.23512.01282.

Kandola, A., Lewis, G., Osborn, D. P., Stubbs, B., & Hayes, J. (2020). Depressive symptoms and objectively measured physical activity and sedentary behaviour throughout adolescence: a prospective cohort study. *The Lancet, 7*(3), 262-271.

Kaplan, S. (1995). The restorative benefits of nature: Toward an integrative framework. *Journal of Environmental Psychology, 15*(3). doi:https://doi.org/10.1016/0272-4944(95)90001-2

Kerr, M., & Schneider, B. (2008). Anger expression in children and adolescents: a review of the empirical literature. *Clinical Psychology Review, 28*(4), 559-577.

Lovell, R. (2009, March). *Physical activity at Forest School.* Retrieved from Forestry Commission Scotland: https://www.owlscotland.org/images/uploads/resources/files/Physical_Activity_at_Forest_School_Research.pdf

Patall, E., Cooper, H., & Robinson, J. (2008, March). The effects of Choice on Intrinsic Motivation and Related Outcomes: A Meta-Analysis of Research Findings. *Psychological Bulletin, 134*(2), 270-300. doi:10.1037/0033-2909.134.2.270

Sackville-Ford, M. (2019). *Critical Issues in Forest Schools.* London: Sage Publications Ltd. 196

Sandseter, E., & Kennair, L. (2011, April). Children's Risky Play from an Evolutionary Perspective: The Anti-Phobic Effects of Thrilling Experiences. *Evolutionary Psychology, 9*(2). doi:https://doi.org/10.1177/147470491100900212

Selhub, E., & Logan, A. (2014). *Your brain on Nature.* Toronto: HarperCollins Publishers Ltd.

Stenfors, C., Van Hedger, S., Schertz, K., Meyer, F., Smith, K., Norman, G., . . . Berman, M. (2019, July 3). Positive Effects of Nature on Cognitive Performance Across Multiple Experiments: Test Order but Not Affect Modulates the Cognitive Effects. *Frontiers in Psychology, 10*, 1413. doi:https://doi.org/10.3389/fpsyg.2019.01413

Tedstone, A. (2018). *Tackling Obesity is Everybody's Business.* Retrieved from NHS: https://www.england.nhs.uk/expo/wp-content/uploads/sites/18/2018/09/14.00-Tackling-obesity-is-everybodys-business.pdf

Tiplady, L. (2018). *Impacting on young people's emotional wellbeing through Forest school: The Breeze Project, pilot year.* Newcastle University, Research Centre for Learning and Teaching, Newcastle. 26.

Tremblay, R., & Boivin, M. (2013). Executive functions: Synthesis. *Encyclopedia on Early Childhood Development [online]*. Retrieved August 3, 2021, from https://www.child-encyclopedia.com/executive-functions/synthesis

Wikimedia Foundation, Inc. (2021, July 14). *Baba Dioum*. Retrieved from Wikipedia: https://en.wikipedia.org/wiki/Baba_Dioum

Chapter 4 – What does a Forest School leader have to do?

Lily Horseman and Francesca 'Froo' Signore

In the last chapter we looked at why Forest School leaders do what they do. In this chapter we'll look more broadly at *what* leaders have to do. We will divide this chapter into three sections, looking at before, during, and after a session.

Before

When you are imagining your Forest School session, 'paperwork' probably is not the first word that comes to mind. However, there is a lot of paperwork involved behind the scenes, and there is a lot of thinking to do, which is why your Forest School leader training is so important: it will help you to confidently commit all of your newly found knowledge to paper. You will need to comply with local legislation and this will be reflected in policies, protocols and procedures, risk-benefit assessments, and your communications with parents and staff. Much of this informs what is known as your Forest School handbook, and will be explored further in your Forest School training. The paperwork also includes certificates such as your qualifications, insurance, First Aid certificates, and checks on suitability to work with children and vulnerable adults (DBS or equivalent safe recruitment checks). Written agreements regarding the use of the land would also feature, if you are using a public space or a privately-owned woodland. Proof of registration with and membership of professional bodies like Ofsted and the FSA may also be necessary.

If you are working within an existing setting, it may look at first glance as though much is already in place regarding policies. But if you look at policies through the lens of Forest School, you will quickly see that almost every policy needs either an addition or an adaptation. For example, most school policies on Health and Safety are entirely lacking paragraphs on sticks or fire; and the safeguarding policy may need a nod to the fact that outdoors, out of earshot of others, you may be more likely to be the recipient of sensitive information (and it may be harder to pass it on straight away). All of this is reflected upon and recorded as part of your Forest School handbook.

Planning will be important before the session if this is a new group. Thereafter, planning is more effective as part of reflection and evaluation after the session. Forest School delivery on school sites may require something of a gear change and a lighter touch from staff than is usual according to the existing school behaviour policy. This, too, will need to be reflected in your handbook.

The Forest School leader also needs to do a site check and litter pick before the session and keep an eye on the weather forecasts, particularly wind speeds.

In Chapters 5 and **12** we will look in more detail at all the documents that need to be put in place.

During

But what actually happens during a session? What does a leader actually *do* from the beginning to the end? It will be different depending on the group, the point in the programme where the session falls, and so many other factors like weather, environment, and the participants' mood. But in general, there is a certain flow to the session.

Resourcing

The Forest School leader is most likely to be the person bringing the resources for the session. This will be in response to requests from the group or based on observations of interest, or even an empathetic guess about what might spark engagement. Getting resources to the site may be part of what the group does at the start of a session, or you may decide to do this in advance of meeting the group.

Putting up some sort of tarpaulin shelter for the group and ensuring resources can be kept dry can often be part of the preparation, especially in areas of high rainfall and where the weather can change quickly. Again, this might be what the group does as part of their arrival and settling in, or it might be done in advance by the leader. On many Forest School sites you cannot just nip and get something that has been forgotten, so having some sort of check list or resource list is really helpful. That said, when seemingly crucial bits of kit have been forgotten, groups have responded with creativity and resourcefulness – like the time when the scissors were forgotten, and so the group spent a long time working out how to successfully cut string with different stones and became really engaged with the process.

Meeting, greeting and transitions

How we meet our groups needs some thought. Their arrival and the Forest School leader's greeting will set the tone for the session. The leader should try to read the group, including the staff, and sense what energy levels are like today. Relationships that need attending to, and any 'baggage' that is being carried in, can often be obvious from the start. The Forest School leader needs to be prepared and willing to meet the group where they are. This may require a change from the planned activities right from the start.

That transition into the site can take many different forms. Will you walk with the group and how far? Is this a long walk or just crossing a school field? Do you meet them in the Forest School area? Do they all arrive at once or do they each arrive at different times? Do you need a holding activity while the group gathers? How will you mark the start of the session? For example, in one school they built a willow arch between the playground and the Forest School area, and participants would 'brush off' school as they went through the arch, metaphorically leaving it behind them to put back on at the end of the session.

Establishing the community of learners

At Forest School – more so than in many other settings – the leader tries to engender a sense of community. This is reflected in a commonly used agreement: 'Look after yourself, look after each other, look after the environment.'

How this is framed and explored is dependent on the attention span and level of understanding of the participants. This can take many forms: a discussion with participants and agreement of what a community might look like in practice; a quick 'wake up your body' exercise; or waving to the rest of the group and greeting the biggest and smallest things we can see in nature. All other questions about how we respond in different scenarios can be framed by the three 'look after' statements. For example, we are often asked *'Can we climb this tree?'* – 'Yes, but how will we do this whilst looking after ourselves, others and nature?'

This agreement starts to set the social and emotional boundaries for the group. Physical boundaries must also be set. How high? How far? How many in a hammock? You need to plan how you will mark boundaries physically – perhaps with ribbons, or by naming the points where we stop and how big the boundary is – recognising that it is much easier to make a boundary bigger than it is to make it smaller.

Building relationships

Building relationships is something we do through the whole session in many different ways, and it is crucial to the group dynamic. How do we build a community of learners rather than just being a bunch of people in the same place all doing things at the same time? We build it through connections and shared experiences. The start of the session may be a good opportunity to build in something like a game, a story, a challenge, a mystery, or a snack – something that draws the group together. This could also be the right time to hear reflections on the previous session: *'Is there anything that was tricky last week that you want to try again?' 'Has anyone got any unfinished projects?'* There might be things in the environment that have changed or developed that the groups want to check on. It is worth recognising that the Forest School leader is trying to find a routine that works for each individual group – no one way is right. The routine needs to be adapted and planned with deliberate intention based on an understanding of the needs of each individual in the group. This might mean that it looks like there is no planned beginning – yet from the leader's point of view, there may be a recognition of, and a respect for, the group's need to expend energy before they can come together to share.

Introducing options

There are various different ways to introduce options and opportunities for the session. The starting points will emerge from hearing the ideas that participants bring with them. Past discussions will inform this. We might also introduce new ideas and help them to discover potential that is outside their current experience. With some groups this can be supported by a visual timetable or menu of options (an example is shown on the previous page) so they can see how the session might flow.

The leader can add in new options by suggestion: *'Today I am thinking that I'll start building the stick hedge around the bluebell patch to protect it, if anyone wants to help.'* That way children who don't arrive with their own ideas can hear options. It may be that available resources are pointed out: *'Over there is the mud kitchen stuff, I've put the bag of pulleys and little animals next to the climbing tree and later I will open up the tool area...'* Having things up your sleeve is vital to springboard participation. It is also worth remembering that your carefully planned starting points might not be needed or wanted and that is also okay. Opening the options up to the group allows them to have agency: *'I'd love to hear what you are excited to do today... Would anyone like to chat with me about what they want to do first?'* Forest School is a long-term process and what a group needs in terms of input will change over time. The facilitation aspect of Forest School is something that is explored in more detail during Forest School leader training. We should always be aware that our suggestions may become instructions to some participants, restricting their freedom of choice. Exclaiming *'You can come and help me spread woodchip on the paths!'* may sound like an invitation to us, but to a participant used to adult-led direction it may feel like a veiled command or instruction and implies a hierarchy. It may even act as a trigger for some participants! Introducing the same task by just getting on and using spades and wheelbarrows allows participants to communicate their desire to join you and opt in if they want to, and affords a greater degree of freedom for play, fun and child-led learning.

Creating flow

It may be that a shared experience is a good springboard into activity, especially at the start of a programme when the participants are less familiar with the environment and its potential. These springboards need to be open-ended in order to give the participants choice – something that allows each individual to leap off in their own way and find their own needs and interests. Some participants might require more individual support to find their flow, especially if there are basic needs to be met first. Once participants are immersed, then Forest School leaders need to ensure the participants have time and space to deeply satisfy their interests.

Maintaining flow

The leader's role at this point is to observe, only stepping in to maintain the different levels of engagement if necessary. We establish flow and then step away. The leader is looking for energy levels, behavioural cues, interests, motivations, signs of unmet needs (e.g. hunger, toileting and cold), and where these needs might lead. As leaders we try to get ahead of people coming out of flow states, having the next springboard lined up in readiness. This role can be seen as 'seeding' or 'strewing': putting something out or placing resources in an accessible and timely way. This is what the play theorist Fraser Brown calls the Portchmouth Principle for resourcing play. Brown (2017) uses a quotation from the artist John Portchmouth to explain this:

'I don't remember how it started. There was me, and sand, and somehow there was a wooden spade: and then there were castles! I don't even remember asking how to do it; the need was big enough, and the way was there. Or maybe I'm not remembering exactly; perhaps I only found what someone had provided ... someone who had anticipated the need. ... It helps if someone, no matter how lightly, puts in our way the means of making use of what we find.' – John Portchmouth.

This way of resourcing participants means that things may be used in a way that you hadn't anticipated, or even not used at all. Forest School leaders need to recognise that the anticipated use often reflects our own play needs (because even as adults we have them). We need to be mindful of the risk of the leader's play needs dominating the session. The Forest School leader is still available as a resource for participants and may model engagement, but with the *active intention* of handing control over to the participants.

Repairing & troubleshooting

The participants might struggle in Forest School for lots of different reasons. What this boils down to is that their needs aren't being met in some way or another. Are they warm enough or hungry? Are they feeling left out or frustrated? Do they not have the resources or time to satisfy their interests, or are external factors impinging on their Forest School experience? This creates conflict, distress, or crises, which may be expressed as withdrawing, lashing out, unkindness, or absconding. How should a Forest School leader respond?

Looking through the lens of the Forest School principles, we are trying to respond in a way that nurtures Emotional Intelligence (holistic learning principle), supports innate motivation (learner-centred principle), and is compassionately responsive to needs (community principle).

A reflective Forest School leader enjoys a different sort of power relationship with their participants. Participants don't do things 'because I said so' – the hierarchy (if that's even the right word to use here) at Forest School can be much flatter. The skill of the leader lies in being able to connect with their own feelings, in order to hold the space for their participants and support them without judgement to develop strategies such that they can make more effective choices for themselves.

There is a difference between natural consequences and punishments. Part of the learning process at Forest School is to experience the impact of actions and the natural consequences that unfold. We have the luxury of time in the woods, to explore and understand the impact of a choice with participants. We can also aid the problem-solving process. Whilst punishing someone may seem expedient (and leave us feeling that we have 'dealt with' something), it can actually work against us in the long term. Not only does it not allow the above learning to take place, it also obstructs us in our quest for connection with our participants. Glasser names punishments (and rewards) External Control Psychology – this is our attempt to control others' behaviours by punishment or reward – and he views this psychology as a relationship-destroying mentality. It leads us to see and treat others as a means to an end, rather than as autonomous agents. He adds that it 'harms *everyone*, both the controllers and the controlled' (Glasser, 1998). Far better that we embrace an approach that fosters connection and supports reflection. From interpersonal conflict to a wet sock, the Forest School leader is there to support the participant's growth through experience.

Accompanying staff and volunteers may find this challenging as they may be used to a different style of management, and they will all arrive with their own needs too. Holding all this in balance can be tricky. This book explores some useful strategies for getting everyone on the same page, but in the flow of a session, narrating your own observations can be helpful – what Magda Gerber describes as 'sportscasting'.

'"Sportscasting" (or "broadcasting") is the term infant specialist Magda Gerber coined to describe the non-judgmental, "just the facts" verbalization of events she advised parents to use to support infants and toddlers as they struggle to develop new skills.' – Janet Lansbury

---

In this example, an accompanying adult points out some children on the far side of the Forest School site. The children are running and screaming and waving sticks.

Accompanying Adult: 'What are they doing with those sticks? I'm going to sort it out. Someone is going to get hurt. I am going to sort it out.

We both turn and face the children.

Sportscaster: 'What is going on there? They all have sticks. They are running towards one another – they are in two groups. They stop when they get close to each other.'

Accompanying adult: It would be that lot! They are being really disruptive. This isn't going to end well.'

Sportscaster: 'It's interesting. They seem to be in two groups. The two groups meet and shout but then separate.'

'This is quite an intense interaction. They run towards one another, stop, shout and wave their sticks, and then return back to the place where they started from. Have you seen who is involved?'

Accompanying adult: 'That is interesting. These children don't normally mix together. We usually try and keep those two in separate groups.'

Sportscaster: 'Everybody is very focused on the game; here they go again, they run, they shout, they stop and wave their sticks at each other.'

Accompanying Adult: 'I've never seen Alex not go too far before. They [the children] can't regulate their behaviour.'

Sportscaster: 'Alex is in the thick of it.'

Accompanying adult: '...and look at Jo! Normally Jo wouldn't say 'boo' to a goose.'

Sportscaster: '...interesting...'

Accompanying adult: 'This is great! Look at all the social interactions that are going on – they are actually self-regulating!'

Sportscaster: [smug mode on]

Sportscasting is usually used to help develop children's awareness, but can also be used to allow other staff and volunteers to understand your perspective. In an environment where experiments are welcome and leaders cannot ever anticipate exactly what children will choose to do, a Forest School leader needs to be adept at dynamically assessing and managing risks so that the participants have agency.

'Sportscasters don't judge, fix, shame or blame, they just keep children safe, observe and state what they see.' – Janet Lansbury

The dance

We have presented these stages of the 'during' part of the session as a linear process. In reality it is not so neat, simple or tidy. The different combinations of activities that are initiated or led by the participant or by the Forest School leader are represented below:

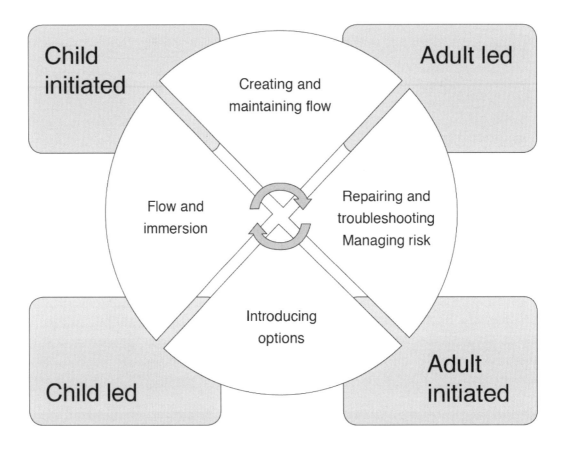

Play Matrix © Lily Horseman

Seeing it as a circle allows for any and all options to happen in any order, simultaneously or not at all. This is the dance of a Forest School leader: stepping forward and stepping back, stepping in and stepping out, partnering with one participant or many.

Winding down

We saw above how key the transition *into* Forest School is. The transition *out* of Forest School needs just as much – if not more – thought. The last part of a session can look and feel completely different to the rest of the session. Perhaps participants' minds are turning to leaving, to change, to less freedom or, indeed, less safety. This can affect participants' choices.

So how do we prepare them for that transition? 'Naming and owning' the difficulty of leaving can lead to fruitful discussions of how to make it easier. It might be sounding a wind chime or blowing bubbles (for a multi-sensory approach); it could be the singing of a particular song. If the tidying away of equipment is something the participants will be doing with you, that is also a clear sign that the session is drawing to a close.

Ending together

Just as with the beginning of a session, the ending may look and feel completely different from Forest School to Forest School, or indeed, from group to group or week to week. Having some sort of shared experience, something that is developmentally and emotionally appropriate for the group, helps the session to end well and can further develop the community of learning. Some groups may take it in turns to pour a cup of water over the fire whilst sharing thoughts or feelings about the session; others may respond to statements read out by the leader (e.g. *'I have felt part of a team today.'*). A song or story of 'our day' may work for others. It should be emphasised there is no wrong or right here – this is an opportunity for the participants to reflect on their session and embed the experience. As participants become more experienced at communicating, we get more experienced at interpreting their contribution. Our empathetic guesses become more informed. This is part of the relationship that builds between leader and participant.

Leaving the site

Who does the tidying? Who does the lift and shift of resources? How you leave the site and what you can leave there will depend on your setting. Who owns it? Who else uses it? What is your impact on the site? A more secure site (like a Forest School within school grounds or a private site) may mean more – a shelter, perhaps, or equipment – can be left in situ. Other sites, including public woodlands or special habitats, may require the Forest School leader to leave no trace.

After

After a Forest School session, one of the most important things a Forest School leader will do is reflect. This might be with other adults who were supporting the session, or it may be a solo process if the other adults have left with the group. There is not one single way to reflect effectively, but over time each leader will find their own style. Reflections will include: their actions, the impact of their interventions, the needs, interests, and development of individuals within the group and interactions between members of the group, the environment, and resources.

As Forest School is a long-term process, there are aspects that need to be held in mind for the next session or sessions. This can be tricky if you are running multiple sessions a week. Some people make notes or record themselves speaking about key events on their phone. Some people write session evaluations and track development for individual participants. This may be part of an existing system in the setting, or it may be separate to this and developed by the Forest School leader. Collecting evaluations, case studies, and monitoring is all part of the planning cycle. In addition, these elements become very valuable should you ever need to advocate for Forest School and your programme.

This is also the time to share any joys or follow up any concerns you may have about individuals. This may require a conversation with them or their families, the school or setting, or safeguarding professionals if you have serious cause for concern. Forest School leaders can become a trusted member of a person's support network, and so it is vital to make sure you have somewhere to take your concerns and that you understand the systems to support vulnerable individuals.

As well as the reflection on the session, Forest School leaders are reflective about their approach, knowledge, skills, attitude and impact. Finding tools to help you recognise your own areas for development is crucial. This might be through peer mentorship, network groups, or reflective tools to explore the possibilities for growth (see the wonky wheel diagram overleaf). We are dealing with the complexities of human development and the rich natural world, and there will always be something to learn. In our learning we need to be gentle with ourselves, mindful that the question *'How could I have done that differently?'* does not stray into self-criticism but is instead harnessed as an opportunity for development and growth.

There is also the part that many leaders find the most challenging – drying out the wet tarps, untangling all the string and storing the equipment until the next session… Even as we write, there is a bucket of wet tarps in the back garden, waiting for the sun to shine.

Wonky wood cookie wheel

. Understanding **Risk** and safe working – including Risk Benefit Analysis and Procedures.
. Knowledge about **Nature** and how to manage the impact on the natural environment.
. **Springboards**– The offers, suggestions and ideas I can give to the groups I work with.
. Understanding and application of the **Ethos** of Forest School.
. Understanding about and ability to facilitate **Play**.
. Hard **Skills** like fire lighting, carving and using tools and knots etc.
. **Theories** of learning, behaviour and development.
. Observing, recording and communicating about **Outcomes**.

www.kindlingplayandtraining.co.uk.

How to use this tool

Each category is something to reflect on. Like a tree, your capacities grow. The smaller it is the more there is to develop.

There is always room for growth but this is about highlighting where you feel you need to focus your attention, your CPD, your reflections and your learning. In the principles it states: *'The Forest School leader is a reflective leader and sees themselves, therefore, as a learner too.'*

Mark dots on the circles to show how well grown that area feels for you. The nearer the centre, the more growth is needed. The nearer the edge, the more it has grown already. Use lots of dots in one category if you feel like there are lots of separate elements. After you have marked all the dots, join them up. You should now have a wonky wheel showing which areas could do with attention (Horseman, 2018).

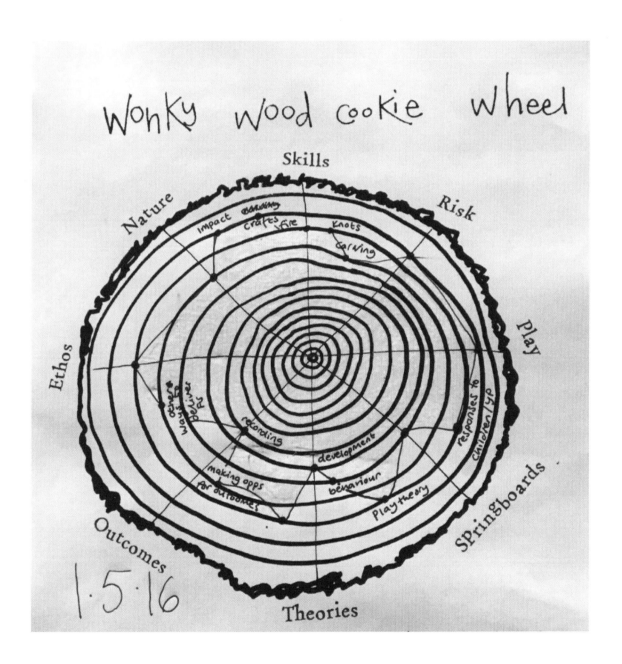

References

Brown, F. (2008). *Playwork Theory and Practice.* Maidenhead: Open University Press. 228

Brown, F. (2017). *What is unique about Playwork?* Leeds: Playwork Foundation. Retrieved from

Glasser, W. (1998). *Choice Theory.* Harper. 368.

Horeseman, L. (2021). *Play Matrix*.

Horseman, L. (2018). *Wonky wood cookie wheel – reflective practice*. Retrieved from Kindling: https://kindlingplayandtraining.co.uk/forest-school/wonky-wood-cookie-wheel-reflective-practice/

Lansbury, J. (2021, July 23). Retrieved from Janetlansbury.com: https://www.janetlansbury.com/2013/04/5-benefits-of-sportscasting-your-childs-struggles/

Chapter 5 – I want Forest School – what are my options?

Nell Seal

Hopefully, having enjoyed reading the first part of this book, you are now at the point where you know whether Forest School is right for you – we hope it is! This chapter sets out to help you choose the next steps on your journey: we will look at different client groups, discuss the Forest School qualifications, and outline five of the most common routes that you or your organisation can follow to become involved in Forest School. Before we begin exploring these five routes, however, it is important to get to grips with the qualifications needed to be a Forest School leader, assistant, or volunteer.

Forest School qualifications and training

Regardless of which route you use, if you are intending to implement Forest School you will need to know a little about the qualifications. The Level 3 Forest School qualification is a fundamental aspect in the success of your Forest School: you cannot set up and run a Forest School without it. It may lead to exciting transformations and opportunities and could even change your life. Whether you are planning on running sessions yourself, hoping to train others to do it for you, or buying in a service or freelance supplier, knowing you have the right person qualified to the correct level is critical. It is also extremely useful for a member of senior leadership to achieve a qualification if you intend to have Forest School in your organisation or setting. We will explore why this is advantageous in **Chapter 8**. Choosing the right level of qualification is important. It is equally important to ensure you have the right trainer. In this next section we will explore the qualifications and then offer some considerations that may help you to find the right trainer for you. There are three levels of qualification for Forest School:

Level 1 – Introduction to Forest School. This qualification gives participants an idea of the Forest School principles and practice, but it does not equip you to lead a group. People who attend this are generally volunteer helpers, managers who do not want to practise themselves but need to know what the principles and elements of practice entail, and people who wish to dip their toes in before committing to becoming Level 3 leaders. Level 1 only involves a total of 30 hours and is worth 3 credits on Qualifications and Credit Framework (QCF).

Level 2 – Forest School Assistant. This qualification enables participants to take a proactive role in helping a Forest School leader plan and deliver a Forest School programme, and also to support participants during Forest School sessions. This course usually takes approximately 60 hours and is worth 6 QCF credits.

Level 3 – Forest School Leader. Once qualified, a Level 3 Forest School leader can set up and run a Forest School programme. The Level 3 course covers: theory and practice during sessions, including a deep understanding of the ethos and pedagogy; how to facilitate groups in a learner-centred way; risk and the value of risky play; and how to environmentally assess and manage a Forest School site sustainably. It also covers some basic practical skills and introduces tool use and cooperative working, all of which will be required of a Forest School leader. Generally, this course lasts approximately 180 hours and is worth 18 QCF credits.

There are certain entry requirements to bear in mind for the different types of qualification:

Level 1
- Aged 14-16 or older (depending on Awarding Organisation)
- Have access to a Forest School programme being run by a Level 3 Forest School leader.

Level 2

- Aged 18 or older
- Hold a current enhanced disclosure (DBS or Disclosure Scotland certificate)
- Have experience working with your chosen client group
- Be able to assist on a Forest School programme being run by a Level 3 Forest School leader.

Level 3

- Aged 19 or older (depending on Awarding Organisation)
- Have a relevant Level 2 or higher qualification
- Hold a current enhanced disclosure (DBS or Disclosure Scotland certificate)
- Hold a current and valid First Aid qualification. NB: some trainers can offer this qualification alongside their Level 3 course
- Have access to a group with whom you will be able to run an introductory six session Forest School programme.

Finding the right training and trainers

Forest School training can be a deeply reflective and transformative process, so it is worth identifying a trainer with whom you gel well. It is also important to acknowledge that the quality of the training you receive, the type of qualification you end up with, and the level of ongoing support that is available all vary hugely in the UK. FSA Endorsed Forest School Trainers have all been through a rigorous, three-stage quality assurance process, are able to demonstrate that they meet a variety of high standards, and are committed to reflective, ongoing professional development. You can find a map of FSA Endorsed Forest School Trainers on the FSA website: https://forestschoolassociation.org/find-a-forest-school-trainer/ **[4]**

The FSA only recognises certain Level 3 Forest School qualifications, so if you or your setting might wish to become an FSA Recognised Forest School Provider in the future, you need to choose a trainer who offers an FSA recognised qualification. All FSA Endorsed Forest School Trainers offer a Level 3 qualification that we recognise. There is also an up-to-date list on the FSA website that details all of the Awarding Organisations currently supported by the FSA and the qualifications: https://forestschoolassociation.org/forest-school-qualification/ **[5]**

We advocate researching different trainers carefully, exploring their websites and social media, and having conversations with a couple before coming to a decision. Different training approaches will work for different people, and different trainers have experience working with different client groups (see the section on 'Which client group do you want to work with?' later in this chapter).

The following checklist, available as a downloadable resource in our online appendix, includes a variety of questions that you may wish to ask about a potential trainer. Though many of these answers will be found on the trainer's website, we would still encourage you to have a conversation with them. There are also a few reflective questions to consider once you have gathered the information.

Your research about or conversation with a potential trainer might explore a variety of questions about the training course, such as:

- ☐ What does the training cover?
- ☐ Does the course include First Aid training with paediatric and outdoor elements?
- ☐ Do I get a recognised certificated award, and from which awarding body?
- ☐ How long have you facilitated Forest School training specifically?
- ☐ How do you model the Forest School ethos and principles in your training?
- ☐ What format do your training courses take? Intensive weeks? Weekends once per month? Days spread over a year?
- ☐ What type of venue is used?
- ☐ How much of the content is delivered outdoors?
- ☐ How much does the course cost?
- ☐ Where does the course take place?
- ☐ If you require overnight accommodation, what are the local options?

Below: A photograph of some of our FSA Endorsed Trainers and Nell Seal

You may also want to find out about the trainer themselves, so may wish to explore a variety of questions such as:

- What experience and/or qualifications do you have relating to ecology and conservation management?
- Do you have past and current experience of facilitating Forest School yourself? With which client groups?
- Do you have experience of working with my chosen client group?
- What sorts of CPD have you been involved in recently yourself?
- How long have you been training educators?
- Have you recently visited a setting like mine that facilitates Forest School?
- Are you connected to any national organisations?
- Are you connected to a local Forest School network through which I can access ongoing support and CPD?
- What Level 4 or equivalent training qualification do you hold?
- What is your own area of interest within the practical skills: fire, tools and/or woodland management?
- How many Level 3s do you train each year? What proportion complete the course? What proportion pass the qualification?
- How can you cater for my particular learning requirement (if relevant)?
- How do you support students outside of the face-to-face days with you?
- What equipment do I need to have? What equipment is provided?
- Do you have your own Public Liability Insurance and Professional Indemnity Insurance in place?

Following your conversation with a potential trainer you might like to take some time to reflect using the following questions:

- Do you feel a connection with the trainer; did you click?
- Do you feel sure that the course they offer is of high quality?
- Do you feel that the course they offer will give you the knowledge and skills you need to be a confident Forest School leader?
- Will you be offered full support throughout (and beyond) your training period?
- If you think you may wish to eventually become an FSA Recognised Forest School Provider, will you end up with a qualification that is recognised by the FSA?
- Does the course format and method of assessment suit your requirements?

One other potentially illuminating way to research who to train with is to speak with other Level 3 Forest School leaders who trained with different people; ask them about their own training experience, perhaps using questions such as:

- Do you feel your training prepared you well for the role of Forest School leader?
- What was the learning environment like?
- How many days did you spend face-to-face with the trainer in the woods?
- What personal qualities did the trainer bring to the course?
- How did you feel after a day of training?
- Was your training fun?
- Was your training challenging? In which ways?
- How have your perspectives altered as a result of the training?
- Did you feel supported during the course and do you still feel supported post-qualification?

In some larger settings you may have a large number of staff or volunteers who wish to undertake Forest School training; in cases such as this it might make more economic and logistical sense to invite a Forest School trainer to facilitate a course in your setting. If you wish to host a Forest School training course, you will find many Forest School trainers are happy to work with you to enable this. If you have several people who require Forest School training but not enough to make up a full cohort, you could consider partnering with similar settings nearby or in your cluster. In the majority of cases, it makes more sense to identify an existing Forest School training course to send your colleagues on. Whether you wish to host a Forest School training course or find an advertised course to send your staff and volunteers on, it is worth investing time to find the right trainer for you and your context.

Qualifications and the Recognised Provider Scheme

At this early stage, whilst you are exploring your options, it is worth noting that many schools, settings and freelancers go on to become FSA Recognised Forest School Providers. FSA Recognised Forest School Providers are able to demonstrate that they are offering Forest School experiences in line with all six principles.

If you decide that your longer-term aspiration is to become FSA Recognised, you will benefit from examining the benchmarks associated with this scheme so that you can establish provision in a way that meets all standards. The FSA Recognised Forest School Provider criteria are freely available, and you can look at the guidance associated with each question on the application form to build a picture of them. In most cases you will need to have been facilitating Forest School for six months in your setting before submitting an application.

https://forestschoolassociation.org/join-the-fsa-as-a-school-and-organisation-member/ [6]

Which client group do you want to work with?

You may already have an idea of the types of group you would wish to work with using the Forest School approach. You will hopefully have already decided this by using **reflective exercise 2** (page23). When considering who to work with it is wise to start with groups with which you already have experience of working, groups within which you have existing contacts, or even with those whom you particularly enjoy working. The Forest School approach is very versatile and can be used with a wide variety of clients:

- Babes-in-arms and their carers
- Toddlers and pre-schoolers
- Primary or Secondary age children and young people
- Young offenders
- Looked-after children (children in care)
- People struggling with communication, or with emotional or behavioural difficulties
- Parents alongside their children
- Home educated children and young people
- Isolated adults and adults requiring support
- Older people
- People with autism, or neurodiverse groups
- Refugees
- People with multiple and complex needs

This is not an exhaustive list. You may be able to diversify and make your business more sustainable by offering Forest School provision to more than one type of group.

Case Study – Forest School and Dementia – Circle of Life Rediscovery CIC (CLR)

Forest School Leader and FSA Endorsed Forest School Trainer – Marina Robb

Circle of Life Rediscovery CIC (CLR) was launched after spending three weeks immersed in nature with the Rediscovery Foundation in Canada and learning about ways of working that respected the land, the cultural traditions, and the wisdom of elders. Right from the beginning, there was always an understanding that people thrive where there is fertile ground. The provision of learning in nature, with all its possibilities, offers a raft of well-being benefits; and in an educational context it can be linked to increasing knowledge and understanding of mainstream subjects.

For over 15 years, CLR has partnered with National Health Service teams to offer nature-based interventions for people with more severe health needs. These people benefit from a partnership containing the expertise of someone trained in an area, for example dementia, alongside someone who has trained as a Level 3 Forest School leader and has experience working with more vulnerable groups.

The Forest School training does not necessarily equip people to work with individuals with higher needs, but it does have highly relevant core essential principles as the foundation of good practice. The principle of long-term relationships, for example – the more time we can use to foster a quality relationship with a person, the more we can build trust and understanding and offer engaging and appropriate activities and inspiration. The relationship is really the ultimate focus, but we have to be willing to unpack our own stories about ourselves and suspend our judgement of others enough to meet the person in front of us. This human-based approach means that we can begin to work sensitively with all kinds of groups, valuing everybody. The natural world makes space for everyone. The ability to listen and see that we may be wrong is quite a skill. The success of the Forest School model relies on the adaptability of the six principles and our responsiveness to the place and the people.

Nature Based Care – Wellbeing in Nature Therapies through nature for people with dementia and their caregivers:

- Circle of Life Rediscovery CIC (CLR) began a pilot scheme in an area of woodland in East Sussex, working with the dementia clients and their caregivers to improve their personal health and well-being by connecting to nature in an informal and friendly environment. Clients were referred through the Specialist Older Adult Mental Health Service (SOAMHS) in August 2020. The pilot scheme ran for a period of 10 weeks.

- Morning sessions included welcome, refreshments, ice-breaking and activities, often with a mindful or meditative component, followed by a choice of place-based crafts and cooking, as well as offering the opportunity to explore the natural environment.

- Six participants (limited by COVID-19 restrictions) attended, with two staff from CLR and support of SOAMHS, giving a ratio of 3:1.

- Consistent with the 2016 Natural England Report's (Bragg & Aitkens) literature review, our therapeutic model combines the following components to bring about benefits to mental health:

  - The natural environment
  - Meaningful activities
  - The social context.

'This has been the best ever and a bit of a lifeline. It's been amazing and has helped to build my confidence. This has been the best thing I've ever done outside since I was a kid. The staff have been great, they've seen the person and not the dementia.'

Dementia directly affects around 850,000 people in the UK (NHS, 2021), and a further 670,000 caregivers. With an ageing population the number of people living with dementia is estimated to double in the next 30 years. Key findings suggest that social interaction and access to the outdoors and nature are important for people living with dementia, and that these activities have an important role in their quality of life.

The flexibility of the Forest School ethos allows a level of structure appropriate to the participant in the sessions. Participants with neurological conditions like dementia can often find it difficult to freely develop play outdoors, and are comforted by choices or structured opportunities. Being participant-centered allows us to follow the needs of the individuals, which is part of the creation of lasting long-term relationships and well-being. This is illustrated beautifully by this participant's feedback from the project.

'I couldn't find any bad points. Just the whole practical aspect of it, it wasn't a course, a thing you go on where somebody talks at you all day, so inclusive and interactive – that's what I loved about it. The fact that we were all included, we were all encouraged, but not badgered into doing things, we were asked, you know we were asked if we wanted to do this, we were given a choice. Sometimes, we were given a choice of two things that could be done and what we wanted to do, it was very much at the beginning where we were asked as a group if there was anything we would like to do in that setting, it just felt very inclusive and it was about US as a group, we were, I certainly felt, we were the focus of what was happening.'

Although this case illustrates a short-term pilot, it is clear that the value of the Forest School ethos and nature connection was beginning to be felt by the participants. This was illustrated by the results from the pre- and post-programme Canterbury Wellbeing scales and participants' telephone interviews: the feedback showed an increase in social connection and the participants even set up a WhatsApp group to stay in touch! The long-term nature of Forest School can really change the world for some people, improving not only self-esteem and self-worth but also quality of life, and the longer the programme the more embedded and effective the outcome. Every participant said that they would not normally do these kinds of activities at home, and it was something they looked forward to every week, which in itself was a huge positive for this group. Forest School's flexibility enables leaders to find funding from a number of streams and forge strong partnerships with other agencies, helping them to reach targets but also to provide wonderful enriching opportunities.

Routes to getting involved in Forest School

This next section explores five routes you might take to get involved in Forest School provision. Each has a different degree of responsibility, from buying in a freelance Forest School leader all the way to running your own business. We will look at each in turn and offer some case studies to help illustrate some different perspectives. The routes are:

1. Setting up and running a new Forest School business/charity of your own
2. Training to become a Forest School leader to work in another person's setting
3. Training yourself or a colleague to become a Forest School leader to work in your own existing setting
4. Finding a Forest School leader to help set up and facilitate Forest School for your existing setting
5. **Offering your site as a venue for Forest School.**

Route 1 – Setting up and running a new Forest School business/charity of your own

One option is for you to establish a new organisation that offers Forest School experiences to your desired client group(s). Organisations that offer Forest School tend to be businesses (sole-traders or limited companies), charities or Community Interest Companies (CICs). It is however rare to set up as a charity from initial conception, as this requires adherence to strict rules, and trustees that are willing to gamble on an unknown product; it is costly (in both time and money), complicated, and often fraught with bureaucracy; and it will most likely be better pursued at a later stage.

Setting up a Forest School business is relatively straightforward, and some of the information you need is covered in your Level 3 training. However, before you embark on setting up your Forest School business or deciding which route to take, you will find the following chapters contain some key information you will need to consider: **Chapter 4 – What does a Forest School leader have to do? Chapter 6 – A business perspective to growing your Forest School, Chapter 7 – Business management, Chapter 8 – Considerations for planning a Forest School and delivering it myself, and Chapter 9 – Considerations on setting up a Forest School in your school or setting**.

Case Study – Little Grubs Kindergarten – FSA Recognised Forest School Provider – Shropshire

Forest School Leader – Jacqui Rowe

Little Grubs Kindergarten is incorporated as a Limited Company. It was set up to run as a separate enterprise on the Oakly Park Estate to fulfil a particular need within the local community: to provide an educational provision on the site. We are enormously fortunate to be offering Forest School and access to nature to our local communities, as well as a wide variety of experience-based learning around food production, nature connection, the environment and sustainability. You can find out more about us and our Forest School delivery in the case study in **Chapter 2** or through our website https://www.littlegrubskindergarten.co.uk/ **[7]**. We offer Forest School and kindergarten to children aged two and a half to six, five days a week.

The decision to set up as a business gave us the freedom to manage our company in line with our passion, to ensure that we operated with sustainable, ecological and ethically sound practice at all times whilst not compromising on the needs of the children in our care or the staff we employ. It also gave us the ability to monitor and adapt to the needs of the clients and the land.

As a small business, it can sometimes be a challenge to get the word out about your provision, and we have found that being a business has allowed us to create a brand and an identity that people have grown to trust as quality and fun provision. Being an FSA Recognised Provider has helped with this too.

There are always worries when you set up in business, and it can be difficult when you feel like you always stand on a see-saw between finding new clients and finding the money to pay staff to cover new sessions. Covering sickness is a particularly difficult issue for us, and is something that you should budget for when you set your pricing and look at your cash flow. As a small business, one of the main challenges we faced was to find people who shared our passion for maintaining quality and ethical provision; and this is critical if you want to diversify or find your niche. Two of the most important aspects of running a successful business are: getting to know your clients, and building your business with the level of interest you get. It is best to take it steady and try not to overreach, but keep moving forward.

Route 2 – Training to become a Forest School leader to work in another person's setting

You may prefer to train to become a Forest School leader and offer your services to other settings; perhaps to an organisation that you already work for, or on a freelance basis to new organisations looking for Forest School provision. The information contained in **Chapter 4** will be of particular interest, so that you have a fuller understanding of what you are signing up to. If you are hoping to facilitate Forest School for your current organisation, you will find the section on writing a business case in **Chapter 6** particularly useful, and **Chapter 8** is essential reading. If you intend to work as a freelancer in other Forest School settings, you will still need to set up your own business, so that you can work in a self-employed capacity. You will likely need to set up and register your business as a sole trader, and you can find more information about this in **Chapter 6**. As a sole trader you run the business, take full responsibility for its debts (should you incur any), and have administrative responsibility to report to HMRC via self-assessment for tax purposes, although you can pay an accountant to do this for you.

Author's Journey – Nell Seal, Freelance Level 3 Forest School Leader

© Sarah Allington

'I was already working in a self-employed capacity as an education consultant offering CPD training in curriculum-led outdoor learning. I had had a period of several years where I had not done any formal work with children outdoors, which did not feel ideal for someone who trains other people how to work with children, so I decided to bring in another aspect to my freelance work. I was fairly certain that I did not want to introduce part-time work as a classroom-based teacher. I had been involved on the edges of Forest School for over a decade and decided this was my favoured route forward: it gave me contact time with children, time outdoors and, most importantly for me, a way of working with children that felt congruent. At that time, I was lucky enough to have the capacity for study and the available money to finance my training. I invested a lot of time researching potential trainers carefully; unfortunately, I found that none offered the sort of course and qualification I wanted local to me. I therefore decided to travel out of the area to undertake my Level 3 training.

The course I chose was modular, spread over nine months, and involved spending up to three days at a time away from home. I identified a Pre-school setting (in the village where I live) who were interested in me setting up Forest School provision for them, so I ran my pilot sessions with them. Gaining my Forest School qualification alongside other work commitments and family life proved challenging at times due to the hours required for independent study, portfolio writing, session planning, and practical skill development. Following the successful pilot, the pre-school managers decided to significantly expand their outdoor provision and train their staff to become Level 3 Forest School leaders. I was nonetheless intent on building one day a week into my work programme for facilitating Forest School with children. I began discussions with my daughter's school. From the outset, I advocated for Forest School in line with all six principles; I wanted to establish our Forest School in a way that met all of the benchmarks set out in the FSA Recognised FS Provider Scheme. I delivered several sessions for senior leaders, governors, staff, and parents and carers to build a picture of the Forest School principles and ethos with each stakeholder group. There were several challenges we had to overcome along the way to reach the point where both the school and I were comfortable with the setup:

- There was no suitable land on the school site so we had to look elsewhere for woodland to use, and that took time to organise.
- There was not much spare capacity in the staffing, yet we wanted to ensure the usual class teacher and teaching assistant were part of every Forest School session. To ensure high ratios of adults to children we also established a small group of parent volunteers to become some of the additional supporters: they participate on a rota to accommodate people's varying commitments.
- The school is a small state school and unable to absorb the cost of Forest School into their usual school budget, so the cost was passed onto parents, who are given various payment options (weekly, half term blocks, or the whole year).

> - From a strategic point of view, the Forest School provision needed to fit well with school priorities. Our eventual agreed focus is linked to the Christian values of the school, supporting the transition to Key Stage 1 from EYFS, and helping children become caring (toward ourselves, each other and the world around us), resilient, and respectful members of the community.
>
> I currently facilitate a 2.5 hour session once a week for Years R and 1, with up to 15 children per session and at least four accompanying adults. We use a small, relatively young piece of woodland (owned by the Parish Council) just five minutes' walk from the school. I try to fit all of the work associated with the Forest School delivery aspect of my job into one day: the session planning, the record-keeping, the reflections, the communications with staff and parents/carers, and the equipment wrangling and maintenance. I learned during my pilot that, for me at least, you can allow Forest School to absorb as much time as you can offer it! As a self-employed person with a varied portfolio of work, I find it helpful to have clear boundaries between my different responsibilities.'

Route 3 – Training yourself or a colleague to become a Forest School leader to work in your own existing setting

If you are working in a strategic role in an existing setting and, following consultation with the Leadership Team, have decided that Forest School would be an effective way of helping you to meet your objectives and the needs of your clients, you may be keen to train a number of your staff to become Forest School leaders. **Chapter 9 – Considerations on setting up a Forest School in your school or setting** contains useful information to consider before you take the plunge.

The FSA and FSA Endorsed Forest School Trainers have observed that the settings which have most successfully embedded the Forest School approach often have three common features:

- Some members of the senior leadership team are Forest School trained themselves, and so have a deep understanding of the ethos and principles.
- The majority of staff have undertaken some level of Forest School training so there is widespread understanding of (and support for) Forest School.
- There is more than one Level 3 leader, so that Forest School provision doesn't stop when staff move on.

To facilitate Forest School experiences, you will need to have at least one Level 3 Forest School leader at every session.   There are however three levels of Forest School qualification that might be worth considering. Forest School qualifications are outlined in the training section at the start of this chapter.

As well as deciding on a course and trainer, it is also important to choose the right staff. When exploring who might train to be a Level 3 Forest School leader, there are some important aspects to consider:

- Who is self-motivated enough to undertake quite a hefty qualification with lots of self-directed learning?
- Who can include the additional work into their professional and home life?
- Who has an existing skill set that fits well with Forest School?
- From an organisational point of view, which staff member will ultimately be able to fit Forest School facilitation in among their other roles and responsibilities?

The Level 3 qualifications are a considerable commitment, so it is advisable to ensure that those signing up for the course have a solid, practical understanding of the Forest School ethos outlined in **chapters 1**

through 4 of this book. There are different ways to acquire an understanding of the Forest School ethos ahead of attending your chosen training:

- Talking to existing Level 3 leaders
- Visiting settings that use the Forest School approach
- Undertaking a Level 1 or 2 Forest School qualification beforehand.

When seeking settings to visit, it is important to acknowledge that the quality of Forest School provision varies hugely in the UK; it is worth spending time to identify a setting that facilitates Forest School in line with all six Forest School principles (see **Chapter 1**). When talking to people and visiting settings you may find some people use terms like 'Forest School Lite' or 'Full Fat Forest School', yet provision is either Forest School or it is not. To be Forest School all six principles must be present, and if just one is missing you are looking at some other (often fabulous) form of outdoor learning. All FSA Recognised Forest School Providers have provided evidence that they facilitate Forest School in line with all six principles, so this is a great place to start your search.

Case Study – The Loddon School's Forest School Journey – FSA Recognised Forest School Provider

Forest School Leader – Emily Clark

The Loddon School® caters for children with severe and complex learning needs, including autism and severely self-restricting behaviours; most of the children are non-verbal. Our Forest School (FS) runs for 52 weeks a year for the 30 children (aged 8 – 19) that call The Loddon School both home and school. Forest School sessions take place within the safe perimeter of a strip of woodland within the school grounds. The Forest School approach and ethos complement The Loddon School's Personalised Learning for Life Using Supportive Strategies (PLLUSS) curriculum. The 'whole school approach' to learning and development eases the child's reliance on restrictive behaviours – the barriers that prevent learning – which then enables children's more settled being, and access to learning. The Loddon School has no classrooms. A child's timetable is made up of their preferred activities. Concentration on activities that motivate the child promotes a positive learning environment and more easily engages the child's ability to learn; learning steps intended to meet personalised learning needs are then intertwined into those activities. The school's ethos is very much akin to that of Forest School and I could see the benefits for The Loddon School children.

I was, however, a little apprehensive about whether FS's strict adherence to the six principles would allow participation of The Loddon School and children with complex needs. After discussing my worries at an FS taster day, regarding how I may implement FS with my cohort, I came away with a newfound confidence that I could make this work for our school and children. Then there was only the barrier of my lack of nature knowledge and low confidence in this area – let us just say, I am more Gruffalo than woodland fairy. I had, however, already realised everyone can enjoy the benefits of Forest School, even Gruffalos!

I completed Forest School Level 3 training and enjoyed every minute. During the journey that ensued, I did stumble on some large metaphorical tree roots – finding a fit for my setting was always going to be a challenge. Although I now totally understood the FS ethos and principles (and wanted to follow them), it was not always easy. However, the positive outcomes far outweighed any negatives, and seeing the benefits of FS enthused me to pursue national recognition through the FSA Recognised Forest School Provider Scheme.

The whole school community began to acknowledge the value of Forest School sessions and they became embedded in what we offer. This encouraged me to work towards becoming part of the FSA Recognised Provider Scheme and show everyone that Forest School truly was for all! Initially we were told that we *would possibly not meet the criteria for the national FSA's quality award badge,'* which was disappointing. Thankfully, it turned out that The Loddon School was a perfect example of how settings that don't 'tick all boxes' can certainly still engage with the Forest School ethos, and so we were offered special consideration. Thus began our journey in seeking FSA Recognised Provider status and supporting the FSA to further their inclusivity.

The children we work with find it extremely difficult to generalise and maintain skills. Numerous factors influence this, such as sensory processing and sensory aspects of their environment (weather, people, time) and difficulties with interoception (the perception of sensations from inside the body), as well as their understanding and the motivation to become involved, alongside their severe and profound learning difficulties, autism, self-restrictive behaviours, and communication difficulties.

The Loddon School children can find it extremely difficult to relate to others, particularly their peers. For example, instead of playing with a toy with a peer in an imaginative or symbolic way like many children, they may perseverate objects (want to keep the item and use it in a limited and repetitive manner); they may use it for self-stimulation or become entirely self-absorbed with it. This example typifies the difficulties children with complex needs related to autism have in their play skills. This does not mean that they do not engage in play – it may just look different compared to other children of their chronological age.

The Loddon School's PLLUSS curriculum, in conjunction with Forest School, enables the children to develop skills that will reduce their struggle to cope in the world and help them to manage their challenges. These are the same skills that enable them to reduce the *need* to rely on their restrictive behaviours to get their needs met, thus allowing them the psychological bandwidth to *begin* to be concerned about their self-esteem. The difference with the PLLUSS curriculum compared to a normal academic curriculum is that the unplanned objectives are already built in as outcomes. More typical mainstream curriculum outcomes are a by-product and are secondary to the psychological-based outcomes.

Most Loddon School children need a degree of adult direction to keep them engaged, and Forest School's child-centred approach fits nicely with this. Forest School sessions are flexible and build in opportunities for potential free play. The planned activities are always set at a challenging but achievable level for my cohort; the children feel able to take part and are motivated to join in. I ensure there are activities and resources available that encourage and stimulate the children; and I have observed, over time, children choosing preferred items and activities from the options available and beginning to engage and enjoy what they are doing with decreased levels of staff initiation and interaction – this is when I begin to observe free, self-directed play emerging. Because of the nature of our cohort, the children must be able to dip in and out of sessions to build on their willingness to engage in any activity. Engagement at The Loddon School's FS is child-led and it is the child that initiates the end of a session – for some children two minutes' engagement is a target and cause for celebration. This clash between two of the six principles was our main issue with meeting the FS session duration criteria. The recognition process was daunting at times, but *so* worth it. I feel, by working alongside the FSA, we have in some sense paved the way for other SEND provisions struggling to meet the criteria.

There have been other challenges, as our children require one-to-one staff support to remain safe – there is a necessity to respond to any sign of increasing anxiety or stress. Staff support has its benefits, but it can be difficult for staff to understand the FS approach and the necessity for their reduced input. We implemented staff mentoring sessions, so they have a better understanding of the core FS principles. It is imperative that staff are on-board and know that, within the FS setting, they need to give the children as much space as is safe to do so. It can be hard for The Loddon School staff to supress the urge to take advantage of a learning opportunity or enthusiastically act to maintain the child's engagement in the activity – they had to step back and let the children lead more than any other school activity. At the same time, staff needed to know the appropriate times to reassure and praise the child, and spot when anxiety, frustration or upset may lead to a behavioural incident. The mentoring sessions became a crucial aspect of maintaining and embedding a quality FS provision.

I am eager to continue developing our FS, knowing I am on the right path with the added reassurance and support from the FSA that we comply with requirements in our own unique way. Forest School really does work for all, no matter a participant's age or ability. I am elated The Loddon School Forest School is on the Forest School map! My FS tutors were right, we are not a typical Forest School, but I now go with the phrase, 'Who wants to be typical?' Our Forest School rocks!

Route 4 – Finding a Forest School leader to help set up and facilitate Forest School for your existing setting

If you are exploring this route you are interested in inviting someone from outside your organisation to facilitate Forest School for your chosen client group. It might be that you work in an existing setting but feel that none of your staff have the capacity to train to become Level 3 Forest School leaders at present, or perhaps you do not have the physical space to deliver sessions suitable for the participant groups. This route is about finding a freelancer or organisations to help you set up Forest School provision for your school/setting.

Case study – Lime Tree Forest School – FSA Recognised Forest School Provider

Forest School Leader – Janet Green

The Lime Tree Primary School leadership decided in 2013 to employ a full time Forest School leader to be part of the school team. Lime Tree has a large area of natural space within the school grounds, which the leadership visualised being used by the pupils of the school not just for playing, but as a place to learn, build confidence and self-esteem, learn to take risks, and of course have fun. After research and discussion, the decision was made to take on the Forest School model and ethos for the children at the school. Looking at the current staffing structure and their abilities and passions, it was evident to the leadership that they needed to employ someone who could take on this element of the learning for the school, giving that person autonomy, as the trained leader, for developing the direction it should take. It was also realised that it was essential to have someone who not only had a connection to the natural world, but also did not mind being outside in all weather, something that not everyone may care for!

These senior leadership decisions have been pivotal in the success of the development of Forest School at Lime Tree. The fact that the leadership understood the ethos of Forest School right from the beginning, and held a vision for what it would look like within the school grounds for the pupils, has meant that the leader has been able to develop it in its true essence. Forest School has featured in the school development plan ever since, and has also enabled the outdoor learning in the school to be developed as a side shoot. There have been the usual battles to fight within the school, including trying to send larger groups out for the Forest School sessions, swapping children in groups, calling Forest School a treat for the children, not letting the children put mud on their faces, and parents complaining that their child has mud on their white shirt, to mention but a few, but due to the vision being held by the leadership, there has been full support to keep the Forest School ethos true to its nature. There has had to be an element of flexibility and learning from both the leader and the in-school staff over the years as this has developed. This involves having honest and open conversations, showing care and compassion for each other's practice, and remembering that ultimately the school is answerable to the governors, the parent community, and of course to Ofsted to show positive learning results for children. But when the school values are not merely based on academic results but also on the well-being and success of every child, then these things can work together.

Forest School fits the school ethos for the well-being of the child. As the Forest School has been developed over the years to become part of the offer of the school, the evidence of its impact has become more and more apparent. Children who may not say much in class find a voice in the woods; children who struggle to focus in the classroom come outside and let off steam and find themselves often more able to go back inside and learn – I could list endless benefits here, but they have already been written about in Chapter 3. The essential key has been good communication between Forest School leader and teaching staff throughout. We have conversations with the teacher after each session about particular children. We also use shared google documents as well as the school CPOMS system to reflect and record the journey of each child. We also link our sharing with EHC plans and SEN where appropriate. Forest School is a shared journey with the whole school staff team.

The school now has Forest School sessions being delivered to children from nursery up to year two. This has taken time, finance, more staffing of leaders, and effort to develop. The school started with one Forest School leader and now has four. It has not happened overnight and required careful investment financially, but has been totally possible. Salaries are supported with money from the main budget and pupil premium, as well as with money raised by external working as staff share practice and provide training outside of the school itself. Ultimately the key ingredients have been vision and determination: where these exist, you find a way to make it work.

The older children at the school receive what we call Earth Adventures – having travelled through Forest School in their earlier years, they now get a slightly shorter session for approximately six to eight weeks of the year. This way they continue to learn through play and adventure in the woods, continue to grow in confidence and self-knowledge, and also have fun as they learn. It has been important to recognise that this is not Forest School, because the provision does not meet all the six principles of Forest School. Although the school now has a team of four leaders, they simply can't provide Forest School for everyone: there are only so many hours in a day and Lime Tree is a two-form entry school! The Forest School team also support the teachers with developing outdoor learning linked to the curriculum, and deliver a number of small intervention groups each week.

When seeking someone to facilitate Forest School experiences for your chosen client group, you might be searching not just for a person but for a location too: your organisation might not have any suitable land. This problem can usually be overcome; in the UK we are fortunate in having an extensive network of green spaces, many of which might welcome a careful Forest School leader. You might identify an organisation which offers Forest School at one of their sites; for example, conservation organisations who have an educational remit. You might find a suitable woodland site that is convenient to your organisation and then identify a freelancer to work with. Or you might work with a freelancer who already has a woodland space that they use for the Forest School sessions; if they do, many will be happy to work with you to identify a suitable space.

Case study – Wirral Hospitals School – using external providers with an external site

Mark Jones, Mentor

Wirral Hospitals School backs onto Birkenhead Park, a 127-acre public park and Grade I listed landscape, and as such we often use it for lessons. After building relationships with the Park Rangers through litter picks and adult directed lessons, we were invited to take part in a Public Health Outcomes Fund Project delivered by the Rangers and supported by the school's mentors and staff. The project offered long-term, frequent, subsidised Forest School sessions run by 2-3 qualified Forest School leaders. Our young people have a variety of needs; being in a different environment and meeting new people challenged our students. These challenges were overcome gradually and our students settled in. The project was a success and the students took an active role in the sessions. The Rangers encouraged students to use all of their senses during the activities and offered the experience of using tools, knives, saws and fire lighting equipment, which helped students to build their fine and gross motor skills and gain a better understanding of health and safety outdoors. The relationship between the students, the park, the staff and the Rangers grew as the sessions progressed.

Overall, the experience was a very positive one; students took part in activities they would never have experienced outside of Forest School. Working with the Rangers raised the students' awareness of the environment and local surroundings, and the Rangers were able to apply for funding to reduce or remove the costs of the sessions. Due to the project, links between the school and other agencies developed and the school staff were offered opportunities for professional development to expand the school's offer to include other outdoor education.

We found that there were a few challenges to overcome with accessing Forest School in this way. Firstly, because of the regular and frequent sessions, the students missed the same lesson every week and this caused some issues for us and our students. The project was funded in blocks of ten sessions during the autumn and spring terms because of the stipulations of the funding, but ideally, we would have created a more holistic and variable experience by encompassing all four seasons.

Choosing a Forest School provider

As discussed in earlier chapters, to have any Forest School provision in your school or setting you must work with a qualified Level 3 Forest School leader who has the depth of understanding required for the role. You may also wish to identify a Level 2 assistant and Level 1 trained additional supporters. The various levels of Forest School qualification are covered at the start of this chapter.

An ideal place to begin your search is the database of FSA Recognised Forest School Providers. By choosing an FSA Recognised Forest School Provider you know that they meet the national minimum standard for facilitating Forest School and that they are working to all six Forest School principles. You can examine the map to establish whether any Recognised Providers are geographically close to you. https://forestschoolassociation.org/find-a-forest-school-provider/ **[3].**

If you are unable to find a suitable FSA Recognised Forest School Provider offering freelance outreach in your area, you can advertise with the FSA to try and identify someone. All FSA members, including individual members, are permitted to place an advert on the FSA social media channels for £25 (£50 for non-members). You can post a call out for a Level 3 leader by visiting the FSA website's job page at: https://forestschoolassociation.org/jobs/ **[8].**

Once you connect with a Level 3 Forest School leader (especially if they are not FSA Recognised), you will want to explore with them whether their skill set offers you what you need and want. The checklist on the next page includes a variety of questions that you could consider posing to a potential Level 3 Forest School leader. Many of these questions might be answered by browsing their website or reading their terms and conditions.

Example questions to ask or find out about your potential Forest School Provider

These questions are available as a downloadable resource at:
https://forestschoolassociation.org/book-resources/ [1]

- ☐ What type of FS qualification do they hold? Which level? What is the name of the qualification on their certificate?
- ☐ Do they hold any additional education qualifications such as a B.Ed. or PGCE (whilst this is not a necessity it might be relevant to your setting)?
- ☐ When did they qualify? How much experience do they have?
- ☐ Who was their Awarding Organisation? Is this an FSA supported Awarding Organisation?
- ☐ What type of client groups have they worked with in the past?
- ☐ What do they consider to be vital components of Forest School? Are you both on the same page? E.g. did they mention all six Forest School principles?
- ☐ Do they have Public Liability Insurance that covers Forest School activities? What are the stated conditions of that insurance?
- ☐ When was their most recent DBS check? Can they bring current documentation in to enable you to conduct a new check?
- ☐ What is their process for planning sessions? E.g. do they approach planning by starting with the needs of the client group?
- ☐ Can you agree on an overarching focus with them for the group you have in mind?
- ☐ Will they conduct a training session for supporting adults before Forest School provision begins? Does this involve additional cost?
- ☐ Will they hold an introductory meeting to share information about the Forest School ethos and principles with parents/carers before provision begins?
- ☐ Do they have an example of an existing Forest School handbook they would be willing to share with you?
- ☐ Which of your setting policies will they need sight of to create a handbook appropriate for your planned provision?
- ☐ Do you have any policies that you need to negotiate or discuss deviating from?
- ☐ What would their approach to behaviour management be? Are you comfortable with the proposed approach to behaviour?
- ☐ Are they comfortable and clear about your school safeguarding processes?
- ☐ Do they have their own woodland space? Can you visit to take a look?
- ☐ If they do not have their own woodland space, are they able to offer other possible locations you could use?
- ☐ Are you confident they are taking care of their woodland space? E.g. do they have a woodland management plan and Environmental Impact Assessment that you can see?
- ☐ How do they charge for provision? How will you cover these costs?
- ☐ Where does their value judgement lie with regards to risk? Are you on the same page?

The following checklist, also available on the online resource from includes a range of other matters you may need to consider and work through:

- ☐ If you are using an external woodland space, how will you deal with transportation logistics and costs?
- ☐ If you hope to use an onsite woodland area, does the practitioner think it could work? What developments might need to be undertaken?
- ☐ Who will organise and pay for a tree survey? Who will pay for any resulting tree work required?
- ☐ In Forest School, there are high ratios of adults to children (before any additional needs are taken into account): who will these additional adults be?
- ☐ Is there any scope for training additional adults to Level 1 or 2 to increase their knowledge and understanding about Forest School and provide enhanced help to the Level 3 leader?
- ☐ Will the clients' usual teachers, carers or key-workers be able to attend Forest School sessions? If so, how will the Forest School leader and usual staffs' roles differ? If not, how will you manage the flow of information that needs to happen (e.g. what happened during the Forest School session) between the practitioner and the staff?
- ☐ How will you support the Forest School leader to get to know the clients and their needs ahead of beginning sessions? Can you enable meetings between the practitioner and the clients' usual teachers, carers and key-workers?
- ☐ To be considered long-term, sessions need to take place weekly or fortnightly across the seasons. How will you fit this into any existing timetables and commitments, and will this work for the Forest School leader?
- ☐ If you are working with a Forest School leader who is not an existing FSA Recognised Forest School Provider, do you wish to aim to apply for this award? It may be worthwhile examining the benchmarks associated with this scheme so that you can establish provision in a way that meets all standards. The FSA Recognised Forest School Provider criteria are freely available; you can look at the guidance associated with each question on the application form to gain a picture of this. You will usually need to wait until your setting has had Forest School running for six months before applying.

Route 5 – Offering your site as a venue for Forest School

This route is specifically for landowners who would like Forest School provision to occur on their site but who do not wish to run it themselves. This is common in Local Authorities, private estates or woodlands, sites that require income from their land to be sustainable, schools with large grounds, wildlife groups, 'friends of' organisations or land use trusts, and community partnerships. Rather than incurring the costs of bringing in a provider, this route allows landowners to create agreements with a freelance business, so that organisations or schools can use their land as a Forest School location. There are some implications which you should consider if you are choosing to follow this route, the most important of which are around responsibilities and agreements; this is covered in **Chapter 10**, where you can find information on land use agreements and information about your responsibility as a land manager.

Case Study – Houghton Hall Estate, Norfolk

Houghton Hall is a stately home built in the 1720s for Britain's first Prime Minister, Sir Robert Walpole. It is still the private home of the 7th Marquess of Cholmondeley, his wife and three children. The Hall is set in over 350 acres of parkland, home to over a thousand white fallow deer.

Houghton Estate has been open for local schools and Early Years settings to visit in a self-guided capacity since 2003. Lord Cholmondeley is keen that local children have the opportunity to explore the beautiful Estate, and so has worked in partnership with Norfolk County Council and Norfolk Wildlife Trust to develop the educational facilities, originally focusing on Early Years and Key Stage 1 children but now welcoming all age groups.

Any Norfolk school or Early Years setting can make a visit to the Estate free of charge on days when it is not open to the public. Groups have access to a range of outdoor spaces including woodland, parkland, and walled gardens, as well as an indoor education center. Many different groups use the facilities for a range of educational visits, including Forest School; the first Forest School pilot program for Norfolk was run on the Estate in 2004. Knowing that transport can often be a barrier to school trips, Lord Cholmondeley provides a free minibus service to groups within a 20-mile radius. There are also a number of kit boxes containing outdoor equipment, as well as waterproof clothing available for groups to borrow. The project is overseen by a part time Education Coordinator, whose role is to train and support school/setting staff through a Group Leader training day which will enable them to make self-guided visits.

This one-day training course provides leaders with all the information they need to make a visit, outlining: terms of use, roles and responsibilities, health and safety, orientation around the site, kit and equipment, booking logistics, etc. In accompaniment to the training day, staff also receive a group leader handbook which contains guidance, risk assessments, and insurance information. There is also a supporting website with a members-only section designed to support the group leaders.

Reflective Exercise 8 – Routes to Forest School

Before we move onto Chapter 6 you may find it useful to reflect on the information so far:

- Which route best serves your long-term vision?
- How does Forest School help you realise your long-term vision?
- How much capacity do you have to commit to Forest School?
- What do you need to make happen before going down your chosen route?
- Have you consulted all stakeholders before choosing a route?
- How can you make Forest School sustainable in your setting?

Whichever route you decide to take to get involved in Forest School I hope that the experience is as enriching and valuable. The following couple of chapters look at the business considerations for creating a Forest School from planning to price point.

References

NHS, 2021. *Dementia.* [Online]
Available at: https://www.england.nhs.uk/mental-health/dementia/
[Accessed 17 August 2021].

Chapter 6 – A business perspective to growing your Forest School

Gareth Davies and Nic Harding

In our experience, the majority of Forest School leaders love delivering Forest School but are somewhat less enthused about the business and management side of things. Unfortunately, you need to get both aspects right if you are to be successful in attracting and retaining clients. This chapter asks you to consider the business and management side of your Forest School endeavour at an early stage. Those Forest School providers who encounter problems often regret not having spent more time on these aspects at the planning stage.

It is worth pointing out that your client is probably not the person who participates in your Forest School programme. The client is the person or organisation paying for your services. If the clients are not satisfied then the participants will stop coming and your Forest School enterprise will fail.

Your clients need to understand the benefits of your Forest School offer. We will assume that, given the choice, clients will prefer a more expensive yet higher quality service over a cheaper service of lower quality. We will cover *price point* a bit later on in **Chapter 7**. The FSA, and this book, are orientated towards high quality Forest School provision. By reflecting on the content in this book you will be able to explain to clients how your Forest School provision is of the highest quality.

Clients will judge you on the basis of their experience of moving through your management processes. They will be particularly sensitive to factors such as your level and methods of communication, and whether or not you have useful policies and procedures in place. However, the financial side of your operation will be known only to you. It will be largely invisible to others, unless it goes badly wrong. Is that a scary thought? Any new enterprise is a risk. In Forest School we like to talk about risk/benefit assessments – we take steps to mitigate the risks and then weigh them against the potential benefits before settling upon a course of action. By reading this chapter, and understanding the importance of the topic, you are already taking a mitigating step. We cannot promise to tell you *everything* that you will need to know about running your business, but we can certainly point you in the right direction. **If you are unsure about anything at any stage, we highly recommend that you DO YOUR OWN RESEARCH and seek expert advice where necessary, whether that be business, financial or legal.**

Making the business case

At some stage you will probably need to explain what you want to do to someone else, as every new enterprise must secure support. This could be potential funders, line mangers, directors, governors, or even family members. How you explain your plans to others is dependent upon your personal context. It is important to be able to do this clearly.

In **Chapter 5** we considered five possible routes to Forest School. These may be split into two broad categories: growing a Forest School as a project or initiative in an existing organisation and growing a Forest School business as a new organisation.

Making the business case within an existing organisation

If you want to establish Forest School within an existing organisation, then you will first need to persuade the decision-makers within that organisation that it is a good idea. These could be nursery owners, school governors or senior leadership teams, etc. A sound business case should be produced. If you do not feel able to do this yourself, you will need the support of someone else in the organisation who can help you to develop and present your case.

A business case should provide a decision-maker with sufficient information for them to appraise the proposal and make a decision. Only you will know how much information is necessary in your particular context.

Your organisation may have a standard format for the presentation of proposals or businesses cases. If not, here is a template with the sort of things you could include. You may want to add more detail using the additional elements found in Part B.

Business Case (Template)

To be used to clearly communicate a proposal to:

1. Line manager

2. Senior decision- maker

The level of detail provided should be proportional to the complexity of the proposal and sufficient to allow appraisal. **Please see part B to consider what else to include in more complex proposals.**

The completed proposal should be passed through the appropriate person (line manager?).

Use clear simple bullet points for each heading.

....

Part A (Basic information)

Your Name:

Date:

NAME OF PROJECT

THE IDEA / PURPOSE

- Outline the problem that this Forest School initiative will address or the opportunity that it will create.

BACKGROUND

- Describe the current situation and why this exists.

PROJECT OUTLINE

- What is needed to complete the project?

CONSTRAINTS

- What could prevent the success of the project?

BENEFITS

- The benefits that this project will bring to the organisation.

Part B (Further detail)

OTHER OPTIONS: Describing alternative options will help decision makers better understand the context and give them confidence that your idea has been well thought through. What are the pros and cons of each option?

FIT: Decision makers want to see how new ideas fit with the organisation's strategy and existing plans. Being able to explain your project's objectives in terms of what else is happening in the organisation will greatly support your case.

WIDER IMPACT: Describe how this project will affect the organisation. Think about other team members and projects that are running. What internal processes or equipment may be affected? This is your internal stakeholder analysis.

ASSUMPTIONS: State if you are making any assumptions about things that could affect the project. For instance, about where the money or time is coming from! Also, is there anything else that must happen first to make your project possible?

TIMELINE: Describe the timeline and time scales for particular stages of the project. This will reflect your key milestones.

BUDGET: Show that you have thought through the financial implications by putting together a budget with the level of detail that is needed. A cash flow forecast (see **chapter 7**) will be particularly important for revenue-generating initiatives.

KNOWN RISKS: What could happen to knock your project off course? Delays? Rising costs? Partners pulling out? What can you do to mitigate these risks?

OPPORTUNITIES AND THREATS: What external forces in the wider world could affect your project? Show the results of your PESTLE analysis (see the following section on business planning). Will you be able to embrace the opportunities and deal with threats?

The dreaded business plan (showing that your Forest School business idea can and will work)

If you want to establish a new Forest School as a separate business, you will almost certainly need to produce a full business plan in order to convince others to support you. Even if you don't need to show it to anyone else, it is a very good idea to produce one anyway.

The business plan is a working document, providing a snapshot of where your business is currently and where you intend it to go. **The important thing to remember is that it is a tool to help you structure your thinking and express this to others**. It's also a point of reference to assess whether your business is performing as expected.

The business plan should reflect your personal circumstances, including your plans to navigate the specifics of these circumstances so that your business can succeed. It communicates your business planning, and so demonstrates to others (and yourself) that you have actually done this planning properly.

A business plan is typically created prior to incorporation and the start of trading. It helps define what the business is and describes your business structure. Your business plan will explore the objectives and strategies that you will follow to achieve your goal. It will explain your own skills, personal drives and aspirations, and the history of how you have arrived at this point – what has driven you here may seem irrelevant at first, yet it serves as a reminder of why you got into Forest School in the first place. Your business plan will describe your market and products, and detail your approach to marketing, financial forecasts, key milestones, pricing, tipping points, and mitigating milestones. It will consider your management structure, policies, and procedures.

> **Mitigating milestones**
>
> These are points in the life of your business where risks are offset by the process of running a business (e.g. reaching a breakeven point in the number of children attending a session). There is more about mitigating milestones in the strategic management section of **Chapter 7**.
>
> **Tipping points**
>
> These are points that you set to warn you that something in your delivery needs to change (e.g. dropping below an operational threshold in the amount of working capital).

Countless templates and examples of business plans exist on the internet. A lot of excellent advice about producing a business plan is also available. We recommend that you spend some time reading around this topic, and that you find some examples that are relevant to your particular circumstances.

Business planning

Business planning skills and knowledge can be developed through experience and training. There are many short courses available online (many of which are free) to help people develop their idea and turn it into a successful business initiative. We recommend that you look into taking one or more of these courses if this is your first time setting up a business or new enterprise. The same skills and knowledge are needed regardless of whether you are growing a Forest School as a new initiative in an existing organisation or as a new venture. If you are not the person setting up the business or project, then you must ensure that whoever is filling the role is fully committed to the enterprise and its goals and needs.

A great starting point for your business planning would be to consider the following questions. Obviously, they are context dependent. **Write down your answers.** Later parts of this book may help if you don't have an immediate answer to some of the questions. If you have completed the reflective exercises in previous chapters, you will already have done some thinking around many of these questions.

- Why am I setting up a Forest School enterprise?
- Do I have the right skills to run this Forest School enterprise? If not, how can I gain those skills?
- What kind of business do I want?
- Who is my ideal customer?
- What specific products or services will my Forest School provide?
- Am I prepared to invest the time and money needed to get my Forest School started?
- Where will my Forest School be located?
- How many employees will I need?
- What types of suppliers do I need?
- How much money do I need to get started?
- Will I need to get a loan?
- How soon will my Forest School services be available?

- How long will it take before I start making a profit?
- What differentiates my Forest School business idea and the products or services I will provide from others in the market?
- Who is my competition?
- How will I price my services compared to my competition?
- How will I set up the legal structure of my business?
- What taxes do I need to pay?
- What kind of insurance do I need?
- How will I manage my business?
- How will I advertise my services?

Business planning is a bit of an art form. The success or failure of your business will come down to how well you manage to answer the questions above and integrate them to inform a good plan. You may not yet be in a position to answer all of these questions in full. This is perfectly normal at this stage, so **_don't panic_**. To help you to break down this process into smaller, more easily achievable tasks, we now present the 'Analysing, Choosing, Implementing' (ACI) framework.

The ACI framework

The ACI framework helps you to consider your business plan from different perspectives. It helps you to explore topics in bite-sized chunks, and it will aid you in uncovering links between different aspects of your business. These are not separate steps that need to be followed sequentially. Each perspective should be considered in the round, to ensure that all your thinking supports the plan and also that the plan supports your business goal. The three perspectives can be outlined thus:

Analysing – Researching and interpreting information about your environment. Look at the internal (what we have and what we can do with it) and external (the world with which the business must engage). What information you will need to find is affected by your choices and by how you intend to run the business (implementation).

Choosing – Exploring your options and deciding what is best for you. This relates more to the high-level decisions that are difficult to change later down the road. Essentially, this is the direction of your business and how you are going to get there (your strategy). What you choose to do will depend on the results of your analysis and your ability to put your plans into action.

Implementing – How you will put your choices into action. This is how you will manage your business. The processes that you create will depend on your strategy, and on your ability to create competitive advantage in the market with the resources and capabilities available to you.

Analysing

Your 'internal' environment

You need to take stock of **your strengths and weaknesses** with reference to what you hope your business plan will achieve. These can be considered in terms of how well your resources and capabilities match your needs. Your *resources* are things you have that make it possible for you to do things. The things that you are able to do are your (or your organisation's) *capabilities*.

To help you work through this you could start by making a list of all your resources. To help you structure this exercise, you could group your resources into:

- **Tangible resources** – your financial and physical resources (land, equipment, etc.)
- **Intangible resources** – such as your reputation and your organisation's culture
- **Human resources** – including skills and know-how, capacity for communication and collaboration, and motivation.

What capabilities do these resources confer?

Think about how your resources come together to create your capabilities. Write this down as a series of statements. These could be things like:

- My existing relationship with the landowner next door to my school, combined with my working capital, means that I will be able to secure somewhere to run my Forest School.
- My working capital will allow me to employ a qualified Forest School leader.
- My reputation, communication skills, and knowledge mean I will be able to attract clients in the local market.
- My working capital and knowledge of this sector will allow me to procure the equipment that I need.
- My prior experience in middle management gives me the knowledge and skills to manage the business.
- My working capital gives me the ability to not starve before my business starts to make a profit.

This exercise should help to highlight any critical assumptions you may be making.

- **Do you have any key capabilities missing or weaker than they need to be?** You will need to refer to the 'implementing' part of the framework to help you work this out. *What are they?*
- **What would you need to do to acquire and develop the resources and capabilities that you need?** Is there scope to outsource activities that would be better performed by other people or organisations? *Make a note of these actions.*
- What interim steps might you take whilst you are building up your resources and capabilities? Remember to refer to the 'choosing' part of the framework. *Make a note of these options.*

Use the above analyses to describe your situation in terms of your strengths and weaknesses. This is an important section in your business plan.

Your competitive environment

Having an understanding of your competitive environment will highlight **opportunities** and **threats** that exist for your new enterprise. To run a successful Forest School business, you will need to have a good understanding of the **key success factors** (KSFs) for the outdoor learning industry, specifically the nature play sector and Forest School in particular. These KSFs come down to understanding what the customer wants and how you will survive competition in the industry.

Words like *competition* and *industry* may be off-putting to you, but it is important that, despite the inclusive, caring, and non-judgemental ethos of Forest School and our community, you understand that your enterprise must be able to stand on its own two feet and survive in the face of industry rivalry.

Although the FSA only recognises provision operating in line with all six Forest School principles and run by qualified Forest School leaders, there is little to prevent unqualified people from offering services that they call Forest School. The term has been used to describe all sorts of activities that do not meet the basic principles laid out by the Forest School community. You may be in direct competition with people who say that they are offering Forest School when they are not.

Clients have considerable bargaining power thanks to the lack of public understanding about quality Forest School, its benefits and what it looks like. Clients also often wish to spread limited budgets for outdoor learning as widely as possible so as to benefit more participants. Trained Forest School leaders, who understand what Forest School is, find that they are often asked to provide services that are not Forest School, such as short-term programmes that fit neatly into half term blocks. Despite not following all the principles and being a different form of nature play with their own values and outcomes, you are in competition with these other sources, as clients will have to make a choice between you.

Even where a customer is sure that they want quality Forest School, the barriers to entry for Forest School provision are relatively low, and so you may find yourself in direct competition with other qualified Forest School leaders who would like that same job or to work with that same client. This has the effect of keeping wages fairly low in our industry.

You do need to understand who your potential customers and clients are and what they want in an outdoor learning scenario. You should allow for the possibility that a potential client may not initially know exactly what they are looking for. You may have the exciting opportunity to introduce them to the enhanced benefits of quality Forest School compared to other forms of outdoors learning. Regardless of the outcome, going through this process should ensure a better fit between you and your client.

A good way to deal with this situation is to treat potential clients as partners working towards a shared goal. This is especially true if you are already offering services to a client that doesn't yet meet the criteria for Forest School. Examples include schools, landowners, community groups, NGOs, and local authorities.

The FSA is orientated towards supporting quality Forest School services in this industry. If you choose to offer quality Forest School provision then you will be able to differentiate yourself from others in the market on the basis of quality, and charge accordingly. The FSA Recognised Forest School Provider Scheme is one way to demonstrate this. As of 2021, the FSA is also developing a portable 'ticket' that Forest School leaders may take from one employment to another to demonstrate their competence.

As part of your analysis, you will need to do some market research to identify your competitors. This will also give you a good indication of the market value for your services, which will help you to decide on your entry price point. In addition, you should remain aware of other Political, Economic, Sociological, Technological, Legal, and Environmental (PESTLE) factors that may present opportunities or threats for your enterprise – for instance, changes to government tax policy or labour laws, interest rates (cost of borrowing), cultural barriers, technological change, environmental laws, or health and safety laws. It is well worth reading about how to do PESTLE analysis.

Assessing stakeholder expectations

It is very important to have a clear understanding of the interests of anyone who can directly affect your Forest School initiative or is otherwise affected by it. These people are called primary stakeholders. Secondary stakeholders are people who may indirectly affect or be affected by your initiative. Tertiary stakeholders have an interest in the initiative but cannot influence it and are not affected by or benefiting from it.

Stakeholders may be internal or external to your Forest School initiative. A stakeholder analysis involves actively considering the specifics of stakeholder interests and consulting with them to find out further details if necessary. It is well worth doing this in a structured way and filling out a table to record your thoughts and findings.

We offer you an example to help you better understand this. There are too many possible scenarios for us to cover them all, but this one should give you some structure and ideas to get you started.

> **The Stakeholder Analysis Table** overleaf concerns a hypothetical new Forest School initiative at a Church of England primary school. A teaching assistant has been asked to produce a proposal for how Forest School sessions may initially be offered to year 1 pupils who have recently transitioned from reception year. This is expected to happen in a nearby wooded area. The school has suggested that they are willing to fund and support Forest School training to Level 3, and the teaching assistant has indicated willingness to study to become a Level 3 leader and take responsibility for establishing quality Forest School provision for the school.

Stakeholder Analysis table – for establishment of a Forest School setting (strategic perspective)

Stakeholder	Internal/ External	Nature of interest	Degree of influence	Primary/ Secondary
Teaching assistant	Internal	Development of a Forest School (FS) programme within the school	Very high	Primary
Head teacher	Internal	Development of quality education offer at the school	Very high	Primary
School governors	Internal	Ensure compliance with legal requirements, congruence with community needs, and appropriate resourcing	Very high	Primary
Diocese	Internal	Maintenance of stated Christian values of the school	Very high	Primary
Parents and guardians of pupils	Internal	Perceived benefits to children. Degree of tolerance to risk, additional cleaning of clothes, and diversion from classroom-based learning	High	Primary
Other school staff	Internal	Degree of acceptance of systemic changes, organisation culture, direct impact on practice	High	Primary
Volunteers FS assistants	Internal	Willingness to support the initiative and undergo appropriate training	Moderate/high	Primary
Pupils at school	Internal	Degree of willingness to engage with nature and leave the classroom	Moderate	Primary
Ofsted	External	Inspection and regulation of educational institutions including state schools, academies, and childcare facilities; inspection of other services for children and young people	Very high	Primary
Landowner	External	Maintenance	High	Primary
Forest School Trainer	External	Commercial, professional delivery of services; satisfied customers; promotion and development of quality Forest School	High	Primary
Funders	External	Compliance with funding criteria	Moderate/high	Primary
Forest School Association	External	National professional standards; provision of marketing and membership services	Moderate	Primary
Site neighbours	External	Degree of understanding and willingness to tolerate the consequences of your FS programmes	Moderate	Primary
Local authority	External	Statutory responsibility for provision of services and guidance	Moderate	Primary
Families of future pupils	External	Choosing the best school and feeder school for their children	Very low	Secondary
Wider community	External	Appreciation of the importance of nature connection on community, health, and well-being	Very low	Tertiary

Reflective Exercise 9 – Stakeholder analysis

The type of stakeholder, their interest, and their ability to influence or be influenced by your initiative, will really depend on your specific context. Imagine if your Forest School setting was:

- A Forest School Kindergarten
- An SEN group in a secondary school
- An adult group at a university.

Who are your stakeholders? Are they inside your organisation (internal) or outside (external)? What is their interest in what you are hoping to do? How much influence do they have? At what level can they affect your plans? (Primary – directly; secondary – indirectly; or tertiary – remotely influence.)

Choosing

Identifying strategic options

You have some fundamental choices to make about what you want your enterprise to achieve (your goal) and how you intend to achieve it (your strategy). This book advocates for you choosing to offer quality Forest School. If you decide to do this, your choices will be narrowed down to strategies that offer something *different,* and what you offer is unlikely to be the cheapest on the market. However, you will still need to decide how focused your offer is. For instance, will you be offering quality Forest School to a wide range of client groups (perhaps all year groups at primary school level), or will you be offering a much more focused service (such as Early Years children with particular needs)? In addition, you will need to think about the following options:

1. **Will you be competing with others who are offering the same services in the same market?** In this case you will need to think carefully about how you can create competitive advantage. Maybe you can do it cheaper? Perhaps you have great marketing and promotion opportunities. Could you simply buy out a rival's existing business? Are your purposes and values more closely aligned with potential clients? Could you offer additional levels of support?

2. **Will you be offering your services to new markets?** Perhaps there is no quality Forest School provision in your geographical area. Is anyone else offering quality Forest School to particular groups, such as adults, or offering entirely woodland-based kindergarten?

3. **Will you be offering quality Forest School services to your existing clients**? In this case you will have the opportunity to sell the benefits of quality Forest School to existing clients, and even work closely with them to ensure a good fit to their needs.

You will need to consider the business structure that will best help you in implementing your strategy.

Business structure

For new organisations you will need to consider your business structure and how you will be constituted.

There are several different ways to structure your business. You must decide which fits best with your business model. Each has a unique set of rules, responsibilities, advantages, and disadvantages. In the UK there are three main types of business structure suitable for Forest School:

- **Sole Trader**
- **Partnership**
- **Limited Company**

Sole trader

This is sometimes referred to as 'self-employed'. It is the easiest business structure to set up and is often used as a start-up structure. As a sole trader you pay income tax on your profits, and you must be registered with HMRC and fill out tax returns from the outset regardless of whether you meet the income tax threshold or earn a single penny. At the time of writing, you will begin paying tax at 20% when profits exceed £12,500 a year. If you are lucky enough to run at a profit of over £50,000 then you will pay 40% tax; and in the extremely unlikely event your profit exceeds £150,000 a year, you will pay 45% tax. You will also need to make National Insurance contributions. You must be VAT compliant and register for VAT if your turnover goes above the VAT threshold (£85k/year). You can find out more about VAT registration at:
https://www.gov.uk/vat-registration/when-to-register **[9]**.

As a sole trader you can employ other people; you are responsible for informing HMRC and will need to operate a PAYE scheme to collect income tax and National Insurance contributions.
https://www.gov.uk/set-up-sole-trader **[10]**.

Advantages

- Low set-up costs

- Relatively simple to set up and register

- You have sole control of the business and delivery

- Your business finances and your own finances are effectively one and the same, making it much easier to draw out money than in a limited company or partnership. (You must still keep records of the money you remove from the business in case of spot checks or other issues.)

- Privacy: as sole trader you need not file your annual accounts at Companies House or file an annual corporation tax return.

Disadvantages

- Any collections of deficits or debts that you incur are not restricted to your business holdings. This includes compensation claims and legal costs. It is therefore of vital importance that you ensure your paperwork, procedures, and insurances are all kept up to date and fit for purpose. Any debt recovery can come from ***your personal assets, including assets which are jointly owned with another person***
- You are solely responsible for the business side of things as well as the delivery. This can mean that you are putting in more work than you can handle. Once you get some working capital, you may wish to look at getting administrative support. This will free up more of your time for prepping and delivering (making money), but it is a balance: administrative support is not free, so you have to be certain that it works for you
- As you earn more money, the sole trader model becomes less advantageous
- It can be tricky to separate expenses for the business from personal expenditure (e.g. cost of phone calls on a mobile shared between work and personal use).

Partnership

A partnership may be formed by two or more individuals who share the running of a business. The business therefore has two or more owners. Partnerships are classed as unincorporated (i.e. not a company) and all partners are deemed to be self-employed.

Like the sole trader, partners share responsibility for the business (good and bad); each partner receives the benefits of the business in line with an agreed split or ratio (e.g. 70:30, 50:50, 60:40, etc). Each partner is also responsible for losses or debts in line with this pre-agreed ratio. An important point to remember when entering into a partnership is that you are responsible for debts and liabilities incurred by your partner, and even for their negligence or misconduct; *their* business liabilities may be recovered from *your* assets (including those owned jointly with another person such as a spouse).

Both partners pay income tax on the shared profits, and follow similar rules to sole traders for VAT, National Insurance and PAYE contributions. Agreements are made about how the partnership will function; these are called **deeds of partnership**.

Advantages

- Partners can share responsibility for decisions and work

- Partners share financial responsibility

- Agreements are relatively easy to alter if circumstances change

- Setting up and registering is relatively easy in comparison to limited companies and limited liability partnerships

- The system is flexible so work can be directed to the partner with the skills necessary to undertake it

- Privacy: As a partnership you need not file your annual accounts at Companies House or file an annual corporation tax return.

Disadvantages

- Sharing responsibility for decisions and work can be difficult if partners do not agree

- Any collection deficits or debts that your partnership incurs are **not restricted to your business holdings**. This includes compensation claims and legal costs. It is therefore imperative that you ensure your paperwork, procedures, and insurances remain up to date, are fit for purpose, and are agreed and followed by all partners

- As a partner you are also responsible for your partner's debts, liabilities, negligence, and misconduct. This can make breakdowns in the business extremely risky (and expensive) if things go wrong

- Partnerships are reliant on good working relationships and trust. If this is lost or broken the business is likely to fail. It is critically important that you have an agreement in writing about how this situation is to be handled, including the division of profits and equipment, before you begin trading.

Limited company

This business is usually identified by the suffix *Ltd*. A limited company is an incorporated entity, which means it is formed and registered as a company at Companies House. Effectively, this process makes you and the business legally separate entities. The *company* is responsible for everything the company does, not you personally. The profits that the company creates are retained within the company after paying corporation tax, and may then be passed on to shareholders as dividends. Shareholders receiving dividends may be taxed on them if the payments exceed their personal allowance (https://www.gov.uk/tax-on-dividends **[11]**). This has the major benefit of protecting your personal assets, at the cost of a potentially higher tax rate. As a limited company you do not pay income tax on your profits or surplus. Instead you pay corporation tax. Limited companies are liable to pay National Insurance Contributions (NICs) for any employee payments above the NI threshold for employees and directors. Directors are classed as employees with their NICs worked out from their annual salary. NICs are not usually paid on any dividends a director receives.

Limited companies **must** file their annual accounts at Companies House and their corporate tax returns with HMRC. In order to be formed or incorporated, a company must register with Companies House and complete their *memorandum* and *articles of association*. These documents detail why a company has been created, how it is managed, and by whom. It outlines the company's responsibilities and states what services members or directors can be paid for. The Memorandum of Association and Articles of Association are submitted to Companies House before company registration.

It is critical to get these documents right, and although it is quite possible to set up a company by yourself for a small fee, it is advisable to get proper business and financial advice from an accountant familiar with incorporation. This will ensure you do not fall into numerous paperwork pitfalls during the process.

Limited Companies follow one of the following two models:

- **Company limited by shares** – the shareholders' responsibility for the company's liabilities is limited by the value of the shares. This means the company has share capital, and that shares can be either kept or given or sold to others in order to raise capital. You must ensure that you retain the majority stake or risk losing control of the company. Shareholders should be considered as primary stakeholders

- **Private company limited by guarantee** – does not normally have share capital or shareholders; instead it is incorporated with *members*. Members are people who act as guarantors; they have ultimate control over the company and are liable to pay a fixed fee if the company fails to meet its obligations. Members tend not to exert direct influence on a company but they do empower the directors to do so. Members should always be considered as primary stakeholders.

Community interest companies (CICs), co-operatives, not-for-profits and social enterprises

'**CICs** are limited companies which operate to provide a benefit to the community they serve. They are not strictly 'not for profit' and CICs can, and do, deliver returns to investors. However, the purpose of CIC is primarily one of community benefit rather than private profit.' [1].

'A **co-op** is a business or organisation that's owned and controlled by its members, to meet their shared needs. The members can be its customers, employees, residents or suppliers, who have a say in how the co-op is run.' [2]. Co-operatives are often created to solve a problem, to protect a community space, or to give better job security to their members. They span all aspects of business but are somewhat complicated to create. You can find out more about co-operatives and how they work at: https://www.uk.coop/support-your-co-op [12].

Not-for-profit companies are, unsurprisingly, organisations that do not earn profits for their owners. They often provide services to cover their costs, and any surplus is either reinvested in the company to further their aims (as outlined in their memorandum) or else used to further other social causes.

Social enterprises are not for profit, but are run a little differently. Unlike other not-for-profits, social enterprises sell products or services in a similar way to normal profit-making companies, to create profits which they can then use to benefit society (as well as covering their costs). The distinction is subtle yet important. For more information on social enterprises, visit: https://www.gov.uk/set-up-a-social-enterprise [13].

Evaluating and selecting options

To help you work through the various decisions that you need to make about your market, business structure, products and services etc, and ultimately select the most appropriate for you, we suggest using the 'suitable, feasible and appropriate' model. These are three core questions to ask yourself with regard to each option. Is it:

- **Suitable** – would this choice allow me to achieve my business goal?
- **Feasible** – can this be done with the resources and capabilities at my disposal?
- **Appropriate** – is this compatible with the interests of all key stakeholders?

Implementing

Your business planning must take into account how you intend to run your business to achieve your business goals. Are you sure that you know exactly how your business choices will affect how you deliver the plan? Is there a good fit between your business choices and your resources and capabilities? Do you understand what impact your business choices will have on the management processes and systems that you will need in order to manage the business?

Remember, this isn't a step-by-step process. Analysing, choosing, and implementing perspectives are simply different ways of looking at the same thing.

Ultimately, you must be able to use your resources and capabilities to create competitive advantage. Your business plan will follow your core strategy. This is true regardless of the business structure you have chosen. Business management or implementation is a huge topic in its own right. We cannot hope to cover the topic in great depth within this book but we do think it deserves its own chapter, and so in **Chapter 7** we will explore some of the most important aspects of business management.

References

[1] Department of Business, Energy and Industrial strategy, *"Information and guidance notes."* Office of the Regulator of Community Interest Companies, London, 2016.

[2] Co-operatives UK Limited, *"What is a co-op?"* [Online]. Available: https://www.uk.coop/understanding-co-ops/what-co-op [Accessed 15 March 2021].

Chapter 7 – Forest School Business Management

Nic Harding and Gareth Davies

In the previous chapter, we explored the process of planning our Forest School business or project. In this next chapter, we will begin to look at business management. You may be wondering: what is business management? Business management is a continual process of working out how your business will work or is working – from planning when you get paid, to how you get the apples and cinnamon for your fireside snack together.

Terminology

Before we begin, we need to look at some of the terms we use. Words are important, and the words we use in this chapter have specific business meanings that can sometimes be unpalatable for those of us who have our roots in the caring and sharing education and environmental community.

Survival – Like it or not, in order for you to change the world for the better your enterprise must survive. All your best intentions and social responsibility will come to naught if you starve in the process.

Productivity – Whilst this is not a word often used in Forest School delivery as it carries connotations of judgement, in business productivity refers to the efficiency and effectiveness of our efforts.

Assets – These are useful or valuable items of property that are owned by a person or company and are available to meet any debts or commitments.

Capital– The word *capital* has a number of different meanings and uses. These include:

- The amount of money your organisation has to start or invest in a business. This is often referred to as *investment capital.*
- The money that you have to run the day-to-day operations of your business is often referred to as *working capital* and is linked heavily to your cash flow.
- *Capital assets* (or *fixed assets*) are assets that are used long term rather than sold by a business e.g. land, buildings or equipment. Your woodland, if you own it yourself, is a capital asset, and so is your composting loo.

Quality Control – As Forest School leaders we strive to be non-judgemental. Often, any mention of quality can irritate and feel like it goes against the ethos. However, in business terms your *quality control* is really a form of reflection on your observations; it is feedback and evidence about your business. How are you performing? Can you perform better? Are you competing well within the market? Do you need to improve your communication or marketing? Is your delivery effective? Do you need more training? Is your business healthy or is your cash flow crippling your ability to cover your costs?

Market – This is the competitive environment in which our clients are looking to purchase our services. As such we are subject to market forces, politics and competition. To survive in the marketplace, we must understand the market's needs and our unique selling points in order to gain a competitive advantage.

Business management

There are many different aspects to business management and you can study for years to get to grips with them all. Indeed, in large companies, each aspect is a specialist field with a team of highly skilled individuals devoted to it. As decision-makers wanting to develop Forest School, we need to look at some of the aspects of business management to ensure that the projects run smoothly and in line with our organisation's needs. As Forest School leaders, we need to consider at least a few branches of business management in order to make the most of our training and skills and ensure the survival of our business on a day-to-day basis.

There are six core disciplines of business management relevant to leading or controlling a Forest School. These are:

1. Operations management
2. Financial management
3. Human resources management (HRM)
4. Knowledge management
5. Marketing management
6. Strategic management.

Operations management

This part of your business management is to ensure that all parts of the business work effectively together and are efficient. Operations management therefore looks at:

- Capacity planning
- Logistics
- Deadlines
- Productivity analysis and development
- Quality assurance.

Figure 1 overleaf shows a simple transformation model. These are used to illustrate and simplify the cycle of operations management. The transformation of resources (inputs) to products or services (outputs) requires different aspects of business management at different times, and the model demonstrates which of those aspects are needed at which point in the cycle. The rest of this chapter will look more closely at each of the different aspects of management.

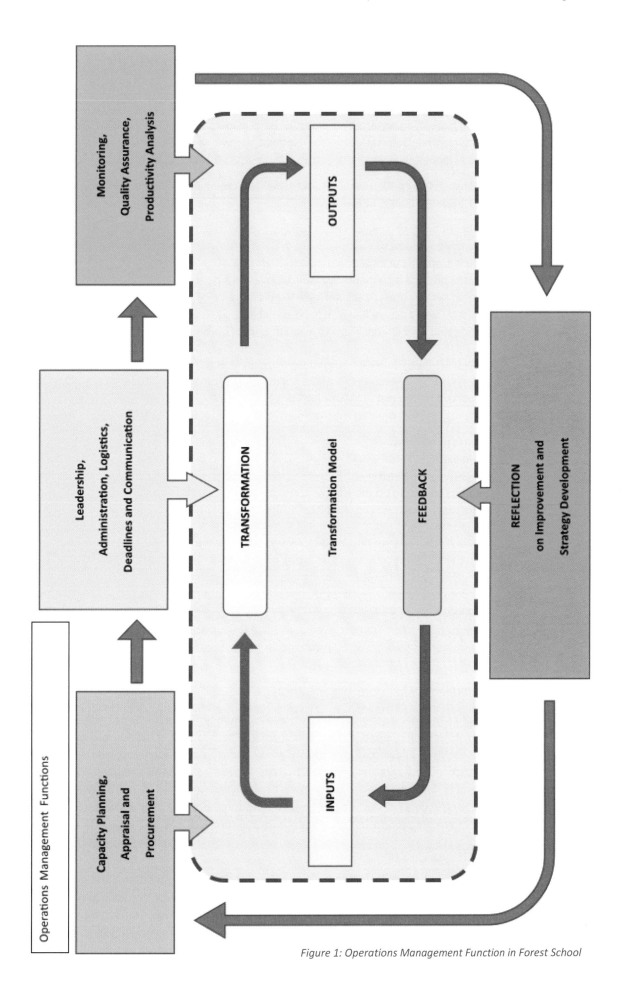

Figure 1: Operations Management Function in Forest School

Capacity planning

Starting a business can be an overwhelming experience. Many businesses fail due to inadequate planning or unforeseen circumstances, and Forest School businesses are no exception. Don't be too disheartened though, as Forest School leaders do have an advantage over many business owners. We are skilled in breaking down activities into smaller, more achievable tasks for our participants; we can assess risk and benefit in a heartbeat; and we reflect without judgement. These skills will prove useful in capacity planning.

Capacity (in a business sense) refers to the resources and capabilities you have available that enable you to deliver a piece of work. These resources may include:

- **Time** – the number of hours you can offer to a project
- **Equipment –** the tools available to you
- **Knowledge –** the information or experience available to you
- **Raw materials –** the physical ingredients available to invest in a piece of work
- **Money** – the amount of working capital you have to invest in a piece of work
- **Staff** – the people, skills and capabilities you have available
- **Energy** – managing your own energy levels to avoid the risk of burnout.

Capacity planning is a way of finding a balance between your resources and the needs of your business. As a Forest School leader, you will need to keep several plates spinning to ensure your business thrives. Capacity planning is therefore important in all aspects of your business management, but it is especially important in the day-to-day operations. Effectively, capacity management is a form of reflection based on five questions:

- Do I need to do this piece of work?
- What do I need in place to do the work?
- Do I have the capacity to do the work?
- When do I need the capacity to do the work?
- If I don't have the capacity, where can I find it?

As Forest School leaders, much of what we do sits squarely on our own shoulders; our time and energy can often be the limiting factor when trying new things or taking on new work. For example, when filling a new Forest School programme, if we deal with every booking and enquiry personally whilst we are also trying to plan, deliver and review our current programme of sessions, it can be busy. As our business grows it can become too much to manage. Capacity is finite, but it is often possible to shift a capacity issue by exploring other resources you have to hand. For example, we could solve the capacity issue in taking bookings by expanding our human resources or staffing, or by providing an online booking system, or even by hiring a virtual assistant to help.

Resources and knowledge outside your organisation

There is a reason we describe the Forest School community as a community. Despite many of us being rivals within a fairly small marketplace, there exists a culture of sharing. The first port of call for information on setting up a Forest School after you have read this book might be the Forest School Association website to locate Recognised Forest School Providers and Endorsed Trainers, in order to get some more information on running quality provision or to find out if there is an FSA Local Group in your area that you could join. Getting to know other Forest School leaders in your area will help you to forge positive relationships and offer a support network, as well as enabling you to identify what quality provision also exists.

Logistics and deadlines

Logistics is the organisation of all the aspects or details of delivering a complex operation. The logistics of delivering a Forest School can be a challenge. Making sure that you have popcorn for your group's mid-morning snack, water for washing hands, shelter in case it rains, rope for swings, knives, fire-lighting materials, and so on – the logistics can test even the most organised brain. Your business is also subject to logistical issues. Ensuring you have purchased the right equipment in time for it to be delivered, employed the staff for the right date and time, and invoiced your clients in good time – these are all really important aspects of management.

Within operations management, it is critical to create deadlines and try to stick to them. Once you know what you need to do to create a Forest School, you can begin to put things in order. There is a simple way to explore this. It is often a good idea to work backwards through a process from your point of delivery. Look at the big things first; they will often take more time. With each step focus on two questions:

- What do I need in place to get to this point?
- When do I need to get it into place?

Your Forest School training will inform a lot of your choices and help you to create a lot of your policies and principles, risk assessments, and an approach for your delivery.

Communication

Another part of your logistics toolkit is communication. Making sure that the right message gets to the right people at the right time is amazingly time-consuming and complex. Building communication into your business management processes will ensure you don't need to waste time and energy chasing errors or mistakes later. Of course, communication is always a two-way street, and you will need some information to ensure your sessions run smoothly. For example, knowing ahead of time that a child is allergic to nuts can help you ensure everything is ready for that child to safely attend. This is the delivery aspect of your session. Knowing when you need to send the request or collect the information as part of your booking system to get the best response rate is the operational aspect of the process, which is tied to both your capacity and logistics management.

Quality assurance, quality control, and productivity analysis and development

Quality assurance (QA) is an important management process which helps you to have confidence in the quality of your product. It looks for potential issues arising from your business processes in order to avoid problems or reduction in quality. This also means the systems attached to your business are more likely to be sustainable.

The QA approach can be used to develop and implement inspection or evaluation activities that help communicate information about potential risks or benefits of your product internally (to shareholders, stakeholders, trustees or staff). It may also provide evaluation and evidence to inform customers or stakeholders about the benefits of using your services, or reassure government agencies, regulators, or certifiers that your service meets the relevant quality requirements. You may find external processes that can help too; the Recognised Forest School Provider Scheme is a great way to check whether you meet the minimum industry benchmarks, for example, and also allows you to communicate this to your customers and clients. QA provides the procedures for the final parts of the operational management process, *productivity analysis* and *strategy development*.

Quality control is a smaller part of the QA process, focused on the product alone. It is often used to identify isolated problems and inform delivery processes, and is performed reflectively after the final product or service is ready or delivered. As such it tends to be a more reactive process, and directly linked to things like session planning.

QA and QC look at the quality of our products on multiple levels. *Productivity analysis and development* uses the QA process to evaluate the *effectiveness* of our delivery. It can help us to look for effective ways to reduce costs or remove barriers, delays or interruptions. To effectively look at productivity you will need to look at when and why things haven't gone smoothly. Look for times when you ran out of resources, or your system of delivery was put under strain, or your service was interrupted. You may even consider looking at times when your workforce was feeling particularly stressed. Once you identify a problem area, try to find a workaround through capacity planning. Anything that can reduce waste (resources, time, or energy expended) can improve profits and enjoyment *and* reduce costs. This means reaching goals and maintaining a sustainable business is easier.

Financial management

Leaders arrive at Forest School from all walks of life. Some were previously in education, child care, conservation or outdoor activities, but all have a love for the outdoors. They are great at delivery but are not always competent in running businesses. They find it difficult and become unhappy, or else avoid the business management aspects, and so the business fails. As leaders we reflect on areas that need improvement in our delivery, and the same should be done in matters of business. Financial management is quite a complex thing to learn and we strongly suggest that you get some specific training in it, if you don't have previous experience.

Financial management is the strategic directing and controlling of the finances of a business, including budgeting, planning and accounting; this part of your management looks at the flow of money or finances within your business. It will link to other aspects of management and often inform what is feasible (or within your means). It may include:

- Financial planning
- Covering overheads (such as insurance, subscriptions or memberships)
- Making everyday purchases (operating expenses)
- Cash flow
- Price point.

Thankfully there are a number of downloadable apps that can take some of the pain out of the process. These often come with a monthly subscription so you will need to weigh up their value to you (this would be part of your capacity management – time versus subscription fee).

Record keeping

One of the most critical parts of financial management is record keeping or bookkeeping. This will include:

- Profit and Loss – a way to explore the amount you make after deducting expenditure and taxes from revenue and income
- Bank reconciliation – a way to check your accounts against the money in the bank
- Balance sheets – a summary of your financial position, including assets and liabilities
- Accounts ledgers – a way to keep track of financial movements in different accounts, e.g. cash account, online bookings account
- Annual statement – usually used for tax
- Sales – a way of measuring your income/revenue and tracking client payments
- Taxation and National Insurance Contributions (NICs)
- Budgeted cash flow.

Financial planning

It is difficult to begin planning your finances until you know how your business will work. Having completed the sections above (and the exercises in previous chapters), you should now have some ideas with which to start pulling together a plan. Your financial plan is a critical part of the business plan and you should consider including:

- How much your services are going to cost you to deliver
- Whether you can deliver alone or whether you will need help, and how much that help will cost
- A survival budget – how much you need to earn to make it viable
- Capital costs and operating costs
- How much you are going to charge
- A financial forecast – especially useful when tied to mitigating milestones
- A cash flow forecast looking at the way the money moves in and out of the company

- Hidden costs (such as environmental management and CPD).

How much do your services cost to deliver?

There is some great advice online for working out how much your business costs to deliver, and you will need to do some estimation and research here. To arrive at your base costs, you will need to work out:

- Your survival budget
- Your capital costs
- Your operational costs
- Your cash flow and cash flow strategy.

What is a survival budget?

A survival budget is quite simply how much you need to earn to live in the way you want. This figure is unique to everyone, and several websites are available to help you calculate your survival budget. The Prince's Trust offers advice on budgets (search for *survival budgets*), as does the Welsh Government.
https://www.princes-trust.org.uk/ **[14]**
https://businesswales.gov.wales/starting-up/finance/personal-survival-budget **[15]**

It is very tempting to just pull a figure out of the air, but this may restrict your business's growth and your aspirations, or worse, give you false hope. It is often easier to work out aspects of your survival budget every month by looking at your current bills. You can easily multiply these values by 12 to get an annual estimation.

It is worth remembering that your survival costs may change if you begin running a business – if you work from home more often you are likely to spend more on utilities but you may spend less on travel, for example.

Capital costs / expenditure

Capital costs are often one-off or irregular costs needed to set up a business or project, or to buy equipment that is used for longer than the financial year in which it was purchased. This may mean that the item is treated as an asset. Typical capital expenditure for a Forest School might include:

- The cost of buying (not renting) premises/site
- Purchasing a vehicle
- Initial equipment cost
- Incorporation cost or registration costs
- Land use agreement legal costs
- Cost of initial Forest School Level 3 training
- Website creation
- Site creation and preparation.

You can often claim allowances on your capital expenditure, but it is too big a topic for us to go into here. You may also need to calculate depreciation for tax purposes. However, https://www.gov.uk/capital-allowances **[16]** contains a lot of information about capital allowances and expenditure.

Operating expenses, overheads, and direct and indirect costs

Operating expenses are regular or semi-regular costs that are paid to keep your business running (in fact they are often referred to as running costs). They may be:

- **Variable** – a variable cost is usually linked to your product and will vary depending on the number of products or services you produce. For Forest School this may be freelance staff costs, or the price of consumed materials (like firewood or string). Because variable costs are based on your revenue they are sometimes referred to as **revenue costs**.
- **Fixed** – a fixed cost is a cost that is not linked to the number of products you produce. Land rent, for example, may be a fixed cost if it is paid as a flat rate per week/month. These costs stay the same each month and do not increase with the amount of product produced.

Direct and indirect costs

Operational costs/expenses are often split into **direct** and **indirect** costs for accounting purposes. A *direct cost* can be traced directly to a specific product like direct labour or raw materials. An *indirect cost* is not directly related to a specific product or process but is incurred in the course of running the business – examples include utilities (electricity for lighting an area) and general marketing for the business (but not advertising a specific programme). This raises a bit of a conundrum, because there is no definitive list of what is a direct or indirect cost; you must decide!

Overheads

The ongoing expenses of running a business are called overheads. Most overheads are classed as indirect costs, as they are usually not related to a specific product, product line, or customer (and as such, do not directly generate profit). They can be fixed, variable or semi variable.

Direct costs, indirect costs and overheads are all types of expenses. How an item is budgeted can depend on three factors:

- How the item is used
- How you pay for an item
- Whether it can be directly costed to a product (our programme of sessions), product line, or customer (school, parent, or organisation).

Expenses can be a challenge to untangle, but a basic bookkeeping course should point you in the right direction. For example: advertising a specific programme would be a direct cost, whereas promoting your company or all your programmes would be an indirect cost. Staffing is another interesting cost – buying in freelance help for specific sessions on an hourly rate would be a direct cost, but employing a person on a salary to work with you would be an indirect cost.

Why do we need to separate out these costs at all? Your direct costs help you to calculate your **gross profit,** whereas your **indirect costs** are used to calculate your **net profit**. Calculating net profit is critical because this is what you are taxed on.

Some of your business costs are termed as *allowable expenses* and can be deducted from your profits to reduce your tax bill. An internet search will provide a wealth of information on allowable expenses and how they work. You can find out more on the gov.uk website:
https://www.gov.uk/expenses-if-youre-self-employed [17]
https://www.gov.uk/simpler-income-tax-simplified-expenses [18]

There are usually relatively few direct costs associated with the delivery of a Forest School programme. Usually these are restricted to staffing costs and consumables or materials.

Overleaf are some common operating costs you may need to consider during your financial planning or management.

Direct costs:

- Freelance staff costs
- Consumables – equipment and materials that are consumed by their use (this might be kiln-dried wood, a packet of elastic bands, or the time it takes to collect the right sticks for a learning opportunity)
- Online booking costs for a specific programme.

Indirect costs:

- Fuel
- Business insurance
- Purchase of uniforms
- Equipment repair
- Utilities
- Site rental
- Legal costs (licence agreement charges)
- Administration costs
- Booking costs (staff time or charges)
- Policy updates
- Chasing payments
- Finances and tax returns
- Marketing and publicity (time and costs)
- Accountancy costs
- Resource building
- Market research (charges from SurveyMonkey etc)
- Website upkeep (monthly hosting/domain fees)
- Transport to site (where applicable).

Cash flow

According to the Office for National Statistics, **90% of businesses fail because of cash flow issues** (cited in Rehman, 2007). In most start-up businesses, cash flow is going to be a major concern. This is especially true with Forest School work, as you may have a hefty chunk to lay out before you get paid (equipment, staff, training, etc). There is a common misconception that cash flow is about profit or how much money you make. This is incorrect: it is about how the money (or cash) flows in and out of your business as income or expenditure, and (crucially) when this happens! It is possible to have large profits yet poor cash flow, or great cash flow but with small profits. This can all get a bit confusing – but don't panic!

Cash flow forecasting

Cash flow forecasting is a tool to help manage the finances of your business. It is principally used to identify potential hazards for your finances and help plan for solutions to them. A forecast can also help us to model scenarios, such as: What happens if a payment is late? What happens to *my* cash with this unexpected expenditure? Cash flow is constantly moving and you will need to modify your budget by allocating or reallocating expenditure at times to suit your organisation's needs. A cash flow forecast will show you potential hazards in your current course of action, or what will happen if you don't take action. This can give you time to change, budget for a solution, or decrease your expenditure.

We all do little bits of cash flow forecasting in our day-to-day lives without even realising it. When we coordinate a direct debit payment to leave our bank to coincide with when we get paid, or when we put off buying that new axe or pair of boots until next month when we have more disposable income, we are working with cash flow. Creating a cash flow forecast for a business is a little bit more involved but uses a similar principle. We need to analyse our income, expenditure, pricing and payment strategies, and ensure that they create a balanced cash flow. We each need to choose a process that works for us and then continue to *observe*, *analyse* and *choose* in order to refine the effectiveness of our process as we *implement* our plan.

There are ways to diminish cash flow problems. One way is to have a considerable amount of start-up capital. The initial investment allows you to delay the onset of cash flow problems until you build enough profit to allocate more working capital to reduce the risk from cash flow deficits. This is a temporary fix and your working capital will ebb away with time if your price point/timings are not set right. Another way is to move slowly and plan ahead, carefully ensuring you do not overreach.

To help you with planning your cash flow, it is well worth estimating (or noting) the dates and times that payments go into and out of your accounts. This will prevent you from paying hefty bank charges or running out of working capital.

Many businesses end up borrowing money to pay for their running costs because of late payments, and expend enormous amounts of energy chasing money held by debtors. This can be a real juggling act and becomes especially tricky if you are paying staff who rely on the money. How you deliver your sessions, how they are paid for and who your debtors and creditors are can also have an impact on the way your cash flows.

Considerations for forecasting a cash flow

This sounds far more complicated than it actually is! Forecasting is simply recording your expected income and expenditure in an easily readable way. There is a huge amount of information online about creating cash flow forecasts, and template cash flow documents can be downloaded to make the task easier. The purpose of a cash flow forecast is to calculate the working capital of your business for a given time frame and to forecast any *pinch points* (places where income drops to dangerous levels) *before* they happen. By estimating the amount of cash on hand you have for a timeframe, you can see the rise and fall of your capital and be forewarned of any problems arising. Cash flow forecasts are working documents which need to be regularly updated. If you get extra sales or if you incur extra expenditure you will need to add this into your forecast and analyse how this affects your bottom line (working capital).

Cash flow and working with schools

Schools are typically reasonably good at settling their debts but do represent a larger risk to your cash flow. They will have a set time frame (four weeks or more) and due process they need to go through to authorise your payments, and no amount of begging will change this. The time they take to settle their accounts can be less than efficient if you step outside their usual processes. I cannot stress strongly enough that the secretaries, administration and finance staff of your client groups are *critical allies* in the success of your business. A friendly one can save your life; an unhappy one can crush your dreams just by being inefficient. Keep the relationships as friendly, professional and supportive as possible and ensure the admin staff have the easiest route to get you your money.

Problems with cash flow can occur with late payments from debtors. To avoid running into any problems, you must make sure *your terms and conditions* stipulate how and when you should be paid. You may need to understand and agree to the financial process of the organisation that you are providing the service for (common in Local Authorities). If your supplier has a 28-day payment delay, consider raising your working capital by charging extra to ensure you cover any issues this presents for your cash flow, or else issuing invoices sooner.

Cash flow and working with parents, carers, and individuals

Individuals such as parents and carers are often less reliable when paying their bills, yet if managed correctly they pose a lesser risk to your cash flow (one lost payment may not cause a critical problem). You should consider how, where and when parents pay, and how their payments are grouped. You may want to consider direct debits (weekly or monthly), and definitely consider payments in advance. Taking payments from individuals after you have provided the service, or on a cash-in-hand or session-by-session basis, could leave you out of pocket – or worse, turning customers away for a DNA (client Did Not Attend). There are some serious implications for your booking procedures and terms and conditions if you are taking payments from individuals, and you should also ensure that the extra admin time is reflected in the charges. There are websites and online services that can help with bookings and payments; these often come with a charge or a % fee and it is important to reflect these costs in your pricing.

It is always worth remembering that as a supplier we also have rights to being paid on time. It may be worth considering communicating this in your invoices regardless of who they are for, using a statement like the example below to focus the mind of the client(s):

'Payment terms: *Payment should be made by cheque or money transfer within 30 days of the above invoice date. Cheques should be made payable to 'Little Friendly Flames Forest School Ltd'.*

'Little Friendly Flames Forest School will exercise its right to claim statutory interest (at 8 per cent over the current Bank of England base rate) and compensation for recovery costs under the late payment legislation if payment is not received within 30 days of the invoice date.'

Seasonal dips and cash flow

Cash flow forecasts or predictions can help you to map out these consistent ebbs and flows in business, allowing you to create strategies to counteract or adapt to the changes. Forewarned is forearmed, and gives you the opportunity to make hay while the sun shines and invest for those quieter periods.

'The other advantage that we have with predicting cash flow is that the school year, with its regular holidays, is a known annual/seasonal factor. I know that August and December are going to be quiet each year – therefore I ramp up the number of sessions, and thus income, during June/July and October/November to account for the dip.' – Geoff Mason, Wood Learn Forest School

---

Example of a six-month cash flow forecast

Table 1 on the following page has an example of a six-month cash flow forecast. We can use this forecast to see our income (revenue) [row 11], our expenditure (costs) [row 35], and our cash-on-hand at the beginning [row 4] and the end [row 36] of each month.

If we look at the cash on hand for each month in a bar chart (below) we can clearly see the flow of cash into and out of the business during this six-month period. We can see a fall in cash on hand in April (in this example) so we may want to avoid planning any big expenditures until May. Cash flows can be useful in locating pinch points before they become problems. Forecasts can give us the time we need to implement a solution. Balancing a budget can be a challenge when pinch points loom. One solution is the ten steps to balancing a cash flow forecast outlined below.

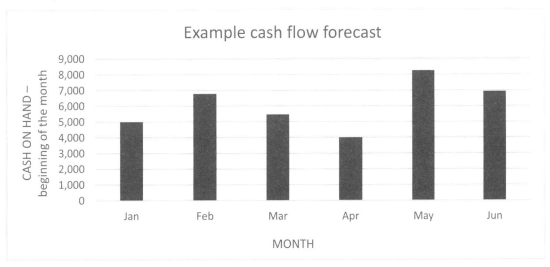

Table 1: Example of a six-month cash flow forecast

	Jan	Feb	Mar	Apr	May	Jun	Total
Cash on hand (beginning of month)	5,000	6,784	5,474	4,002	8,248	6,932	
CASH RECEIPTS - REVENUE	Jan	Feb	Mar	Apr	May	Jun	Total
Cash sales							0
Income 1	3,600			3,600			7,200
Income 2				1,800			1,800
Income 3	600	450	600	450	600	600	3,300
TOTAL CASH RECEIPTS	4,200	450	600	5,850	600	600	12,300
CASH PAID OUT - EXPENDITURE	Jan	Feb	Mar	Apr	May	Jun	Total
DIRECT COSTS							
Contracted Labour - INCOME1 @ £13/hour	312	234	390	156	312	234	1,638
Contracted Labour - INCOME 2 @ £13/hour	156	117	195	78	156	117	819
Contracted Labour - INCOME 3@ £13/hour	156	117	195	78	156	117	819
Direct costs total	624	468	780	312	624	468	3,276
INDIRECT COSTS							
Advertising	10	10	10	10	10	10	60
Telephone	10	10	10	10	10	10	60
Insurance (public liability)	17	17	17	17	17	17	102
Materials and supplies	60	60	60	60	60	60	360
Home Office expense	15	15	15	15	15	15	90
Rent or lease (site@ £130/MONTH)	130	130	130	130	130	130	780
Salary	1,000	1,000	1,000	1,000	1,000	1,000	6,000
Travel	40	40	40	40	40	40	240
Utilities	10	10	10	10	10	10	60
Indirect costs total	1,292	1,292	1,292	1,292	1,292	1,292	7,752
SUBTOTAL	1,916	1,760	2,072	1,604	1,916	1,760	11,028
CASH PAID OUT -	Jan	Feb	Mar	Apr	May	Jun	Total
Capital purchases (tools, clothing and equipment)	500						500
TOTAL CASH PAID OUT	2,416	1,760	2,072	1,604	1,916	1,760	11,528
Cash on hand (end of month)	6,784	5,474	4,002	8,248	6,932	5,772	

Balancing a cash flow forecast in ten steps

Unless you are exceptionally lucky, you are likely to run into cash flow issues in your business from time to time. Your cash flow forecast should help you to prevent these issues from becoming nightmares. You may find you can easily reduce or remove problems by considering these ten easy to follow steps:

1. Discover (using your cash flow forecast) how long the effect of an event will last (timeframe)
2. Estimate the income you will receive within that timeframe
3. Identify when your income is expected
4. Identify and calculate your expenditure
5. Work out what your surplus or deficit is
6. Review your sales to see if they could be increased (perhaps with a marketing strategy offering a one-off discount, for example)
7. Explore the timing of your sales income – can you speed up a payment, invoice corporate clients early, or offer incentives for cash up front or early bird payments?
8. Explore timings of expenditure – could payments out be deferred, reduced, split or avoided altogether?
9. Apply any appropriate alterations and recalculate your expenditure, surplus/deficit, and cash on hand
10. Revisit steps 1 – 9 until you are able to reach a solution to your cash flow issue. Once resolved, finalise and print your cash flow budget. (Victoria State Government, 2021)

There is a short cash flow exercise looking at balancing a cash flow using these ten steps on our online resource https://forestschoolassociation.org/book-resources/ [1]

Contingency Planning

However well you forecast you are likely to occasionally be surprised by life's curve balls. You may want to devise a contingency plan and budget into your pricing in case of illness or injury. This will give you a buffer for any minor mishaps or emergencies.

Price point: how much am I going to charge?

The FSA cannot just give you the answer to this question. Only you know what your costs and expenses are and how much you want to earn. However, there are some interesting points about price that are worth considering.

It may be worth running your figures hypothetically to establish a baseline that will secure you a minimum or living wage, and then increasing the price from there until you reach a sustainable price. There is a danger in pricing your services too low – your business may tick along but never be able to grow past the first set of capacity problems (e.g. you do not have enough hours or stamina to run more sessions yourself but you do not make enough to employ someone to help). Forest School delivery is never going to command the kind of volume (numbers of sessions) that make price a competitive advantage unless you run a national franchise. It is best to price for what you need, not your customers' perceived pockets. There will always be someone wanting to undercut your prices but they will probably not be sustainable, or else will be of poor quality.

There are many methods for setting a retail or actual price for your sessions, and it is always worth seeking professional advice if you can. However, this advice can be a considerable outlay at set-up and it is often worth crunching some numbers yourself first in order to test whether your business is likely to be sustainable. I use this three-stage process in my business and it may prove useful for you too:

- **First**, work out how much your services cost you to deliver, taking into account all of the factors in financial planning above and allowing for a degree of surplus that will offset at least part of the effects of cash flow, and also an amount for *slippage*. This will give you your estimated base cost.
- **Second**, you need to work out the amount of product or service you can realistically offer in your chosen time frame (monthly or annually). You can then divide your base cost by the number of sessions to work out your minimum price or breakeven price. This is the point at

which you break even, and it is important to remember this breakeven price is the price *after* you have been paid, not before!

- **Third**, research the market and look for the maximum price that your sessions can achieve. You can then set your price somewhere between the breakeven or base cost and maximum prices.

Human resource management (HRM)

This section is about the management of your employees/staff and volunteers. It is often thought of as *hiring and firing* but it is much more than that. Every Forest School setting is set up slightly differently, but you will need to consider the following in your staff management:

- Health and safety
- First Aid
- Training
- Staff communication and logistics
- Hiring
- DBS checks
- Staff well-being
- PAYE and national insurance
- Pension scheme
- Holidays and rotas.

Human resource management is really about the strategic planning, controlling, organising and directing of the business's workforce. It looks at how workforces are best deployed and where individuals are best situated to play to their strengths. It will look at support for the workforce, from access issues to sickness. Employee retention is an important aspect of HRM. There is a handy mantra to remember when dealing with your workforce:

'People leave managers, not companies.' – Brigette Hyacinth

Ultimately HRM is about relationships, expectations and processes that enable your workforce to do their jobs well. Your HRM processes should facilitate good practice and not create barriers and blockages, and should always support your policies and procedures. How you treat your staff will impact on how they treat your customers: treat them well and train them up, and you will have a great workforce that will want to stay with you.

Knowledge management

Knowledge management is about the skills and resources that your business holds. Like all other aspects of business, this should be regularly reviewed. Level 3 Forest School training should provide you with the policies you need to have in place to begin delivery, but you may wish to create policies and procedures that deal with specific things depending on your chosen client group. For example, you may need to create and communicate your policy on the challenging of behaviour outdoors, stick fighting, or river walking activities.

Marketing management

As you may expect, marketing management is about getting the word out to your potential clients; it is also about learning what those clients want to hear, see and experience. This part of your continued management will be fluid and should diversify as you choose different clients or pick up new skills and experiences.

Market research

The first part of any marketing strategy is to do some market research. You will need to:

Identify your customers

- Are you aiming at a specific age group or groups, or a particular community? Your potential customers may be a mix of business and individual clients, and you will need to consider the following:
- How are they likely to access your services and what will you need to put in place to help them? (e.g. online bookings system)
- Where are they based – locally or do you need to travel?
- Are they likely to buy your service at a specific time? (e.g. weekends, summertime, or term time)
- Are they likely to buy your services under specific circumstances? (e.g. behavioural interventions)
- Why buy your service over someone else's? (e.g. the quality of your provision, a prior relationship, your ethics, your site or skills)
- Have they bought similar products elsewhere in the past?
- Do you have a portfolio of customers waiting for your service?

Find out about what or who is already in the marketplace

Before you get too far down the line in planning your business, it is a really good idea to conduct some simple market research into what already exists in your area in terms of Forest School provision. How much do your possible competitors charge and what gaps might there be in the market that you could exploit with your new business (using your resources and capabilities)?

If your business idea is similar to other providers that are already in the marketplace locally, you might want to consider if there is room for your business too! You could do this by finding out how popular their products are. For example, how quickly do spaces at their parent and toddler group or holiday club sell out? Do they have any availability/capacity to take on new groups? Do their courses regularly get fully booked?

Whilst competition in a marketplace can be healthy, cooperation can be beneficial too. Find out where you could help others, and work with them or coordinate your cover for mutually beneficial cooperation. For example, a business that works exclusively with Early Years could coordinate with another that concentrates on provision for ages 5 and up, creating a mutually beneficial pathway for clients as they age. This is a form of mutual *product positioning* (see below) or finding a gap in the market. It works for both businesses and is great for your clients too, as they are not abandoned as they turn five but instead have a ready-made signpost to where they can carry on exploring. Younger children who cannot attend the sessions designed for older children can be signposted in turn to the business running for younger children.

Once you have done some market research and know what the market is like, you will need to design a message to promote your service for the audience identified in your research, and you may also think about finding your specific niche (see *market segmentation* below).

Marketing

There are at least eight ways to get your message heard nowadays, and each has its pros and cons. As we heard in **Chapter 5**, Forest School has a habit of swallowing any time you give to it, so be mindful of how effective your marketing is. It is always worth asking people where they heard about you; keep a tally chart, and this will indicate where to put your efforts or where your strategies are working. It is a widely-held idea that in order to reach customers and convert sales you must use more than one method of communication in marketing – some experts recommend using seven! These may include:

- Word of mouth
- Social media

- Advertising
- Direct marketing
- Leaflets, pamphlets, or business cards
- Articles in the local paper
- Websites
- Exhibiting (shows, schools or summer fairs)
- Blogs

It is worth noting here that *everything* you do is sending a message. If you fit around the client's systems and ensure that you tick the boxes they need ticking, with a pleasant, fun and tolerant demeanour they are likely to remember you before your competitors (even if they charge less). You are not the only one for whom time is money and stress is a factor. Saving the client time and effort is a great way to build rapport. Better yet, they will advocate your service to others and word of mouth is one of the most potent marketing tools at your disposal!

It might be worth contemplating adding an extra amount to your pricing so you can jump at the offers of summer fairs, or give extra sessions with parents without carrying the cost. In business terms this is called *slippage*, and it allows you to deliver quality service while being seen to go above and beyond for your client. This is always a good way to win hearts and minds. There is a business mantra that reflects this:

Under promise and overdeliver

Marketing strategies

Before we move onto strategic management, it seems wise to include some of the accepted marketing strategies in this section. To get your message to the right place, to have it seen and understood and elicit a positive response, you may need to employ a marketing strategy. This can be done using the STP marketing model, which is explored in depth in this YouTube video:
https://www.youtube.com/watch?v=iGOw39GWDaI **[19]**

- Segmentation
- Targeting
- Product positioning
- Differentiation

Segmentation

This is the process of dividing the marketplace into smaller groups based on similarities.

You can easily break your potential market down in four ways:

- Demographically (by age, income, gender etc)
- Geographically (by postcode, county, city or rural/urban)
- Psychographically (values, attitudes, interests, lifestyle etc)
- Desires or needs (e.g. a family activity, quality Forest School)

As we all want Forest School to be for everyone and we value inclusion and diversity in our leaders and participants, we need to be sensitive to how we split our groups and ensure that our marketing exercise does not detract from the inclusive nature of our delivery. The segmentation of markets can increase our capacity, productivity and marketing reach.

Targeting

Once we have chosen a group, we need to target them within the market. This can be done with specific messages for that group. Forest School has a huge raft of benefits and outcomes but not all aspects of Forest School will be as interesting to everyone within the market.

For example, a marketing campaign to attract under 5s will not work if it is aimed *purely* at the under 5s as they don't yet make purchasing decisions. However, it may be more successful if the information is aimed at parents, and the imagery shows children having fun, loving their parents and being supported. Well-being, fun, development and safety are often primary concerns of parents.

A marketing campaign to attract teenage participants is unlikely to work if the children in the literature are 3–5 years of age. They may, however, be attracted by images of other teenagers fire lighting, laughing, in social situations, learning new things and having fun. However, unless the teens are very independent you will still have to convince the parents or carers to part with their hard-earned cash, and so education, skills, wellbeing, safety and reliability are still important in your campaign.

People are likely to be attracted by images or messages from people who look like them, have similar styles and have cultural relevance to them.

Product positioning or finding a niche

There are several steps you may want to consider to find your niche:

- Step 1 – identify your competitors
- Step 2 – look at what they offer and identify their strengths and weaknesses (the company size, the ethics, the products, the services, price, their marketing etc). Identify who their customers are
- Step 3 – Look at your strengths and weaknesses, opportunities and threats; work out what your unique value is to the market and identify whether you can offer something your competitors do not.

It is important to realise that, just like the other processes in business management, this is an ongoing process and you must be prepared to keep up to date with the changing needs, demands and desires of your market.

Differentiation

This is the ability to adapt within the marketplace and the marketing of your willingness to do so. If a group of people do not feel they fit within your current provision and they cannot find a service nearby that fits their needs, you may find that with a degree of flexibility and negotiation you can help them get a Forest School experience which is personal, effective and lucrative. This is an important part of your *strategic management*, changing to stay relevant within the market.

Sales

Sales is another discipline that takes a lifetime to master. As leaders we often find discussing money uncomfortable, especially because we are entering Forest School for the social good it does, but if we do not complete our sales then we don't get to eat.

Selling a quality product is tricky because every person and their dog will claim they do the same for less. Often our urge is to provide potential clients with as much information about ourselves and our businesses as possible, and then give the client the prices. Then we sit and wait for the phone to ring … only to find the client has gone somewhere cheaper.

We do this because we feel that the client needs to listen to why we are different. This is not always the best option, because we are helping them in realising what to look for elsewhere. Forest School leaders are great at forming relationships in challenging situations. If we turn our thinking on its head for a moment and use those skills, we may be better placed to complete that sale.

What we do is not important to the client, at least not yet. What *they* want and who *they* are is far more important to them. We must therefore ask questions, find out the *why*s, *how*s, *when*s and *who*s, and even ask about the client's budget. Find commonality and form that relationship, and they may not bother to look for cheaper elsewhere, because you listened and created something bespoke just for them. Have a line in the sand prepared, work out what you will and won't accept, and stick to your guns; remember you *know* how it works! They just *think* they do.

Strategic management

Strategic management is the thinking and actions around moving your business forward. It is predominantly concerned with **where you want to be as a business** and **how you get there**! Many of the other areas of management revolve around your strategic management. By far the most important aspect of strategic management is to create the aims, goals and values of your project or business in line with the expectations of the industry (regulations, professional standards, technology and competition).

Strategic management quite simply produces policies and procedures that allow you to reach your aims and objectives and then allows you to allocate resources to get your plans rolling.

Part of your strategic management will be the creation and observation of milestones, sometimes called mitigating milestones or risk-mitigating milestones.

Mitigating milestones

As we said in the previous chapter, these are points in the life of your business when risks are offset by the process of running a business. Strategic planning of milestones helps us to identify points at which our business or project can move forward. From a funding point of view, each milestone reached means our business is more likely to succeed.

More importantly, they can be tested and plotted as part of the growth of your business. They are indicators that your current strategies are working (at least in part) and your business is moving forward. Often, in business, they are financial, such as selling ten doughnuts a day for ten days to cover this month's stall rental or building a working capital of £3000 to offset the current cash flow issues.

Where now?

Now you have got to grips with some of the business aspects of running a Forest School, the next two chapters are designed to help you with specific ways of delivering Forest School, as a business or within an organisation as a project.

References

Rehman, A., 2007. *Impact Of Cash Flow Forecasting On Growth.* [Online]
Available at: https://chacc.co.uk/small-business-advice/cash-flow-forecasting-for-growth/
[Accessed 18 August 2021].

Rowlands, R. & Rowlands, G., 2008. *Good Small Business Guide.* 3 ed. London: A & C Black Publishers Limited. 576.

Victoria State Government, 2021. *Prepare a cash flow budget.* [Online]
Available at: https://business.vic.gov.au/business-information/tourism-industry-resources/tourism-crisis-management-guide/respond/prepare-a-cash-flow-budget
[Accessed 31 July 2021].

Chapter 8 – Considerations for planning a Forest School and delivering it myself

Nell Seal

Now that you have decided to deliver Forest School sessions yourself, this chapter will help you to consolidate what you have read in previous chapters and to explore what things might look like in reality. A lot of the decisions you make from here onwards will be guided by your level 3 training, especially if you choose a quality training provider; we will therefore concentrate on aspects that may not be covered in detail on your level 3 course. Planning your Forest School provision is a reflective process, and this chapter has been created and compiled from the experiences of many Forest School leaders. In Forest School we value mistakes and failures; in business, however, each mistake costs time, effort and money, and so it is worth investing some energy at this early stage to set yourself up for success. In this chapter we will explore the mechanics of your sessions, consider adult helpers and ratios, and look briefly at the importance of your handbook, as well as introducing you to the FSA Recognised Forest School Provider Scheme.

How well does Forest School fit with me and my organisation?

You may choose to deliver Forest School to participants directly or work through an existing school or organisation, either from inside an organisation as an employee or else as a freelance contractor. Sometimes your clients will be the participants and their parents or carers, and sometimes your client group will extend to include leaders in organisations too. You will have already looked at the pros and cons of who you deliver sessions to from a cash flow point of view in **Chapter 7.**

When working with organisations, it will be important to establish how your Forest School provision will fit into the wider agenda of the organisation or group. All organisations will have core aims and objectives that are important drivers at any given moment. It is therefore sensible to establish what the organisation's priorities are at an early stage, and take some time to think about how the Forest School experiences you can offer might complement them. It is often handy to ask for a description of the organisation's aims and objectives at the point of initial contact.

Once you have had time to draw together your thinking, you may benefit from having a meeting with senior leaders and stakeholders. The stakeholders you may need to liaise with will vary from place to place but may include: owners, governors, heads or assistant heads, well-being leads, behaviour leads, SENCOs, trustees, mentors, heads of department, directors, and parents.

Any meetings with the wider team will generate a wealth of information and will help you plan future delivery with your new clients. Initial meetings can sometimes be a little daunting for new Forest School leaders, so the following list contains some reflective questions you may wish to consider:

- What are the drivers that led to the organisation having an interest in Forest School?

- What are the hoped-for outcomes of introducing the Forest School approach?

- Are the above congruent with the fact that the main overarching aim of Forest School programmes is to develop self-esteem among participants?

- Do the above drivers and desired outcomes match your own?

- What would the areas of compromise be?

- How well do stakeholders in the organisation understand the six principles of Forest School?

- Do you feel you have good 'buy in' to the pedagogical approach of Forest School from the organisation leads?

- Do you feel you will be able to uphold all six principles in your Forest School work?

- Is it likely that Forest School will be effective in meeting the hoped-for outcomes?

- Is any resistance present? If so, what is the nature of the resistance? How can you address these areas of resistance? Is there a compromise that you can envision?

- Do you feel you have widespread support for taking Forest School forward?

- Have you considered resource implications and communicated these? How much time will you need? What additional costs need to be taken into account?

What size groups will I be working with and how many adults will we need?

Once you know a little about your client group, you can begin to consider the mechanics of how your Forest School group will work: how many children will there be and, therefore, how many adults will be required?

The additional adults who help you in your Forest School sessions might already be Level 1 or 2 Forest School qualified, or they might not. If the adults who will be helping you are not Forest School trained, you will need to work with them to develop their understanding of the Forest School ethos and principles to enable them to be effective supporters. There are different ways of doing this: as a cyclical informal CPD session; as a standard part of inducting new staff; as a Forest School session in the woods just for the adults; in a document designed to meet their needs; or by watching the content available on the FSA website (link below) along with a follow-up question-and-answer session. It is also good practice to set out somewhere in your handbook what the role of an adult in Forest School is and how this may differ from 'normal' home or school life and values.

https://forestschoolassociation.org/what-is-forest-school/ [2]

Relative to other forms of nature play, we expect there to be higher numbers of adults present in Forest School. We expect ratios to be appropriate to the needs and experience of the group and the site to enable higher risk activities, allow for child-led play and enable supporting adults to undertake individual planning, observation, and reflection.

Blanket ratios according to age or developmental stage are not appropriate – to establish an appropriate ratio for your setting you will also need to consider all of the following factors:

- experience of the participants

- additional needs

- the sort of activity you wish to enable

- the specifics of your chosen site.

It is good practice to extend any usual classroom 1:1 provision into Forest School as well. The adult acting in a 1:1 role would not be included in the overall ratio as they should not have a responsibility towards any other child.

It is also good practice to adopt the 'plus one' rule, whereby you work to the ratio you have risk-assessed as appropriate and then add in an additional adult. By adopting this rule, you are ensuring that you have safe ratios in place even in the event of an adult becoming ill, being injured, or having to work 1:1 with a child (for example, to administer First Aid).

To work in accordance with all six principles, you will likely find that smaller groups work best. The FSA advocates for as small a group as you can manage, with no more than 15 participants. Larger groups become hard to manage in a way that remains true to the Forest School ethos because of the individual planning, individual observations, and risky play elements that are required. When considering working with a large group you may wish to reflect on the following questions.

With one Level 3 Forest School leader and more than 15 children:

- How do you safely facilitate child-led risky play?

- How do you plan sessions that cater for the needs of individual children?

- How do you routinely record individual observations of each child?

- How are significant relationships built to enable self-esteem gains?

- How do you manage each child having the opportunity to try the exciting 1:1 whittling project they saw another child engaged in?

- How do you maintain a child-led practice with more than 15 children and thereby avoid adult-directed sessions?

- How do you provide individualised and tailored sessions that meet the needs of more than 15 children?

- What is your fire circle protocol with more than 15 children?

- Are you able to do the deeper emotional work when the group size is more than 15?

  With groups of over 15 you will also need to consider:

- How does the Level 3 leader clearly and effectively communicate with the other adult supporters to ensure a consistent approach?

- What is the impact on the woodland environment of more than 15 children using the space for Forest School?

To work with smaller groups, school settings may need to split classes. The FSA generally believes it to be preferable to split a group and work with them fortnightly, rather than to take a whole class to the woods each week.

On rare occasions, some Forest School providers can demonstrate that group sizes over 15 are appropriate because:

- They have multiple Level 3 Forest School trained staff

- Supporting adults each have a core group of children for whose observations they are responsible

- Other supporting adults have been trained to Level 1 or 2 Forest School

- Sessions take place in a large woodland, the use of which is rotated to spread the impact of the greater footfall.

Who will your adult supporters be?

To enable individual observations, planning based on the needs of individuals, child-led play, and the use of tools and fire, you will need a crew of enthusiastic adult supporters in your sessions. Every Forest School session is led by a Level 3 qualified Forest School leader but you won't be able to do it without other adults being present too: who are these adults going to be?

If you are working with a nursery group you may want the children's key workers to be present. If you work in a school you may wish for the usual class teacher and teaching assistant to be present. Having these familiar adults present can offer great continuity for the participants, and also affords the adults a more holistic insight into the children in their care. By being a part of the Forest School experience, these adults can build on the events that occur and the relationships that develop in Forest School when the children are back in their regular classroom.

Supporting adults could be other staff, such as those in administrative roles, caretakers, or teaching assistants. You may also choose to recruit volunteers. Volunteers might be people interested in gaining experience in working with children or outdoor learning; they may be people who recognise that helping in a Forest School session might benefit their well-being; or they may be parents or carers of children and young people participating in the session. You may wish to consider how you will manage the impact of children having their parents or carers present: might those children operate in a slightly different way, become dependent, or feel judged? You may also wish to explore how to keep the goodwill of kind volunteers: can you have a pool of volunteers and use them on a rotational basis so that they have some flexibility? Can you offer CPD to those who want it? Do you want to establish a way of enabling regular check-ins?

At this point it seems wise to mention that adult helpers should know a little about the Forest School ethos, as well-meaning yet uninformed helpers can be disruptive to the Forest School process. This can be easily achieved by a short training session, or by getting them to watch the FSA five minute *What is Forest School?* video, or even by providing a handout with what is expected of them whether they be teachers, teaching assistants, volunteers or senior leaders. Many organisations choose to train their regular supporting adults to Level 1 or 2 Forest School. If you refer to **Chapter 5** you will find information about selecting an appropriate trainer and course. By ensuring everyone is Forest School trained to Level 1 or 2 you will ensure that all adults present have a similar foundation on which to base their practice: a sound understanding of the Forest School ethos and principles.

Applying for National Recognition from the FSA Recognised Forest School Provider Scheme

For Forest School providers wishing to obtain national recognition, the FSA manages a Recognised Forest School Provider Scheme. The scheme is for those who wish to publicly demonstrate that their practice meets the necessary national minimum standards for Forest School. If you are likely to apply for national recognition and become an FSA Recognised Provider in the future, it is sensible to establish your practice in a way that meets the benchmarks set out in the scheme. As well as the national recognition, FSA Recognised Forest School Providers receive a range of benefits from being part of the scheme:

- Your organisation is included in our online, searchable map of Forest School Providers for use by people wishing to identify Forest School provision local to them

- Up to four individuals in your organisation are eligible to become individual members of the FSA (this gives access to the password-protected membership area of the website, as well as member discounts and full voting rights)

- You can use the FSA logo and Recognised Forest School Provider badge/certificate on your materials

- You become part of a network of Forest School Providers so that you can reflect on and develop good practice with like-minded peers

- You can demonstrate to others that you have national recognition and that the FSA recognises your organisation as providing Forest School programmes in line with the six core Forest School principles

- You receive validation relating to your Forest School practice

- The scheme promotes the FSA's purpose of working toward quality Forest School for All.

If you would like to investigate what the benchmarks are, you can visit our Recognised Provider webpage and refer to the Self-assessment Checklist.
https://www.forestschoolassociation.org/join-the-fsa-as-a-school-and-organisation-member/ **[6]**

The key benchmarks that you may wish to consider when setting up your practice can be summarised as:

- All Level 3 Forest School leaders have an FSA recognised qualification

- All Level 3 leaders have a current 16-hour First Aid qualification with outdoor and paediatric elements (i.e. have adopted the IOL statement of good practice for Outdoor First Aid at Band 3)

- Use a session planning format. This format needs to cover agreed areas. These areas are outlined later in the chapter in the **Session planning, recording and reflecting section.**

- Make routine observations of all participants, to inform planning

- All Level 3 leaders undertake at least one day of CPD specifically related to Forest School each year

- Offer at least one long-term Forest School programme, in accordance with the Long-Term Principle. This approximately translates to at least two hours weekly across the year (but refer to the document above for more details)

- Have a site risk assessment, a stated approach to dynamic risk assessing, a series of activity risk assessments that take a risk-benefit approach, and undertake daily site checks

- Have a Forest School handbook that includes sections on the role of supporting adults in Forest School, health and safety, emergency planning procedures, safeguarding, confidentiality, behaviour in Forest School, bullying, complaints, and sustainability

- Have a document that shows how you conserve and manage your woodland space and that you have permission to use it

- Provide evidence that you prepare parents, carers and supporting adults for Forest School experiences by explaining the Forest school ethos and principles.

If you want to apply for national recognition and become an FSA Recognised Forest School Provider you will need to:

1. Visit our Recognised Provider Scheme webpage (see link above **[6]**)

2. Read the Preamble document

3. Review your practice against the quick reference Self-assessment Checklist to ensure you meet our benchmarks

4. Complete the short online form to notify us of your intention to apply and make your initial payment (which is lower for existing FSA members)

5. Undertake an approximately 45-minute-long informal video consultation with an FSA Development Officer

6. Complete an Application Form, compile evidence demonstrating you meet all benchmarks (using an online Teachable resource to support you as required), and submit these to the FSA.

Your status as an FSA Recognised Provider begins when you have demonstrated that you meet all benchmarks, and lasts for 12 months. To maintain your status as an FSA Recognised Forest School Provider you need to maintain standards, complete a short annual declaration each year, and pay the ongoing membership fee.

Where might your Forest School sessions take place?

Following the Nature Principle, sessions ideally take place in a natural environment with trees. Identifying which woodland environment you might use is therefore vital. You will find lots of helpful information in **Chapters 10 and 11** about site use and maintaining a site, and about land use agreements and other site considerations in **Chapter 10**, but here are some initial considerations to work through:

- Do you have anywhere suitable on your or the organisation's current site?

- Do you have an area on site that could be further developed to make it suitable?

- Do you have any existing relationships with landowners?

- Is there anywhere within walking distance that might be suitable? If so, who owns the site?

- Do you have transport to travel to sites further afield? What is the time impact of using distant sites and is that manageable?

- What type of Forest School provision can your site accommodate whilst maintaining the ecological health of the space? How does this impact the extent of the provision you offer?

- Will the site enable sustainable harvesting of woodland materials for activities such as fire-lighting, cooking, shelter-building and crafts? If not, how might you be able to import such materials to your chosen site?

- Is the site safe, e.g. has it had a tree safety inspection?

What equipment might you need?

There is a comprehensive equipment list in **Chapter 13** that sets out ideas for equipment that other Forest School leaders have found helpful. You may have identified your core equipment needs as part of your business plan in **Chapter 6** and this list should be explored as part of your level 3 training. However, even at this early stage, whilst you are making plans and considering possibilities, it may be worth revisiting the issue of equipment briefly.

Wet-weather gear

Spending extended amounts of time outdoors in the UK, all year round, requires decent clothing to ensure leaders and participants are comfortable. You will be able to provide your own clothing as a business expense, but who is going to provide the clothing for participants? Will the organisation provide kit that can be shared between different groups, or will you ask parents to supply it? Will you rent it to participants or provide it free of charge? Who will ensure other leaders have comfortable and appropriate clothing: might the employer have a responsibility to provide this? Will you need to find creative solutions, perhaps through fundraising or establishing a kit donation scheme? Are there any organisations who might be able to help you, such as parent-teacher associations? Remember that FSA members receive a discount with many suppliers and this could reduce your outlay considerably.
https://forestschoolassociation.org/member-benefits/ **[20]**

Emergency rucksack

All Forest School leaders need to have an emergency rucksack that includes an array of items to help manage a variety of situations, including an appropriate First Aid kit. You can find a suggested starting point in **Chapter 13**.

PPE

You will also need to ensure the provision of Personal Protective Equipment (PPE) for adults and participants as appropriate. Things you may wish to account for will be hard hats, steel toe cap boots, fire gloves, fire blankets, plunge buckets, and high visibility jackets if walking on roads to the site. You may need to provide PPE for infection control.

Fire circle

Are you going to create a gathering space in your woodland, such as a fire pit and log circle? If so, where will you source the materials that you need for this? Who can help you get them? Do you have access to the tools that you will need and will you have the correct training to use them?

Fire equipment

Over time you will likely work towards using fire in Forest School, both in a central fire space for heat and cooking, and also with individual children as they develop their skills. On a cold, wet day you may need to get your fire lit efficiently, so having a wood store, matches and various firelighters is desirable. You may also wish to collect a range of natural tinder, fire steels and bow drills with which children can experiment. Many Forest School sessions involve using fire to cook. If you wish to cook or prepare drinks using a fire you might consider achieving a Level 2 Food Hygiene certificate and gathering a set of equipment to use, such as a tripod, grill, Dutch oven, storm kettle, kettle, or popcorn popper.

Emergency phone

Forest School sessions are blissfully tech-free but you will need to ensure that you have a mobile phone for emergencies. Remember to test reception at your proposed Forest School site.

Observation recording

You may also wish to consider how you will make routine observations of all children during Forest School sessions. Some leaders use a tablet; while others prefer the low-tech but effective option of paper and pencil, which can be on a clipboard or in a notebook with some sort of waterproof cover.

Tools

The acquisition of tools may be a significant cost associated with Forest School provision. Tool kits can be developed over time as you become more confident in their use or as skills develop within the group. Things to consider could be scissors, hammers, mallets, bushcraft knives, folding saws, bow saws, junior hacksaws, axes, billhooks, hand drills, palm drills, gimlets, secateurs, loppers, and trowels. If you envision ever doing any sawing it will also be worth considering what you will use as a sawhorse. Having invested in tools, it would be prudent to ensure you also have appropriate storage for them, and you must ensure you have the correct equipment and the skills to maintain them.

Shelter

Forest School sessions happen all year round in all weathers. You will need to have a wind and rain shelter of some sort; some people choose permanent structures if their site allows, whilst others choose to rig a shelter when required. Indeed, valuable outcomes can arise when a group works together to erect a communal shelter. You will likely need tarpaulins, ropes and paracord to create shelters, and you will find these types of resources also get used by participants during participant-led elements.

Toileting equipment

The call of nature is inevitable, so an important question to answer is: does your Forest School site have any existing toilet facilities? If not, how will you support participants and leaders to maintain dignity when answering a call of nature during Forest School sessions? Creating a toileting solution may require you to source some equipment, negotiate with landowners, and even check nearby water sources. You might choose to establish a more permanent composting toilet, or perhaps rig a 'ship out' set up using a portable potty in a changing tent. Whichever solution you decide upon, you will need to consider how you will offer handwashing facilities with soap and running water, and how you will deal with the waste.

Hoarded goodies

You will probably develop a huge range of ideas for activities that you might offer during Forest School sessions and, depending on what these are, these may require equipment of some sort. Forest School leaders are often accused of being hoarders because so many objects might serve a purpose during Forest School sessions. Keeping an eye on local free or selling sites and visiting car boot sales can prove fruitful. You may wish to gather a variety of receptacles that participants can use in an open-ended way, such as metal bowls and baskets of varying sizes. Connecting participants with nature is a key benefit of Forest School and you may find having identification guides and charts, minibeast kits, and books with a nature focus helpful. If you or your participants are interested in woodland crafts you may wish to collect wool, clay, twig pencils and tree cookies. You may also wish to consider how you will provide safe, cosy locations for rest or de-stress: hammocks can be helpful.

You will make your own value judgement about what sorts of materials you view as appropriate in Forest School sessions: some leaders choose not to use plastic, for example, whilst others only use things that are available in the woodland or which can be made from woodland materials.

What paperwork do I need to have in place?

During your Level 3 training, your trainer should provide comprehensive guidelines relating to the various pieces of paperwork you will need or want to have in place. At this early stage, you may wish to consider what you will need to work towards so that you can allocate reasonable time to preparing these.

Land use agreement, lease or licence

Unless your Forest School provision is happening on land owned by you or the organisation for whom you work, it is sensible to establish an agreement with the landowner that sets out the terms of your partnership and the responsibilities of each party. Things to include might be:

- The precise geographical location (the what3words app, address, grid reference) including maps, to show the extent of the space that you have permission to use

- Any limits on the number of people to whom you may deliver

- Agreed access points/parking/storage/water points, to include management of keys or gate codes

- Contact details for both parties in the event of emergencies

- The escalation procedure in the event of an emergency (i.e. who will be informed and when)

- When access is allowed, i.e. when you expect to be using the site (remember to discuss and include how you will manage access outside of agreed session times)

- Whether access is granted for tree inspections and tree work, and who has responsibility for organising and paying for this

- What will be checked before each session and to whom results should be escalated as appropriate

- Who has responsibility for the participants whilst on site (you, not the landowner!)

- Situations which might result in the site temporarily becoming unusable for Forest School (extreme weather, tree harvesting, or shoots, for example)

- Where responsibility lies for adhering to an agreed Health and Safety policy

- What risk assessments will be undertaken and with whom they will be shared

- Which party has responsibility for which aspects of insurance, for example, Public Liability Insurance and Employer's Liability, including which enhancements might be required

- Conservation management agreements

- What ecological monitoring will happen and how often it will take place

- Acceptable activities

- How water, waste and toileting will be managed

- Any financial arrangements relating to the use of the site

- Whether any signage is allowed or required

- Space for the landowner and Forest School provider to sign the agreement.

You can find out more about licence agreements and land use in **Chapter 10**.

Site safety and risk assessment

There will be a variety of risk assessment activities to undertake, both initially and on an ongoing basis. The site risk assessment will detail all of the hazards, and associated risks, presented by the site itself, such as by fencing, water bodies, trees, areas of nettles, toxic species, and stings or bites from fauna.

Activity risk-benefit analysis

Activity risk-benefit assessments (RBAs) will weigh up the hazards and associated risks presented by certain opportunities against the potential benefits for participants. You may have RBAs for opportunities such as tree climbing, ropes, minibeast hunts, woodland crafts, tool use, cooking and fire-lighting. You will need to establish a process for undertaking and recording dynamic risk assessment too: this is how you and participants will approach new hazards that present themselves during sessions, perhaps through participants using equipment in unexpected ways. One final aspect concerning risk is to create a pro forma for 'daily checks'. This is a list of everything that needs checking before each session. This ensures new hazards are identified and any newly-apparent potential seasonal learning opportunities are noted.

Communication and consent

In addition to devising an effective way of communicating the Forest School ethos and principles to parents or carers of new participants, you will need to create and circulate a consent form, and gather details about medical and additional needs. There are a variety of permissions and consents that you may need to gather:

- Permission to participate in Forest School as outlined in your Forest School handbook (to include tree climbing and the use of tools and fire perhaps)

- Permission to be included in a communication group for sharing information about what happened during Forest School (e.g. closed Facebook group or WhatsApp group)

- Taking images/videos/audio recordings of participants

- Sharing or storing the above for a variety of purposes

- Administering First Aid treatment, including the application of plasters

- Applying insect repellent, sting relief, and sun-screen

- Removing ticks

- Removing splinters.

You may also need to gather the following data (information):

- Medical needs

- Learning/additional needs

- Dietary needs

- Emergency contacts (at least two)

- Other information parents/carers would like you to have.

You will need to reference the confidentiality policy in your Forest School handbook for information relating to how you will keep this data safe and use it appropriately.

GDPR compliance

GDPR compliance is an important topic and requirement for all Forest School leaders and educational establishments. ICO (Information Commissioner's Office) is the regulatory body for GDPR and has some really useful downloadable guides as well as a helpline for you to access free of charge. https://ico.org.uk/ [21]

Care for your woodland space

An important aspect of Forest School is the care of, and consideration for, your woodland space. If you refer to **Chapter 11** you will find a wealth of information about how you can approach this. In brief terms you will probably want:

- Information from the landowner about what the woodland management priorities are
- A management plan that you can work to
- An Environmental Impact Assessment that assesses the impact of Forest School activities and how to reduce them
- A document detailing the geographical location of your site, species present, and a summary of its history
- A discussion with other users, so that you can construct a full picture of how a site is used when you and your groups are not there and create policies and procedures accordingly.

Many Forest School leaders choose to establish a dynamic document where they make an ongoing record of all site management, site conservation and ecological monitoring.

Emergency procedures and reporting incidents, accidents, and near misses

Before beginning any Forest School provision, you will want to think through any emergencies that might occur. These may include injury or illness (of a participant, an adult supporter, or yourself), lost participants, uninvited guests, or dogs. You will need to clearly set out the agreed procedure for each scenario and have a means of communicating this to all key stakeholders (fellow adult supporters, participants, parents/carers, landowners, and SLT in setting). You will also need to think through what reporting is required for incidents and near-misses that occur during Forest School sessions.

Safeguarding

The safeguarding of participants during Forest School sessions is as important as at any other time. Disclosures may be more likely during Forest School sessions due to the more relaxed timetable, the secure attachments made with trusted adults, and the possible non-judgemental approaches taken. You will need to set out what will happen in the event of disclosure and ensure that all adult supporters are aware of the procedure. How do adults in Forest School talk to participants during the disclosure conversation? How will the information disclosed be recorded in the woods? To whom are safeguarding concerns escalated? Within which other wider safeguarding policies do you need to operate?

The Forest School handbook

During their training, every Level 3 Forest School leader will create a Forest School handbook. This is a personalised, written document that sets out how you do Forest School. Handbooks can be in a variety of different formats and include a variety of information; you will need to ensure that your handbook works for you and your own, likely unique, set of circumstances. Here is a list of possible content (asterisks denote content required to meet minimum benchmarks of the Recognised Provider Scheme):

- An explanation of the Forest School ethos and principles*
- Health and safety policy*
- Emergency planning and evacuation procedures*
- Safeguarding policy*
- Confidentiality information*
- Your approach to behaviour in Forest School*
- How you deal with instances of bullying in Forest School*
- Complaint's policy and procedure*
- Sustainability or Environmental policy*
- The role of the Forest School leader and other adults in Forest School*
- Brief biographies for Level 3 Forest School leaders and other adult supporters
- Contact details for Level 3 leaders
- How Forest School fits with the wider work of an organisation (where applicable)
- Your particular Forest School vision
- The location and a description of your woodland site
- Information about what clothes and personal items to bring to Forest School

- Information about what participants might be doing during Forest School sessions
- The typical flow of a Forest School session
- Your approach to assessing risk versus benefit
- Information about consents
- Cancellation procedure
- Communications regarding Forest School sessions
- Photography and digital media policy
- Environmental Impact Assessment
- Equality, diversity and inclusion
- Ratios of adults:children
- Insurance
- Emergency equipment
- First Aid
- Medication
- Emergency information summary (location, contacts, procedures, access points, etc.)
- Tools
- Toileting
- Other welfare matters (meeting basic physiological needs)
- Food Hygiene and Safety
- Personal Protective Equipment (PPE)
- Manual handling
- Fire
- Working at height
- Session operating procedures
- A sign-off page that details when the handbook was updated and who has signed to say they have read it.

If you are a member of the FSA and you would like to access more information relating to Forest School handbooks, you can visit the FSA website and search for 'Handbook Guidance Note'. https://forestschoolassociation.org/the-forest-school-handbook-fsa-guidance-note/ **[22]**

Session planning, recording and reflecting

Something to explore before sessions begin is how you will plan for, record and reflect on each Forest School session. Most leaders choose to establish a written format with sections that can be completed for each session. For example, the benchmark set out in the FSA Recognised Forest School Provider scheme is that when session planning one should consider:

- Date and session number (e.g. 7 of 34)
- Special and additional needs
- Current needs of the group
- Outline of possible plan/activities in response to needs (to include use of natural materials & free play)
- Session start and end times
- Names of supporting adults
- Number of children
- Age of children
- Special kit required
- Associated reflection (what went well, what didn't, considerations for next time).

In addition to the general reflections made by adult supporters following the sessions, observations of individual participants will also be made. These observations help Forest School leaders to plan subsequent sessions that cater for the needs of those individuals. Established settings may have existing ways of recording observations that you can adopt or adapt. Possible methods include a clipboard with a single sheet of paper with each participant's name and a blank space to make notes in; post-its or stickers; or recording directly onto tablets or voice memos.

Who should I be liaising with?

Forest School stakeholders might include participants, senior leaders, fellow Level 3 leaders, other adult supporters, teachers, key workers, teaching assistants, educational or child psychologists, one-to-one supporters, landowners, and parents or carers.

You will invariably bring your value judgements to your Forest School practice but, at an early stage, it is really important to explore these with the Senior Leaders attached to your setting (where applicable). These early conversations are an opportunity to set out your hopes for what the Forest School provision might look like. It will also establish the needs of the setting and the participants so that you can identify synergies and the overarching aims. Preceding sections of this chapter cover other important conversations you may need to have.

Working with others

If you will be working alongside other qualified Level 3 Forest School leaders, it will be helpful to have meetings with them before Forest School provision begins. You may wish to discuss:

- What you each bring to the role

- Where your specialisms lie

- Areas in which you lack confidence

- Whether and how you can help one another to become more confident

- How your initial training differed

- Whether you all have the same understanding of what Forest School is and is not.

Due to the need in Forest School to have high ratios of adults to children, you will most likely need to rely on other adult supporters during Forest School sessions. You may be fortunate enough to have a pool of people qualified in Forest School to Level 1 or 2. These colleagues will generally have an excellent understanding of what Forest School is, but if your helpers do not hold such qualifications, how will you help them to develop their understanding? To enable everyone to facilitate Forest School in a unified way, having an informal training session will probably help. You could gather for a few hours, perhaps going over the Forest School ethos and principles indoors and then moving to the woodland space to explore a little more deeply. It may be helpful to spend some time discussing how Forest School might differ from the approaches typically used in schools and homes. To record that this training occurred you could come up with a list of aspects you wish to cover, or even a retrospective one, that would come in helpful in future when inducting new adult supporters. Some providers include a section in their Forest School handbook that sets out the role of an adult in Forest School. During conversations with your fellow adult supporters, you will also benefit from exploring the specific role of individual adults: who takes responsibility for what?

If you will be working with participants you do not usually work with, you will find insights from their usual teachers, teaching assistants, key workers, and one-to-one supporters very helpful. Before having any conversations, you will need to understand confidentiality and how to look after data appropriately. The setting with whom you are working will probably require you to sign a confidentiality agreement. When deciding the overarching aims for your Forest School provision, it is helpful to have some information from people who know participants well so that you can build a picture of the general needs of the group. For example: do they gel well; do they need support with listening; do they need to develop respect for one another; and might they benefit from time exploring boundaries? The assembled group of adults will also be able to help Forest School leaders by sharing information about each participant. You will probably be informed about the participants with stated additional needs, but what about all of the other individuals? You may wish to find out about each participant's likes and dislikes, character traits, friendship groups, areas of interest, strengths, and areas for development. This could be achieved by using a baseline assessment. A simple form that prompts responses in these areas may be completed with the participant (if appropriate and practical) and the other knowledgeable adults.

Working with landowners

If you do not own your own woodland space you will need to meet with landowners. You can find a brief summary in this chapter outlining some important considerations for land use agreements and you can dive to a much greater depth in **Chapter 10**, where you will find lots of information on finding a site and talking with landowners. Aspects to discuss will include: which areas you may or may not use; the nature of activities that are allowable on-site; access arrangements; limits on the harvesting of materials; notice needed for additional ad-hoc visits; where responsibility lies for tree work; Public Liability Insurances; site risk assessments; emergency access; and reporting.

Working with parents and carers

If you are working with children, young people or vulnerable adults, you will need to liaise with parents and carers. Collaborating with parents and carers from the early stages of establishing Forest School provision will help you to develop good relationships. Parents and carers may or may not have heard about Forest School before; they may even have preconceptions or misconceptions about Forest School. In the same way that you worked with senior leaders and supporting adults, you will need to paint a picture of the Forest School principles and ethos for parents and carers too. You will need to convey information about clothing needs, the year-round, all-weather nature of Forest School, child-led play, risky play, and risk-benefit approaches, whilst also allowing them to ask questions. Parents and carers might also be interested in what their child might end up doing during Forest School and the sorts of activities participants might choose. Once Forest School provision has begun, parents and carers may find it helpful to receive ongoing communications that help them build a picture of what has been happening during sessions from week to week; you could create weekly newsletters, use WhatsApp groups, Tapestry (or similar) or closed Facebook groups to do this.

What other tasks need to be undertaken ahead of starting sessions?

Effective Forest School provision requires careful preparation that can feel cumbersome, but don't lose heart! Thinking things through carefully before you start and working collaboratively with others to establish your Forest School provision will reap rewards, and the burdensome feeling will then lessen considerably: soon enough you will be in sessions with participants, enjoying your role and having fun. At this point you are nearly there, but in this final section, there are a few last things that require your attention.

Long-term delivery

One of the six principles of Forest School is that it is a long-term process. Following a consultation in 2017, the FSA defined long-term as running for either: a minimum of two hours per session, for 24 consecutive weeks (or the equivalent of two full school terms) in one year, covering two seasons with the same core group of participants; or a minimum of two hours per session, for 12 consecutive weeks in each year over two years, covering two seasons with the same core group of participants.

With this in mind, you need to explore how often and for how long you will meet, and over which parts of the year. If working with school classes, the FSA generally considers it preferable to work with smaller groups fortnightly rather than the whole class together every week.

Structure and freedom

Whilst Forest School is a participant-centred approach that allows for plenty of participant-led activity, it is likely that establishing a regular and routine 'flow' to your sessions will be helpful. You may wish to think about: how you travel into the Forest School space; whether there are any songs, characters or rituals you would like to use; what you do as you first gather for each session; how you revisit boundaries and safety agreements; how equipment gets put out and put away again; how tasks are shared; when any adult-directed inputs might be offered; where the significant chunk of participant-led activity can occur; when you offer refreshments; how you routinely put out your fire; how you express gratitude; and how you reflect at the end of the session. You can share a copy of this routine in your handbook and with parents, carers, and adult supporters.

Insurance

You must ensure you have the relevant insurances in place before beginning any Forest School practice. There are specialist insurers who understand the nature of the Forest School approach, who will ask you the correct questions and who know what kind of cover you will need. It is worth researching an insurer or broker before deciding to use them. You may find it very frustrating trying to arrange appropriate insurance with an insurer who doesn't properly understand the Forest School ethos, the activities that might happen, or the risk-benefit approach taken in Forest School. It is worth noting that all FSA members get a discount with Birnbeck Insurance Services, a long-standing, UK based insurance broker with experience in arranging insurance for Forest School leaders. You will need to have Public Liability Insurance (PLI) in place. If you are a freelancer you will need to ensure that i) the landowner has PLI in place to cover accidents that are a result of the trees or the site itself and ii) you have PLI to cover accidents arising from activities that happen on the site. If during Forest School sessions there are adult supporters present who are employed by the attached setting, they will also need to be covered by Employer's Liability Insurance. Before having conversations with insurance providers, it is worth having a careful think about the types of activity you envision occurring during your Forest School sessions. To enable risky play in accordance with the Risk Principle, you will require insurance cover for activities such as fire-lighting, cooking with fire, climbing, balancing, tool use, foraging, and the use of ropes. It will be helpful to decide on where your value judgement lies about each. For example, will you be comfortable with tree climbing? At what height might you become uncomfortable?

Tree safety

In accordance with the Nature Principle, Forest School takes place in a woodland or natural environment, hopefully with trees. The condition of those trees will need to be assessed before sessions start and then on an ongoing basis. Trees can become dangerous through age, disease, weather, or wind damage. Qualified and experienced arborists will be able to conduct a tree survey, in which they assess the health of each tree and make recommendations about required actions. Forest School leaders will also check for changes before each session to ensure ongoing monitoring. You will need to have discussions with your landowner about where the liability sits for carrying out any tree work recommended after a tree inspection.

Safeguarding training

Safeguarding the children, young people and vulnerable adults in your Forest School sessions is extremely important and you must have a safeguarding policy. Forest School leaders need to have an up-to-date understanding of safeguarding matters, be vigilant for signs of abuse, and know what to do in the event of a disclosure. With small groups in a large woodland space, there may be occasions when adult supporters are alone, or working one to one, with participants. Forest School leaders will therefore benefit from regularly updated safeguarding training. Ensuring that each adult supporter in Forest School sessions has also had a recent Disclosure and Barring Service check (or equivalent) is good practice.

First Aid

The Health and Safety Executive (HSE) states that First Aid provision must be 'adequate and appropriate in the circumstances', meaning you must provide sufficient First Aid equipment (First Aid kit), facilities, and personnel at all times. The Institute for Outdoor Learning (IOL) publishes a best practice guide for what 'adequate and appropriate' First Aid looks like for various types of outdoor learning. The level of First Aid qualification that the IOL suggests for Forest School leaders is that the course is at least 16 hours (excluding breaks) in duration, with an outdoor element, and covering paediatric First Aid (if you are ever likely to have prepubescent children or infants in your Forest School sessions). There are a huge variety of courses, trainers and awarding organisations to choose from when identifying an appropriate qualification. You may find the person with whom you undertook your Forest School training can signpost you to a good course, or perhaps people in your local Forest School network may be able to do so. You will need to plan to ensure this level of qualification is renewed every three years by attending a new course. 'Adequate and appropriate' First Aid doesn't just mean ensuring you have an appropriate First Aid qualification: you will also need to think carefully about what you need to have in your First Aid kit for the environment you are working in, the type of participants in your sessions, and the likely activities. You should also ensure that you, as the Forest School leader, have access to First Aid treatment in the event of an accident or illness.

Continuous Professional Development

The Leadership Principle highlights that Forest School leaders should continuously maintain and develop their professional practice. Once we are qualified to Level 3 we are by no means the finished article. We might consider ourselves to be a work-in-progress on a co-learning path alongside our participants. As your woodland site evolves and your participants become older and more experienced, you may find your areas of interest and curiosity shift. Being part of effective local Forest School networks might expose you to ideas and techniques that are new to you. You will probably wish to identify and participate in new courses each year. You might identify courses following recommendations at conferences or in books, or from communications circulated by the FSA or your original Forest School trainer. By considering yourself a co-learner, you are modelling an effective way of being to your Forest School participants: you are not the teacher or fount of all knowledge. By undertaking CPD each year you will be helping to maintain a fresh approach and will also increase your chances of meeting the needs of your Forest School participants.

The following chapter looks at **Considerations on setting up a Forest School in your school or setting.**

Reflective Exercise 10 – Future visions

Imagine your provision in five years' time: you are being paid, it is running smoothly and you are loving every minute.

- How did you get there?
- Is there anything missing from your business case or plan?
- Do you need to amend your plan to increase your chance of getting to where you wish to be?

Chapter 9 – Considerations on setting up a Forest School in your school or setting

Charlotte Atkinson

Having made the decision that you want to introduce (or re-introduce) Forest School to your school or setting – what do you do next? This chapter aims to support leaders to plan the best way forward, not just to establish Forest School, but to do so *sustainably,* in order that it becomes an integral part of your school or setting rather than something that you just 'do' (or even worse, something that you *used* to 'do'!).

There are too many examples of schools and settings who have invested heavily in trying to establish Forest School, only for it to fall by the wayside once a member of staff moves on or another priority takes precedence. This might be the situation that you are in, or you might be right at the start of your journey. Whichever, I am very excited that you have taken the step of reading this book, as time invested in research and reflection at this stage will be time well spent.

The decision to establish Forest School as part of your curriculum is not one to be taken lightly. Undoubtedly there will be costs involved, both financial and in terms of staff time and energy. Even if you have not yet tasted Forest School for yourself (something I would highly recommend to all headteachers, managers and leaders on this journey), you are already convinced that the benefits, for those young people who will get to experience Forest School, will outweigh those costs.

I am therefore making the assumption that you have made the decision to establish Forest School, and in this chapter I intend to give you some practical steps and guidance (based on my own experiences as a headteacher, as an independent Forest School leader, and as an FSA Endorsed Trainer of Forest School leaders) in order to help you on your journey.

Step 1 – Establishing a vision

In order to establish a vision for Forest School, you might find it helpful to discuss the following questions with your leadership team:

1. **What is your motivation or rationale for introducing Forest School, and how does this link to the vision and values for your school and setting?** It should be noted here that by introducing Forest School to your school or setting you do not 'become a Forest School'. There is no Forest School badge that then entitles you to call yourselves a 'Forest School'. However, those schools who have established Forest School through adopting practice based on the six Forest School Principles (see Chapters 1 and 2) can apply to become a Forest School Association Recognised Provider (Chapter 5).
2. **What do you want to achieve for your learners and for your school or setting through establishing Forest School?** How does it fit in with your curriculum aims? Think about the impact that you want Forest School to have on your learners. How does this align with your curriculum aims? In five years' time, do you see Forest School as being something that all learners experience – every year, once in a key stage, or perhaps just once during their time at your school or setting? It is worth considering the Long-Term Principle here when setting your vision for your Forest School provision. Remember the FSA definition of long-term: regular sessions lasting at least two hours, over no less than 24 sessions and covering two or more seasons, for each group of participants.

3. **What is your timescale for this achievement?** It is worth considering here what is achievable and on what sort of timescale. If you are starting from scratch, there is no reason why you can't get things up and running within a year, but 3-5 years might be a more realistic timescale to have Forest School firmly established as part of your curriculum.
4. **What are the budgetary implications?** Costs of different options will be explored in more detail later in the chapter, but it is worth bearing in mind that in addition to staff training costs, there may also be expenses involved in establishing your site, buying equipment and resources, and the day-to-day running of Forest School programmes.
5. **What is your staffing capacity to lead the project and to lead programmes of Forest School?** I cannot stress enough how important it is to have a member of the leadership team who takes overall responsibility for Forest School. I firmly believe that one of the key reasons why the establishment of Forest School may fail is lack of prioritisation by the school or setting. Whichever option you decide on for getting Forest School up and running, having a named person on your leadership team (and ideally a named governor too, if appropriate) is a must!

Step 2 – Developing a strategy

Once you have established your long-term vision, it might be useful to consider what you want to achieve by the end of each year. For example, if you are a one-form entry primary school:

- By the end of the first year, a 12-week pilot programme of Forest School has been run with one group of learners (e.g. one class or one group of mixed-age learners)
- By the end of the second year, Forest School sessions run with one year group every week throughout the year
- By the end of the third year, Forest School sessions run with two year-groups every week throughout the year.

This set of goals can be developed into a more detailed action plan once you have considered your options in more detail. Overleaf is an example of how the first year of your plan might look:

Key Objective for First Year – Introduce Forest School	
Objectives	**Success criteria**
Identify a member of the leadership team to take overall responsibility for Forest School. Commit to training to develop their understanding of Forest School (e.g. Level 1 Forest School Leader training, a 'Taster Day' and/or individual research). Identify a member of the governing body as a 'Forest School Champion'. Develop a vision for Forest School. Identify Forest School as a priority on the School Improvement/Development Plan. Identify an external provider to lead a programme of Forest School sessions. Provide a Professional Development Day for staff to introduce Forest School. Identify a class teacher plus one or two other members of staff/parents/governors to work with and assist the external provider. Identify Pilot group/class. Establish policies and procedures, set up site and organise resources through induction/training/meetings. Inform parents and children through website, newsletters, Forest School leaflet. Deliver a pilot programme of Forest School (12 weeks) taking place with the same group of learners – weekly sessions of two hours.	All staff, governors, parents and children have a basic understanding of what Forest School is all about. A safe and fit-for-purpose site for Forest School is created. A suitably trained and qualified Forest School leader is appointed. Two additional adults are identified as Forest School assistants and undertake an induction or training. Policies and procedures (including risk assessments and a site management plan) for running Forest School are all in place, with a review process and timeline. Sufficient basic resources are in place to enable a pilot group of learners to start investigating and exploring. A pilot programme of Forest School sessions with a particular year group or group of learners takes place.

Step 3 – Getting it going: what are my options?

There are two main ways that most schools or settings get Forest School established. One is by training a member or members of your own staff to set it up and run it, and the other is by getting an external provider in to do this for you. In this section I will explore both of these options in detail, identifying some of the benefits and limitations of each and providing context through case studies. I am making the assumption with both options that you have access to a potential Forest School site, either within your grounds or nearby. See **Chapters 10** and **11** for more information about Forest School sites.

If you do not have a site to use, you might want to send your learners off-site to another provider. This model (Option 3) is outlined later in the chapter.

It is worth considering that you might decide to go with one model initially, because it is the best option for your situation at this time, with a plan to use a different approach in the future. Weighing up the relative costs of the different models, I would argue that they are likely to be similar (at least in the short term), as each option has its own associated costs and savings.

It should also be noted that if your long-term aim is to become an FSA Recognised Forest School Provider, you could do this either by training a member of your staff to deliver Forest School (Option 1) or by working with an external provider responsible for delivering (or co-delivering) programmes of Forest School for you (Option 2).

Option 1 – Train staff to run Forest School within your school or setting

There are many benefits to this option, but it will not be a quick fix: it will involve your staff undertaking a recognised Level 3 Forest School Leader qualification, which will take a minimum of 10 months to complete (see **Chapter 5** for more information). As a longer-term solution, provided you have the capacity within your staff, the benefits of this option far outweigh any limitations.

Benefits:

- You know the person who will be leading the Forest School sessions (their capabilities, strengths and limitations) and they know (or are known to) your learners and wider school community.
- It will be good professional development for the staff member and should have a positive impact on their classroom practice.
- Behaviour management is unlikely to be an issue because of the already established relationships between the leader and the learners.
- There may be a strengthening of relationships between adults and learners as a result of Forest School, which in turn may have a positive impact on the wider school community. This can be exploited effectively: the leader is part of your school community and therefore available for support and guidance at times other than during Forest School sessions.
- The member of staff's up-to-date knowledge of both the curriculum and any new initiatives is likely to embed the links between learning at Forest School and learning back in the classroom.
- If the leader is also the teacher or key worker for the group, there may be additional opportunities to take learners out on an ad-hoc basis as well as for scheduled sessions. If they are not, there may still be flexibility in timetabling of Forest School sessions, e.g. by swapping PPA time. This will enable the leader to make the most of any learning opportunities, e.g. a snowy day.
- If you use a member of your staff it is more likely that they will have a stronger connection to your school or setting. They will be more invested in making it work, able to communicate more effectively with other members of staff and parents, more likely to follow things through, and more likely to look at longer term strategies rather than quick fix solutions.
- It will be easier for senior leaders to quality assure the practice of the Forest School leader, for example through linking the role to their appraisal objectives.
- The Forest School leader will already be DBS checked and should be familiar with the safeguarding policies and procedures of the setting.
- The Forest School leader will be covered by the insurance of the school or setting.

Limitations:

- It will take longer to set up initially, as there will be a period of training (incorporating the establishment of policies and procedures) followed by a pilot programme.
- There is the potential of additional workload for the member of staff both during training and on an ongoing basis, as they are unlikely to have a relevant specialism and so will have new learning to take on board. Furthermore, they will not only need to plan, resource, lead and evaluate the sessions, but also ensure that they manage the site sustainably, keep their policies and procedures up to date, manage any adults supporting the sessions, and keep up to date with Forest School-related CPD (see '**Considerations**' below).
- There may be challenges in balancing the needs of the school and maintaining the Forest School ethos and principles, which could result in the latter being diluted.
- Systems for managing behaviour that are in place in your school or setting might not be appropriate for Forest School sessions. Having to adapt between different systems at different times could create an issue for some members of staff or participants.
- It might be more difficult to achieve appropriate adult:participant ratios due to the expectation that a class teacher or key worker leading Forest School must involve their full class. This can be addressed by roping in teaching assistants, parent helpers or governors as additional assistants, and delivering to smaller groups on alternating weeks.
- There may be additional costs involved, e.g. buying resources and supply cover for completing assignments during training.
- Staff might move on, taking the qualification with them (consider succession planning).

Further considerations if you are thinking of training a member of your staff

1. Choosing the right person

If you choose this route, the single most important thing for you to do is to make sure that you select the right person to undertake the training. This may make the difference between success and failure for your Forest School project. If you have someone in mind, consider the list of entry requirements for a Level 3 Forest School leader (**Chapter 5**). The following questions may also help you to decide if they are right for the role:

- Do they want to do it? Are they aware of what is involved in both the training and the role of leader?
- Do they like being outdoors? In all weathers? Do they have any fears or phobias that could affect their ability to embrace the outdoor learning environment (such as a fear of spiders or wasps)?
- Do they have a good level of physical fitness? If they have any medical conditions or disabilities, could modifications be made in order to enable them to undertake the role?
- Are they a reflective leader? Are they interested in learning new things and working in new ways? Are they flexible and adaptable to change? Are they willing to embrace their own and other participants' holistic development?
- Are they able to lead a group of learners and manage all aspects of a programme of Forest School? Consider planning, resourcing, observation, assessment, evaluation, behaviour management, safety. See **Chapter 4** for more detail on the Forest School leader's role.
- Do they have the ability to lead and manage a group of adults?
- Will they be prepared to put in extra time to complete the qualification?
- Do they have the ability to complete the written work that may be required as part of the Level 3 qualification (equivalent to an A-Level)?
- Are they able to work to deadlines and complete what they have started?
- Are they planning on staying in post at your school or setting for long enough for you to get Forest School up and running (ideally at least three years)? If you don't already have one, you may wish to consider introducing a clause within your CPD policy stating that, should a member of staff undertake a training course costing more than a certain amount, if they then leave the setting within a certain timeframe they may be liable to repay some or all of the course fees.

When choosing who will undertake the training, a key consideration is their current role and position within your establishment. For example, a teacher is likely to:

- Have more experience of leading and managing groups of learners and adults
- Be better placed to exploit the links between learning at Forest School and learning in the classroom
- Be accustomed to devoting their own time to studying, putting policies and procedures in place, and planning, resourcing and evaluating sessions
- Be able to complete the written elements of the course to the required standard.

But they are also more likely to cost more, as you will need to pay for cover to attend training and lead sessions (if not with their class), as well as for ongoing professional development. Teachers may also be less likely to fully embrace the six principles as they run against standard classroom management practices.

It may therefore be more difficult to run Forest School sessions with smaller groups if you opt to train a teacher rather than a teaching assistant or member of support staff. Furthermore, a teacher without experience of the Early Years Foundation Stage may find it difficult to adapt to the Forest School approach to learning, which is much more closely aligned to the approach used for teaching children aged 3-5 years. Once they do, however, you may find that you have a member of staff with a whole new skill set! Learners may also struggle initially with their teacher being somewhat 'different' during Forest School, and this may impact on the special relationship between leader and group that is often evident at Forest School.

Often schools and settings opt to train a teaching assistant or member of support staff, rather than a teacher, due to the perception that it is a cheaper option. However, a teacher's pay and conditions mean that they may have more flexibility in their directed (but non-teaching) time to take on the additional responsibilities associated with the Forest School leader's role; it may be unreasonable to expect a member of non-teaching staff to contribute the necessary hours to complete their training and establish Forest School for no additional pay. Furthermore, this new leadership role may be above and beyond the remit of a teaching assistant. For example, if they are employed as a Level 2, it may be necessary to upgrade them to a Level 3 for the hours they work as a Forest School leader, or perhaps to pay them for planning, preparation, and assessment time in addition to the session itself. A 2-hour Forest School session can easily require an additional two hours of planning, setting up for the session, tidying away afterwards and evaluating the learning.

Once Forest School is up and running, there is likely to be a need for ongoing time (and associated additional expenses) for the leader to maintain the Forest School site, maintain and replace resources, and attend training in order to develop their skills.

Whatever your situation, the most important factor is that the person you train has expressed a desire to do the training and take on the role.

2.   Training more than one person from your school or setting

If you have the capacity to do so, it is worthwhile training at least two members of staff at the same time to become Forest School leaders. They will be able to support each other during the training and beyond, and will face a reduced workload during the training as certain elements of it (e.g. production of the handbook of policies and procedures for running Forest School in your school or setting) can be co-authored rather than having to produce two separate documents. There will be two people to help establish Forest School and to share the ongoing responsibilities associated with the role. It also means that if one person does leave, it will be possible to continue running Forest School sessions whilst you train someone else to take their place.

3.   Training staff to work across a network of schools or settings

If you are part of a federation, academy chain, or other network, it may be worth training one or more members of staff to run Forest School in multiple settings. Not only could you split the cost of training and establishing Forest School, but there is also the potential to develop one or several sites that multiple schools and settings could access (although the potential environmental impact of large numbers of people accessing a small number of sites also needs to be considered – see **Chapter 11**).

You might have the capacity within your network for the Forest School leader(s) you train to specialise, perhaps just leading Forest School sessions rather than class teaching. This is likely to lead to a higher quality Forest School experience, particularly if class teachers or key workers are able to assist during the sessions (rather than being removed from the experience, e.g. if the sessions are used for PPA cover).

Option 2 – Buy in the services of an independent leader or organisation to run Forest School in your setting

The second option that most schools or settings consider when setting up (or re-establishing) Forest School involves buying in the services of a Level 3 Forest School trained and qualified independent leader or organisation to run Forest School in your setting. Reasons for choosing this option vary, but for some it's a short-term solution to get things up and running before training their own staff further down the line. As with Option 1, the key to the success of this option is getting the right person, and there is further guidance in **Chapter 5** on how to do this. There is also guidance on points you may need to discuss and agree with the contracted leader before the sessions start. This section outlines some of the key benefits and limitations of buying in Forest School provision.

Benefits:

- As a leader of a school or setting, it will be less time-consuming for you to contract someone to run Forest School for you. You will need to invest some time initially, but once things are up and running, little ongoing support should be needed.
- The person (or company) that you contract to run the sessions is likely to be a specialist who enjoys working outdoors, is passionate about Forest School, and has a good level of understanding about how to set up and run Forest School sessions. This passion and enthusiasm should have a positive impact on your learners and any staff who assist. Their knowledge will be an asset when setting up your site and preparing for the sessions.
- An external person will be able to facilitate the sometimes challenging change in relationships between participants and members of staff when moving between the classroom and the woodland. The leader is able to support staff, at times alternating their role between advocate and sounding board.
- They are responsible for their own ongoing CPD, including Outdoor/Forest School First Aid, Food Hygiene, etc. They should have their own personal liability insurance and be DBS checked, and will be covered by the insurance for your school or setting if running sessions on your site.
- They are likely to have their own equipment they can bring to support the sessions (you may need to provide consumable resources). This will reduce the time and cost of resourcing the sessions.
- You may have more flexibility to choose the day/times, groups and location(s) for the sessions if you are not having to fit in with existing timetables.
- You may have more flexibility on group sizes if the leader is going to be an additional person, so it may be easier to adhere to the recommended ratios for Forest School.
- If the class teacher, key worker, or teaching assistants are able to assist the leader during the sessions, it will give them a good understanding of what quality Forest School is and what the role of leader involves. It will also be good CPD, as they will be able to learn about the woodland environment and its opportunities alongside the learners. This may lead to a member of your staff being keen to train as a leader and take on the role, which may prove a more sustainable long-term solution. Furthermore, this member of your staff will be in a good position to make detailed and accurate observations during the sessions, enabling effective adult interventions during the session as well as supporting planning for future learning, both at Forest School and back in the classroom.

Limitations:

- If your site needs to be set up for Forest School, you may need to pay extra for the external provider to assist you. They may not be available for ongoing maintenance of the site, and a member of staff may need to liaise with the provider over this.
- It might take a while for relationships to become established between the leader, the participants, and the adult helpers. This could affect behaviour management in the early days of using an external provider.
- Day to day communication is likely to be more difficult if the person delivering the sessions spends a limited time onsite. The leader may not be able to follow up easily on issues arising during the session if they are only with you for a few hours a week. You may need to nominate a link member of staff (ideally the class teacher or key worker) to meet regularly with the provider in order to facilitate communication or (even better!) involve your staff in the delivery of Forest School so that they are able to follow up on any issues that arise.
- Although any external provider will want the sessions to be successful, they are unlikely to have the same connection to your school or setting, and will have less influence within your organisation than a member of staff. This means that the impact of the sessions may be less widespread than if a member of staff leads the sessions.

Further considerations if you are thinking of buying in the services of an independent leader or organisation to run Forest School in your setting

Chapter 5 outlines some of the questions that you might want to ask of an external provider before engaging them to run Forest School for you. Once you have identified the right provider, you may also wish to consider PPA cover, policies and procedures, and introductory sessions.

1.   Planning Preparation and Assessment (PPA) cover

Buying in the services of a specialist external provider to run Forest School for a class (or classes) of your learners may allow you to cover PPA time for class teachers and key workers. This can certainly save some money, but it may not be the ideal solution as the wider benefits of the sessions may be somewhat limited by the absence of the class teacher or key worker. If you are thinking of using Forest School sessions to cover PPA time, you might want to consider the following questions:

- Who will cover the class if bad weather prevents the session from taking place?
- Who will check that learners are properly clothed for the sessions, and what will happen if they are not?
- Could a teaching assistant support the sessions to provide a link between the classroom and the Forest School site?
- Who will be responsible for behaviour management during the sessions?
- What communication is needed between the Forest School leader and the class teacher or key worker? Consider planning, behaviour, outcomes of observations, and curriculum links.

How can this communication be facilitated and what will it involve? For example, through any members of school staff supporting the sessions, via email or through regular meetings.

2.   Policies and procedures

An external provider should take responsibility for creating and maintaining the documentation that needs to be in place for running Forest School. However, it is not a case of 'one size fits all' – although the external provider might have a handbook for their organisation, the policies and procedures within this will need to be adapted for your setting and updated on a regular basis. The following questions might help you to clarify roles and responsibilities related to policies and procedures.

- Are they prepared to adapt their handbook for your setting? Will they do this in their own time or will you need to pay for this? Will you be able to keep an electronic copy of this for the future?
- Are they prepared to undertake a site survey and environmental impact assessment and use this to develop a management plan for your site? Will they do these in their own time or will you need to pay for this? Will you be able to keep an electronic copy of these for the future?
- Are they prepared to do a risk assessment for your site and update it seasonally? Will they do this in their own time or will you need to pay for this? Will you be able to keep an electronic copy of this for the future?
- Will they carry out a check of the site before each session? How and where will this be recorded?
- Do they have risk-benefit (or benefit-risk) assessments for any 'risky' activities? How will these be shared with the adults accompanying the sessions? Will they perform assessments in their own time or will you need to pay for this? Will you be able to keep an electronic copy of these for the future?

3.   An introductory session for supporting adults and for the learners?

Before starting any programmes of Forest School as an external provider, I always encourage the school to invest half a day (minimum) for the class teacher (or other supporting adults) to meet with me. This enables me to find out what their aims for the programme are, share information about the group, discuss roles and responsibilities, and look at the site and its possibilities. This is not a substitute for the Level 1 (Introduction to Forest School) or Level 2 (Forest School Assistant) training, which provide a more in-depth understanding of the Forest School ethos and principles, but it is invaluable in ensuring that the programmes of Forest School I deliver run smoothly. I use the outcomes of our discussion to draw up an agreement (see below) which sets out clearly where responsibilities lie right from the outset.

I also like to meet the group of learners before the first session if possible, as this gives me an opportunity to talk to them about what to expect from the sessions. I explain how they need to prepare themselves (including what they might need to wear and bring) and answer any questions they might have. The outcome is a happy, excited group of learners who are well-prepared and ready for learning!

Example of an agreement between external provider and school/setting

Role and responsibilities of the Forest School leader

The Forest School leader will hold and maintain appropriate qualifications, certification, and insurance for running Forest School (Level 3 Forest School Leader, Outdoor First Aid, DBS and Public Liability Insurance).

Prior to a Forest School programme starting the leader will:

- Liaise with the school to agree the number and ages of children within the group, number of adults needed, and dates and times of sessions.
- If requested, provide the school with guidance on transport, equipment and funding.
- Agree with staff the aims for the sessions, and if requested, provide information and consent letter to send to parents/carers.
- Agree and communicate an appropriate approach to behaviour management that will be adopted during Forest School sessions.
- If necessary, liaise with landowners and support the school with requesting permission to use land.
- Carry out and provide the school with a site risk assessment, a general welfare and weather risk assessment, and an emergency action plan.
- Provide training for staff or parent volunteers if requested.

During the Forest School programme, the leader will:

- Produce an outline plan for each session and share this with class teachers (who can then share with other adults if appropriate).
- Carry out risk assessments for activities and share this with class teachers (who can then share with other adults if appropriate).
- Carry out a daily site check, take any remedial actions as appropriate (e.g. removing litter), and inform the school if there are any major concerns that could impact upon the safety of the group.
- Unless otherwise agreed, provide the equipment needed for running sessions.
- Provide a First Aid kit (although the school may take responsibility for First Aid) and carry a mobile phone.
- Provide consumable resources where necessary (school to reimburse).
- Take responsibility for the learning, behaviour and welfare of the group, in consultation with school staff.
- Observe children's learning during sessions and involve other adults in using observations to plan subsequent sessions.

Signed: **(Forest School Leader)**   **Date:**

Role and responsibilities of the school/setting

Prior to the start of the Forest School programme the school/setting will:

- Ensure that the site is safe and prepared for the sessions.
- Ensure that staff and parent volunteers supporting Forest School sessions are appropriately briefed and trained to support.
- Arrange transport to and from the site and carry out the necessary risk assessments for this.
- Brief any adults supporting the sessions about relevant school policies and procedures (e.g. use of mobile phones, smoking, etc).
- Ensure that the leader is aware of relevant school policies and procedures for behaviour management, safeguarding, bullying, etc.
- Provide the leader with relevant information about the group, such as a class list identifying any medical or behavioural needs; and information about any medical needs of adults supporting the group.
- Ensure that any adults supporting the sessions are made aware of relevant and necessary information about the children's needs.
- Agree a procedure for toileting.
- Agree the roles and responsibilities of the adults during 'Normal Operating Procedure' (taking into account the need for safeguarding).
- Agree the roles and responsibilities of the adults during 'Emergency Action Procedure'.

During the Forest School programme, the school will:

- Ensure there are sufficient adults to satisfy minimum ratio requirements for school visits, if going offsite. The suggested ratio for Forest School is a minimum of one adult per six children in Y1-6 (not including the leader). The minimum number of adults recommended is three for any group.
- Ensure that adults supporting the sessions adhere to school policies and procedures.
- Ensure that the key member of staff carries a mobile phone and is responsible for contacting the school (and perhaps parents) in case of emergency.
- Ensure that children and adults are appropriately clothed for the sessions.
- Provide spare clothing for children (and adults if possible).
- Provide refreshments for the sessions (if required).
- Be responsible for bringing, safely storing, and administering any medications.
- Provide a First Aid kit and take responsibility for managing First Aid (if agreed with the Forest School leader).
- Support the Forest School leader in managing the learning, behaviour and welfare of the group.
- Take responsibility for managing any unacceptable behaviour displayed by pupils.
- Take an active role in sessions – ensure that staff join in with games, support the learning, model positive behaviour, and make observations.
- Take responsibility for regular head counts and instigating the lost child procedure if necessary.
- Take responsibility for the group in the event of a fire drill or evacuation.

Signed: **(Class Teacher)   Date:**

Option 3 – Learners from your school or setting to go offsite to another provider for Forest School

Options 1 and 2 rely on you having a suitable site within your grounds (or within easy access) for you to use or develop for Forest School. If this is not an option, you may consider using an external provider who has their own site for the sessions. This removes the need for you to take any responsibility for site management, but may incur additional costs for transport. It will also mean that Forest School opportunities are limited to a set day and time, and that it becomes something for your participants to go and 'do' rather than being incorporated into your school culture.

Case study – Wirral Ranger Service – Forest School sessions run by an external provider on their own site

Context – From 2013 to 2018, in Wirral, 15 local schools visited Forest School sites in a number of public parks within walking distance of the school for their Forest School sessions. The sessions were run by park rangers, park staff, and freelance assistants and volunteers on a long-term basis. There were a number of benefits for the schools involved.

Benefits:

- The sites were all managed and developed as part of the park landscapes by the Forest School staff and this meant that schools did not have to pay for additional hours for site checks, site assessments, or environmental surveys. The staff surveying the sites had extensive knowledge of them and of the hazards they were looking for.
- Work on the sites could be completed quickly to make safe, as the park staff had the skills to do repairs/management in house. This was done without cost to the school.
- The schools and many of the children developed strong relationships with the ranger team and we ended working together much more closely. This meant that use of outdoor spaces increased (both by children and by their families) and problematic behaviours decreased due to the respect for and relationships with staff.
- The staff were massively knowledgeable about the environment, flora and fauna, and their enthusiasm for it carried the children with them.
- The teachers became participants and learned while they attended the sessions. Many schools went on to set up their own sessions and train staff as a result; some negotiated a cooperative model of delivery.

Limitations:

- Travelling to the site took some organising, and whilst some schools walked to Forest School others used taxis or relied on a free minibus service (funded by a corporate partner).
- Communication of changes to the school's plans, e.g. last minute flu shots on a Forest School Day led to postponed or cancelled sessions which ultimately cost either the school or the setting.
- Joint planning between the school and FS providers was limited and opportunities for better joined-up thinking were missed because of this.

Grant funding

Using grant funding is a great way to get Forest School up and running. There may be grants available from lottery funds or through your local authority, or even from smaller organisations such as local supermarkets and housing associations, that you can access to support your Forest School set-up. Through these you may be able to apply for funding for training, equipment, and site development work. When applying for grants from a particular organisation, a good strategy is often to start with a small-scale bid (perhaps for a set of waterproofs or tools) before applying for larger amounts, as organisations with a funding history are more likely to be successful in future bids for larger amounts. There is a knack to writing grant applications; it can be time consuming, and very frustrating if you are not successful. If you lack prior experience, it may be worth allocating the job to someone who has plenty (perhaps an interested parent), or else getting some training – there are lots of short courses and tips online to help you to write a successful bid.

Allocating resources from the central budget

In order for your Forest School provision to be sustainable, the funding to keep it going must also be sustainable. How you allocate your budget to this will depend on your vision for Forest School – account for both the model of provision that you will adopt and your plan for which learners will access this and when.

For example, if you are planning on training your own staff to run Forest School, relying on annual grant applications is unlikely to be sustainable. Instead, you will need to build that role into your core staffing structure. You might want to consider creative ways of deploying your staff; could the Y3 teacher you have in mind as a leader run Forest School for all four classes in key stage 2 by adopting a model of subject-specialist teaching in the afternoons, in which key stage 2 teachers swap their classes and each teach their specialist subject to a different class each afternoon?

Many schools and settings use targeted intervention funding (such as Pupil Premium or Sports Premium) to support their Forest School provision. This could be particularly appropriate if you plan to use an external provider.

Fundraising

Small-scale fundraising is a great way to get your Forest School project off the ground. Not only does it engage your local community and let them know what you're planning, it is also a great way of getting funds for specific purchases, such as equipment, resources or training. Many schools and settings involve their parent associations in fundraising activities like cake sales, non-uniform days, or sponsored events; and if your site needs improvement work, parents and carers are often keen to support with practical tasks too.

Current Forest School participants could be actively involved in raising funds for the next class in a 'paying it forward' system. This is hugely beneficial for both sets of participants and conveys a value for each child. Children could fundraise by selling things they have made at Forest School, or by running the games they have learned there at school fayres or lunchtimes. This takes a degree of supervision, but is hugely rewarding and creates a real sense of pride.

Step 4 – Keeping it going

Developing a long-term strategy for your Forest School provision at the outset is the best way of ensuring sustainability for the future. Here are some considerations that might help to inform that strategy:

1. Ensure that Forest School is part of the annual Improvement and Development plan for your school or setting, and use this to keep your governing body or trust up to date. This will help to ensure that regular funding is allocated and that leadership and accountability for Forest School development is clear.
2. Check in with your Forest School leader or provider on a regular basis. This could take the form of a termly catch-up meeting or visit to a session. If your leader is part of school staff, encourage them to keep up to date with their professional development through attending meetings of their local FSA group, visiting other schools/settings, and attending training events. It might be useful to have an objective related to Forest School Leadership as part of their annual appraisal agreement.
3. Consider ways of measuring the impact of your Forest School provision on your learners. Some schools and settings use pre- and post-programme surveys, case studies based on observations, or ongoing assessment and tracking through specialist programs or online

applications. This evidence is invaluable when helping to justify spending allocations or when reporting to external bodies (such as Ofsted).

4. Ensure that the quality of education provided through Forest School is monitored on a regular basis by someone who is familiar with the Forest School ethos and principles. This could take the form of a learning walk, where half a day is spent reviewing policies, procedures and planning, observing a session, and talking to all those involved. The outcomes of this will help to inform your self-evaluation and to identify improvement priorities for the future.

5. Consider succession planning so that you do not end up with a gap in your Forest School provision if someone leaves. Some schools and settings train a new leader every year or two, to build capacity in case the leader moves on. You may wish to find out about local organisations offering Forest School sessions, just in case. Checking in with your leader or provider on a regular basis, and showing them that you value their work, should help to ensure that you are not left in the lurch by a last-minute decision for someone to leave.

6. Finally, and most importantly, promote what you are doing! Let parents and the local community know what you are doing (and get them involved wherever possible); include regular updates in your newsletter and on your website; and let the local press know about the wonderful opportunities that you are providing for the learners in your care.

The following chapter deals with getting to know your site and landowner agreements, this is a critical part of a successful Forest School.

Chapter 10 – Getting to know your site and landowner agreements

Jon Cree

In this chapter we look at land ownership, explore the considerations for choosing a site, and outline the process of creating land-use agreements. In the UK, nearly all our land is privately owned by individuals or organisations. Thousands of years of cultural, religious, economic, and social practices – such as laws, deeds, battles, enclosures, communal space, and conservation policies – mean that the landscape is a fascinating patchwork of land ownership systems. Deeds of ownership can sometimes date back as far as the Domesday book, but land changes hands every day and the map of ownership in the UK is constantly evolving. Operating successfully on land owned by someone else requires the building and nurturing of understanding. The agreements and relationships established during the agreement stage may mean the difference between the success or failure of your business later on.

Landowners and what they own

A landowner could be anyone, from a group of friends buying a small plot of woodland to a stately home managing vast acres of ancient woodland over centuries. Most of the land in the UK is owned by somebody. This is a general overview of landownership in England in 2019, as identified in an article in Countryfile Magazine.

Below: A diagrammatic representation of landownership in the United Kingdom.

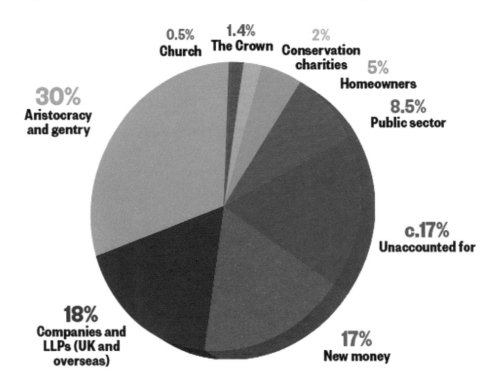

(Countryfile Magazine, 2019)

'Contrary to what we used to think the memory of the Forest is not of one, two or three centuries but at least 2000 years' – Etienne Dambine and Jean Luc Dupouey

---

As a percentage of the total land area in 2019, woodlands accounted for:

- 13% of the UK
- 10% of England
- 15% of Wales
- 18% of Scotland
- 8% of Northern Ireland

Conifers account for approximately half (51%) of the UK woodland area (Office For National Statistics, 2020).

It is worth noting that the UK is one of the least wooded countries in Europe. As of 2019, the ONS reports that 73% of all woodland (2,325,000 hectares) is privately owned, with the remaining 27% (863,00 hectares) in public hands. An encouraging statistic from this report shows that woodlands are becoming increasingly accessible for recreation and education – the estimated percentage of the UK population with access to 20 hectares of woodland within four kilometres of their home increased from 61% in 2007 to 74% in 2017.

The land and our responsibility to it

Our Forest School practice is of the land. As leaders, we are of the land and have the privilege of being given the responsibility to care for it. We are role models to all the people in our sessions and we help them connect to nature. This is one of the reasons why Forest School is so special: we re-build our community's relationship with their local land.

One of the most rewarding aspects of being a Forest School leader is developing a long-term relationship with our Forest School sites. This begins with understanding the past and present stories and uses of the area, and any plans that the landowner may have. This understanding can be developed and recorded through the woodland management planning process (see **Chapter 11**) to create a strategy for the sensitive and sustainable use of the site.

How to find a wood?

'All great adventures start with a map.' – G.K. Chesterton

Start with a map! Maps are fascinating – they give so many clues to a woodland without even visiting it. On a map you can tell which way a wood is facing and if the land is flat or sloping; if south-facing it will receive more light, may have dense vegetation and may be warmer and brighter on dull days. Streams, ponds, and spring lines give clues as to water supplies, and tree shapes indicate whether it is coniferous, deciduous or a mix of both. Footpaths are marked, and (perhaps most importantly) you can see what access is like and what type of land and buildings are your potential neighbours. Before finding out about ownership, always check the site's viability on a map. You will need to think about: distances for travel to the site; access; parking; other public access like pathways, tracks, and bridleways; and you will need to identify any barriers that may restrict access for your learners.

You will then need to find out who owns the wood. This can be done by looking at the local records office, knocking on doors, talks in the pub, or contacting local or national networks and organisations. The obvious first port of call is the local authority (regional, county, or parish). Local Wildlife Trusts, Forestry England, Royal Forestry Society, Small Woods Association, Woodland Trust, Countryside Landowners Association, Forest School Association (especially FSA local groups) and Forest School networks (there are a number of social media FS groups) may also be able to help you locate the landowner. If all else fails, you could even ask

166

parents and local community groups. If it proves tricky to find out who owns your desired wood and you have exhausted all the above channels, then it is worth approaching owners of the land adjacent to the wood.

Getting a 'feel' for a site

When you have found a site and identified its owner, the next thing to do is to get to know your site first-hand. This is to see what shapes the space, its history and its place in local memory, and all the things that make it special. You may have some places already in mind, or you may have found a site using the methods outlined above. Once you have found a site, we suggest that you visit it and sit in it for a while. If there are no public rights of way you will need to get permission to do this. Look at it from as many perspectives as possible, and 'feel' into it, before you decide whether it is worth pursuing for your Forest School delivery. As we have seen in **Chapters 2**, **3** and **4**, the feel of the Forest School site is an important aspect for participants, and plays a crucial role in forming lasting connections with nature. As a person who wants to work outdoors, you are likely to be sensitive to the atmosphere of natural spaces and how they make you feel, so explore it on behalf of your future participants and ask yourself:

- How does it feel to be amongst the trees?
- What can you see outside the wood?
- How many different spaces are available for play?
- Is there a structure to the vertical layers?
- Is there birdsong?
- Are there insects flying?
- How are the elements intermingling? Consider the wind, the light, and whether there is water – any streams, ponds or puddles?
- What's the soil like? Use the thumb test: is it clayey, loamy, sandy?
- Are there any visual clues to who or what may have interacted here and changed its physicality?

Write down or draw your initial impressions and feelings, and then visualise how your learners might be in this site. You might want to think about:

- Where would you put a basecamp and fire circle?
- Is there any access to toileting facilities?
- Are there any possible water supplies?
- Where is the main access into the site? Will it be shared with other users?
- Have you got a safe place for tool use or crafting?
- Does the site contain enough potential space for risk-taking and play?
- Are there areas of calm or stillness within the site?

The importance of site history

Once you have found a site that feels right to you, you may want to look into the history of the site – the tithe maps of the 1800s are often a great resource to get you started (see https://tithemaps.co.uk/about/ [23]), and the local records office is also a good starting point. The history of the site can give participants a source of inspiration or connection and improve their sense of place. Participants often need to know where they are in the world so they can begin to work on who they are within it. Other sources of information for woodland use are **MyForest** and the Small Woods Association.
https://myforest.sylva.org.uk/ **[24]**
https://www.smallwoods.org.uk/en/advice-and-information/ **[25]**

The local Biological Records Centre can be another good starting point. Talking to local people, local farmers, rangers, historians, and council members can often reveal a lot of fascinating insights about your little patch of woods. Local Authorities often have a countryside or conservation department, or even a tree officer, who can help direct you to the right people.

We would highly recommend the following books to get a good grip on the general history of woodlands and land ownership in the UK:

- *Woodlands*, by Oliver Rackham (a classic of the genre)
- Trees and Woodland in the British Landscape, by Oliver Rackham
- *The Common Ground*, by Richard Mabey.

The history of the site should also help you to identify whether it has any specific designations. The landowner should be able to let you know about these and if any restrictions may affect your delivery. A comprehensive list of designations and what they mean can be found in Appendix 1 in **Chapter 11**. The search for local memory and history is a good exercise for building a picture of how the area has been used in the past. The land may have been subjected to traumatic *wild clearance;* or treasured and nurtured for many years, increasing its biodiversity and societal value; or perhaps heavily mined, leaving the ground unstable or unsafe to use. You might even discover that your site was a sacred place for people who lived in the area in the past – you could find a way to honour that in your Forest School practice, and you may want to ensure that you do not offend people who continue to hold the woods sacred.

Below: A picture of Ash Grove

Case Study – Jon Cree– My experience of getting to know a site – Ash Grove in Worcestershire

We were offered caretakership of a small wood called Ash Grove. Immediately my ears pricked up: ash is my tree, the one I identify with and have had a long relationship with – its straight grain is great for carving; the woods of ash are often filled with light as they gain their leaves later than other trees and lose them earlier; ash is THE coppice tree for me; and it is the Celtic 'Tree of Life'. As I suspected, its name was a big clue to its makeup and I was overjoyed. We immediately looked on the OS map and soon noticed a public footpath running through it: great, at least there is access! We found a small stream coming from half way down one side: water too! We could also see that it was surrounded by fields yet close to other small parcels of woodland, and it was on a slight northerly-facing slope.

We wasted no time in venturing out. On arrival our first thought was that the nearest road and parking was quite a walk, and we wondered if the owner of an adjacent woodland would let us use his track and space in the wood… and made a note to do some research into this. On seeing the wood for the first time during our approach from the grazed pastureland in the west, our hearts skipped a beat – no conifers; boundary oaks and hawthorn hedge; hazel understory and lots of ash! We climbed the rickety stile and (having previously sought permission from the wood's owner) strayed off the path and found a glade. Both of us instantly had the same feeling: *'This is it!'* It felt light, and had many open spaces interspersed with clumps of hazel coppice and overgrown ash coppice. There were lots of cherry trees. We both decided to treasure this moment, and as we paused to reflect on our good fortune a robin settled next to where were standing. This was a good sign, we felt, as many Forest School sites I have visited have the obligatory robin companion. Wrens, buzzards, blackbirds and blackcaps also tuned into us!

As we explored the site, we found a bank going across the wood, halfway down the slope – perhaps an old trackway. And then right in the middle there was a large old holly. Maybe, we thought, this had been an important woodland for coppicing in the past and the holly had been planted to protect the land (holly is often an indicator of human connection in the past). We gently moved down through the wood (which covers four acres) and came across a copse of sweet chestnut coppice, and then a little area that had obviously been planted with ash, probably about fifty years previously: obvious lines of trees. This would be ideal for thinning and using for building a shelter, and for firewood!

As we wandered further, we stumbled into a sweet area of open hazel coppice – this felt like a space where the children would be comfortable playing. What's more, there was a dry ditch that might have water flowing in it at some times of year (it was where the stream was marked on the map), but not now. There were also a few birch trees. At the bottom of the wood, the stream appeared: it followed a line of trees beyond the wood, running between two fields before disappearing into another small wood. We moved back up the site, rubbing the soil between our fingers at various spots… Red clay – some more sticky than others! Plenty of raw materials for a Forest School. Having explored, we imagined a space for the basecamp in the middle where we could see both sunrise and sunset… It just felt so right!

We still had some access issues and a lack of water to overcome, which we would need to look at further. Lots of spaces to play and hide, and unexpected diversity.

Over the next few weeks, we met the owner and talked to the neighbouring farmer and woodland owner. We took time to look in local records and found that this wood has been worked as a coppice for many years, but never used for pheasant shoots (unlike many of the other woods in this vicinity). There were still some access issues regarding getting wood and equipment in and out of the wood, but these could be overcome – maybe we would have to purchase a four-wheel drive or acquire an extra robust trolley (the bane of all Forest School leaders!). Not having a constant supply of water could mean lots of lugging. But on the map there seemed to be a spring line along the middle of the wood, so maybe a little digging would reveal a groundwater supply we could possibly tap into eventually. We would need to check with the environment agency on this one.

All these initial explorations took place over winter, and we visited a few times from October to March. As spring rose, we suddenly saw the woodland floor was readying itself for a covering of wood anemone, bluebells, and yellow archangel, plus that indicator of old woodland, dog's mercury. We decided we were so glad we had waited and that our initial impression of the wood had been confirmed.

Once you have a feel for the site and are sure it is for you, you are ready to make an agreement with a landowner, and (if your organisation already owns the land) with the other key stakeholders, such as colleagues and other users of the site.

Below: the approach to Ash Grove.

Making a Landowner/Forest School Agreement

Once you are armed with both your 'felt sense' of the site and some facts about its past and present, then you have some inkling and knowledge of the site with which to start negotiating with the landowner over siting your Forest School. Demonstrating that you understand the land, being able to talk through how you may care for the site (and involve the participants in this care), highlighting how you will minimise the impact of Forest School activity – all this is grist to your mill when having that first real conversation with the landowner. This latter is particularly important when approaching a land maintenance team. In many instances on school sites, for example, if this is not clearly articulated to 'property services' at the start (and on an ongoing basis) the site can be poorly managed, to the detriment of both the practice of Forest School and the wildlife of the space.

Once the initial conversation has been had and both parties agree in principle that Forest School can happen on the site, then you will need to get into the nitty-gritty of a detailed agreement. The following section outlines key things to think about when formulating an agreement with the landowner, and details the main types of agreement used in the UK. Even if your organisation owns the land (as at many school sites), you will still need to have some sort of internal agreement with the board of governors, the senior leadership team, the rest of the organisation, and the maintenance team. It may help to know some of the terms that woodland agreements may include, and an extensive list can be found on the online resource:
https://forestschoolassociation.org/book-resources/ [1].
For an up-to-date glossary: https://ukwas.org.uk/standard/glossary-of-terms/ [26]
UK Forestry Standard terms: https://www.gov.uk/government/publications/the-uk-forestry-standard [27]

Landowner agreements

What is a landowner agreement?

A landowner agreement is a licence to operate, an official confirmation that you are allowed on this land, an agreement about who is responsible for what, and a crucial piece of paper for your final Forest School portfolio! Yes, a landowner agreement is all these things, but most importantly it is a *process*, and it enables you to start and continue conversations and build a relationship with the landowner. It is a two-way process: informing and educating a landowner on what Forest School is, what you will be doing, and how you are doing it safely with care of the land aforethought; and understanding what issues landowners may face with managing land and how we can work together. There will be within all landowner agreements certain aspects that are dictated by legal requirements. Examples include: insurance, nature/heritage conservation and land legislation, planning and access law, and deed restrictions

Building relationships with landowners

As we have said before, ownership is diverse, like a thriving ecosystem! As Forest School leaders, we need to understand what kind of landowner we are working with. We need to discover their motivations and how we can best align with them to build a partnership. There are pros and cons for each type of owner: a small woodland owner might be easy to meet and chat with but may be nervous about insurance and liability; a national park may have a Ranger for you to work with, yet have a lot of restrictions to follow because of the site's designation; a school may require you to work with someone in the council or Local Education Authority, with the complications of organising times to meet them and undertaking complex applications. In the remainder of this chapter, we will explore Forest School agreements with different types of landowners.

Recent surveys of woodland owners have revealed a strong commitment to education and access. With increasing awareness of Forest School and the need for everyone to benefit from the outdoors, a growing number of landowners are sympathetic or even proactive about Forest School happening on their land.

Mindsets and motivations

When approaching a landowner there will be a whole host of mindsets you may encounter, and you, as a Forest School leader, will have several things in mind too: education and community engagement; nature connection and conservation; and even economic considerations (this may well be your livelihood, and there may be ways of making products from the wood which could be sold). You will need to gauge the whys and wherefores of the landowner's wish to have a Forest School on their site – it could be anything, from meeting the requirements to access certain grants or a desire to help educate children on the value of woods and how they are managed, to simply needing a cost-effective means of managing the wood!

The landowner may be someone who has always been involved in the land because they feel they have 'dominion' over it. If this is the case then there may well be an agreement featuring many rules and restrictions on what can and cannot be done. This may conflict with the freer and more emergent processes that the Forest School leader seeks to evoke. There will probably have to be a compromise, and you may have to think hard about how the more participant-centred and participant-led process of Forest School may coexist with these restrictions. Alternatively, you may encounter a mindset of *'I am a temporary caretaker of this land for nature and people'* – this gives scope for a more open agreement, with fewer rules and driven by a few principles with hard and fast agreements. In the end this is about building a relationship with the landowner, whoever they may be, and understanding many different perspectives on landownership. You also need to have the principles of Forest School always in your mind, to see how to accommodate the perspective you are encountering. It is very much a two-way meeting and learning process for all parties involved.

Insurance

All Forest School leaders and organisations will need their own public liability insurance to conduct Forest School activities and programmes. Public liability insurance for the land is also required, where the Forest School organisation or leader owns the land. If there is a separate landowner, the landowner will need their own public liability insurance when allowing people onto their land for education or recreation. If the Forest School leader is also running training and consultancy services for other providers or educators, they will also need professional indemnity insurance. There are a number of insurance providers who specialise in education and Forest School provision; the Institute for Outdoor Learning, the Forest School Association, and landowner bodies such as the National Farmers Union can provide further guidance and advice.

Restrictions to land use

Land often has restrictions conveyed within the deeds. Common restrictions include: no camping; no structures; limited access; shooting rights; mineral extraction rights; water use; and rights of way. Your landowner may not be able to alter these and would then need to insist that you (as a tenant or licensee) also follow the instructions on the deeds. This can sometimes present a problem if neither side can reach a suitable agreement because of historical dictates. These restrictions can seem odd or even weird – the deeds to my house feature a covenant stating that I cannot grow strawberries on my land; nor may I open a teashop, keep geese or sell marmalade!

Types of landowner agreement

Landowner agreements can come in several forms. Some, like leases, are formal contracts; others are more informal, such as a Memorandum of Understanding. Both can be used if there is a disagreement. Each gives different levels of protection based on the type and content of the agreement. The agreement will have a formal-style structure that is signed by the landowner and the Forest School organisation or tenant.

Memorandum of Understanding (MOU)

The more informal Memorandum of Understanding is self-explanatory, and includes agreed ways of working together. MOUs are not legally binding; they are statements of intent and do not create legal obligations. Considerations for items to be included in an MOU include:

- A fee, if required, for using the land, and how this will be paid.
- Who is responsible for what, regarding management, ecological monitoring, access, car parking, toileting, wood and material supplies, and so on
- The geographical location (address, grid reference, what3words) of which parts of the site are accessible to FS. Include maps of the site in the landscape and the extent of FS access.
- What legislation may cover the wood and whether there is a management plan to consider.
- Insurances required (see previous section for details).
- Details on car parking, access to and from the site, and access points and gates (including locking procedures).
- Water and storage facilities, temporary shelters, toileting – who is responsible for maintaining these infrastructure features?
- Waste, toileting, and water procedures
- Risk assessments each party is responsible for, e.g. daily site check, activity risk/benefit assessments, risk management processes, annual and ongoing tree health checks, etc
- Procedures for reporting issues with the site
- Number and size of groups permitted (perhaps including adult:learner ratios)
- DBS, First Aid, and Forest School certification
- Times and periods the wood access is required, and if required outside these agreed times how this will be negotiated
- Emergency procedures and access for emergency services; include emergency contacts (e.g. the main responsible adult with the groups if different from the main FS leader/organiser)
- Communication and contact details
- Permitted and prohibited activities
- When the site is not available (e.g. shooting season or during tree work)
- What notice is needed by the Forest School group (e.g. if the site is temporarily unavailable)?
- If the FS groups are temporarily not using the site (due to extreme weather or change in group circumstances, for example), how much notice is needed, and will they be reimbursed where a block of sessions is paid for in advance?
- Behaviour agreements that may relate to the countryside code (UK Government guidance, 2014)
- Date and signature of both landowner and FS organisation
- Date of review.

Generally, MOUs are regularly reviewed and are more flexible than other, more formal agreements; they are also cheaper to produce. You can find guidance on writing MOUs with schools on the government website and a good internet search engine will uncover free templates and guidance on their creation. You can find an example of an MOU in the book's online resource.
https://forestschoolassociation.org/book-resources/ [1]
https://www.gov.uk/government/publications/setting-up-school-partnerships/guide-to-writing-a-memorandum-of-understanding-mou [28]

Leases

Leases are legally binding contracts between two or more parties, and unlike MOUs and licences they *do* create legal obligations. The agreement is designed to protect the rights and obligations of both parties. A lease will identify all relevant parties and formalise the rights and obligations of each party. Although this is often solely between the landowner and the tenant or leaseholder, there may be rare occasions where leases include clauses from other interested groups or individuals. For example, there may be a dormant mineral extraction agreement, or a timber harvesting agreement with another agency. The lease will often stipulate the agreed rent or costs. Because leases are legally binding, once you have agreed the terms in principle it is worth instructing a solicitor to advise on them and on any relevant laws. The solicitor may also wish to check the status of the landowner and that they have the right to lease the land to you. Leases can be expensive to create so it is important to make sure they cover a realistic time frame. Typical woodland leases contain:

- Landowner's and tenant's name and address
- The full site address
- A plan of the site indicating its size, boundaries and key features
- A start and end date
- Details on continuation or dissolution of the lease
- Rent amount, frequency, and payment date, e.g. monthly or yearly, and whether this rent will alter over time
- Access and parking arrangements
- Permitted uses of the site and restrictions on that use, e.g. fires must be off the ground and contained in a solid fire pit
- Insurance – whose insurance covers which aspects
- Maintenance responsibilities and who is responsible for what
- Problem reporting
- Erection of buildings, e.g. composting loos
- Responsibility for legal costs
- Break clause (i.e. a clause in the contract that allows it to be terminated early)
- Date the lease is signed and by whom (e.g. it may signed by a land manager on behalf of the land owner or by the landowner themselves) (The Woodland Trust, 2021).

There are many organisations that offer great advice to woodland entrepreneurs on leases and agreements; an online search will uncover many interesting facts to help you work out what yours need to contain.

Licence Agreements

Although usually used in a different context, a licence agreement can be modified to pertain to land-use. A licence is an informal agreement giving someone permission to use a site or do something with property owned by another. These are often used by local authorities seeking a more informal or controlled agreement with a person or organisation in order to test the logistics of an idea or concept. They are often halfway between a lease and an MOU agreement, and are much cheaper to produce. The main difference between a licence and a contract (or other agreements) is that licences are unidirectional. This means that the licence affects you (as the user or licensee) and will contain restrictions and permissions affecting how you may use the site – but you cannot force the licensor (the person who gives the licence) to do anything in return. For example, you could get a licence to use a site for Forest School, but find that some trees need safety work doing. With a licence, you cannot force the licensor to do the work, nor can you force them to let *you* do the work. Negotiation is key, but you are often in the weaker position. Licence agreements are often used to trial new ideas or arrangements before more substantial agreements are reached, especially with new partners.

A note of caution when using licence agreements: they may be revoked by the licensor at any time and with very limited notice, leaving you and your participants in a tricky spot with no legal recourse. This is especially risky when the licensor is influenced by political or economic factors or complaints.

Benefits of the landowner agreement

There are many benefits of a landowner agreement. It serves to:

- Provide a checklist for landowner and FS leader to go through annually
- Provide evidence to anyone asking a Forest School leader if they have permission to use the site
- Set expectations for use of the site
- Aid clarity around who does what on the site
- Communicate the practice of FS and how it is sustainable
- Identify sensitive areas for plants and wildlife on the site
- Agree who will manage what on the site
- Build trust between the landowner and FS leader
- Enable a partnership between the landowner and FS leader
- Show landowners that the Forest School community is a professional group of leaders trained to a high standard in sustainability, with an understanding of woodland management and practical skills to care for the land.

Some may view a landowner agreement as an administrative chore, but it is far from it! Conversations between landowner and FS leader can be most rewarding experiences – both share a love of the land, and can see the value of working together for the benefit of nature and society. Many landowners come to understand and respect Forest School, realising that having Forest School *enhances* their land, rather than damaging it! Forest School leaders come to understand the challenges of landownership and appreciate the help an owner can provide. **See our online resource for examples of landowner agreements.** https://forestschoolassociation.org/book-resources/ **[1]**

Working with maintenance teams and contractors

Your paper agreement is only the beginning. Often the best laid plans and management operations by the Forest School leader and their community can be thwarted in one blow by contracted maintenance being unaware of the management plans – where to mow and where *not* to mow! Many young tree whips and meadow habitats have been lost to the mower, and even trees felled. The latter has happened on many sites without notice being given to the Forest School team. Often the Forest School leader has no say in the felling of key trees on the site. A key step during the management planning and scoping out of a site is establishing who does the maintenance. Maintenance teams can include local authority contractors, private contractors, or the landowner themselves.

The best way to communicate with maintenance teams is both face-to-face when they are on site (to show exactly which spaces need to be left and which might need a different mowing regime, for example) *and* by letter to the maintenance team explaining a change of regime. You may even need to review the contract between the organisation and the maintenance team. The Forest School leader needs to have keen eyes on this one: check each time the maintenance team visits the site to start with, until the new regime is embedded. Contact with whoever is responsible for site maintenance may need to be handled by the organisation you are working for, and their backing and support is essential. In some cases, taping off areas with positive and friendly signage may be the best way to ensure your plans and plantings are protected.

Buying your own woodland

Buying your own woodland can be a major undertaking, and it is worth talking to others who have gone through the process. We recommend contacting the Small Woods Association, or even becoming a member, giving you access to some of their resources. If you do choose this route then you can take one of two paths: either employ the services of a solicitor with land acquisition expertise, or do it yourself. You will first need to talk to the vendor and let them know which path you intend to take, so they know where to send the paperwork. If you opt not to instruct a solicitor, you can process all the paperwork yourself, with the vendor, through the Land Registry – you will need to fill in a number of forms (that aren't too taxing), namely a TP1 and ID1. The Land Registry helpline will give you some assistance with this. For more information, visit: https://www.gov.uk/government/organisations/land-registry **[29]**

Change of land use and planning permission

Planning permission in Forestry is a little vague. Many Forestry operations do not require planning permission. Most Forest School practice will not be classified as Forestry, with the exception of sites managed for their timber as part of the Forest school programme.

The erection of buildings for Forestry may be classed as a Permitted Development (PD) under the General Permitted Development Order (GDPO), but the definition of what constitutes *Forestry* is very vague indeed. Permitted developments for Forestry, including buildings that fall within certain parameters (tool stores, toilets, offices, etc), paths and roads with access to a highway (Part 2 Class B of the GDPO), and fences (Part 2 Class A), will still require you to notify your Local Planning Authority (LPA) in advance of erection. This is usually in line with the 28-day rule (i.e. you must inform the planning authority of the changes 28 days before the work commences) to allow the LPA to comment or ask for further information. This may address a few pertinent questions or lead to a request for a full planning permission application.

This means buildings (excluding caravans) and changes in land use for purely educational activities are often subject to full planning permission applications. This can be a major problem if you already have sessions running, because processing planning applications for Forestry sites can take a long time.

Forest School is allowed under the temporary use of land in planning law, but unfortunately there are time limitations on 'temporary use'.

'The use of any land for any purpose for not more than 28 days in total in any calendar year [...] and the provision on the land of any moveable structure for the purposes of the permitted use.' – General Permitted Development Order, Part 4, Class B.

This means that after 28 days of use you may need full planning permission to use the site. The LPA has the right to restrict any development rights in woodland under article 4 of the GDPO. Although the 28-day rule is frequently breached and tricky to enforce, complaining neighbours (especially those with cameras) can cause a big problem if you don't follow the rules.
https://www.legislation.gov.uk/uksi/2015/596/pdfs/uksi_20150596_en.pdf **[30]**

Interpretation of the regulations set out in the General Permitted Development Order is a matter for local planning authorities. It is imperative that you **do your own research**, as each LPA will be different in their approach and their views about the area's woodland. Not all areas have the same development rights in the UK, and you are likely to find the following areas have greater restrictions on development rights:

- Conservation areas
- Areas of Outstanding Natural Beauty
- National Parks
- World Heritage sites.

You can find out more by visiting:
https://www.gov.uk/guidance/when-is-permission-required **[31]**.

Access, lighting of fires, and noise are often the common issues brought up by neighbours. We therefore highly recommend contacting your local planning authority if you are concerned or unclear about change of use, to satisfy any planning regulations. You may be able to apply for mixed use for example Forestry and Education depending on your Local Authority.

This book – and this chapter in particular – is somewhat UK centric. Often the same principles are likely to apply in other countries, but you will need to find the relevant sources and publications as every country is different and has different considerations and laws. As we indicated earlier, the history of a site's use is important when considering land ownership or agreements; and this is especially important where there are ancestral, community or historical relationships with the land.

Resources to support you in landowner agreements and searching for sites

The **Royal Forestry Society** has an excellent education team, who can advise on accessing and managing woods. They run many training opportunities for individuals as well as projects with schools and community organisations. Their Teaching Trees programme has been running for many years and they have regional officers to support with anything woodland related, including accessing sites.
https://rfs.org.uk/learning/ **[32]**

Community Forests are also excellent to contact, as they work with many landowners and educational institutions. To see if you have one in your area, visit:
https://englandscommunityforests.org.uk/about-ecf **[33]**
https://heartofenglandforest.org/ **[34]**
https://www.nationalforest.org/ **[35]**

Other organisations who manage woodlands and are worth considering are the various government agencies:

- Forestry England

  https://www.forestryengland.uk/learning [36]

- Natural Resources Wales

  https://naturalresources.wales/permits-and-permissions/plan-an-event-activity-or-project-on-our-land/?lang=en [37]

- Scottish Forestry

  https://forestry.gov.scot/forests-people/woods-for-learning [38]

- Woodland Trust:

  https://www.woodlandtrust.org.uk/ [39]

  http://treetoolsforschools.org.uk/menu/ [40]

References

Chesterton, G. (2011). *All is Grist.* Read books Ltd. 120.

Countryfile Magazine. (2019, June 10). *Who owns England? History of England's land ownership and how much is privately owned today*. Retrieved from Countryfile Magazine: https://www.countryfile.com/news/who-owns-england-history-of-englands-landownership-and-how-much-is-privately-owned-today/

Forestry Commission. (2020). *Tree felling getting permission.* Retrieved from www.gov.uk: https://assets.publishing.service.gov.uk/government/uploads/system/uploads/attachment_data/file/876642/Tree_Felling_-_Getting_Permission_-_web_version.pdf

Office For National Statistics. (2020, February 28). *Woodland natural capital accounts, UK: 2020*. Retrieved from ONS: https://www.ons.gov.uk/economy/environmentalaccounts/bulletins/woodlandnaturalcapitalaccountsuk/2020

The Woodland Trust. (2021). *Leasing a wood*. Retrieved August 24, 2021, from Woodland Trust: https://www.woodlandtrust.org.uk/plant-trees/community-woods/acquiring/leasing-a-wood/

UK Government guidance. (2014, August 19). *The Countryside Code*. Retrieved from gov.uk: https://www.gov.uk/government/publications/the-countryside-code

University of Hertfordshire. (2018). *Basic Glossary OF LAND LAW Terms*. Retrieved from StuDocu: https://www.studocu.com/en-gb/document/university-of-hertfordshire/land-law/lecture-notes/basic-glossary-of-land-law-terms/1235466/view

Chapter 11 – Considerations for choosing, developing and maintaining a Forest School site

Dawn Preston

Our Forest School ethos is entwined with nurturing a sense of place, stewardship, and connection to nature, fostered by long-term relationships with a woodland or other natural space. This is not just a tick list exercise against the Nature Principle and its criteria but should be at the very core of what we do.

The Nature Principle: Forest School takes place in a woodland or natural wooded environment to support the development of a relationship between the learner and the natural world.

For me, considering this **relationship** as a two-way, mutually beneficial, sustainable one from the outset is key – our woodland or other green spaces are not there just to be *used* or to provide us with resources; they are spaces into which we can feel invited as part of the dynamic and ever-changing natural world around us. I know that a rich, exciting, and varied space, full of constantly changing elements that offer opportunities for exploration, play and learning, can also be a biodiverse space benefitting our native wildlife. We do need to actively consider, plan, and manage our spaces carefully, to ensure our programmes are ecologically sustainable. This also naturally impacts on whether a Forest School business, enterprise or project can be economically or culturally sustainable.

The understanding of our ecological impact is covered in all levels of Forest School training. Those looking to take on a Forest School leader role will need to be actively involved in acquiring the knowledge and skills to sustainably manage their sites, and the L3 training will equip you with some of the starting point skills and resources to do this.

In this mainly practical chapter, we will first touch briefly upon why Forest School is an outdoor-based pedagogy and the benefits it brings, before looking at what Forest School sites need to start with and how to develop a site, as well as considerations for sustainably managing and maintaining our spaces longer term.

Getting outdoors – Forest School isn't just a name!

Our UK Forest School ethos evolved into its current form out of over two centuries of European outdoor education approaches *(Cree & McCree, 2012)*. Frustratingly, as we discussed in previous chapters, the phrase 'Forest School' has become synonymous with outdoor learning (OL), particularly amongst those not working within the outdoor learning or education sector. However, one of the fundamental ways in which Forest School differs from other outdoor learning is the focus on long-term **relationships** between the Forest School community member and our natural sites. As Forest School leaders, we become advocates for ensuring this relationship is a positive one, both for our Forest School communities and for the wildlife and wild places we connect to.

'Henrik Ibsen's meaning with "Friluftsliv" might best be interpreted as the total appreciation of the experience one has when communing with the natural environment, not for sport or play, but for its value in the development of one's entire spiritual and physical being. At its heart is the full identification and fulfilment of body and soul one experiences when immersed in nature.' – Dag T. Elgvin

---

Connection to nature is embodied in our principles and criteria as a long-term process of regular sessions – and we recognise that spending time and immersing ourselves in the outdoors is not just for sunny summer days but for *every* day, in every season, experiencing the dynamic, constantly changing world around us. This has a bearing on the land we choose to run our sessions, the management of those sites, and the agreements we have with landowners (see **Chapter 10**).

Physical and mental health benefits and connection to nature

There is an ever-increasing wealth of research providing evidence of the wide range of benefits human beings gain from spending time in the outdoors, and specifically in woodland or wooded areas (Goodenough & Waite, 2020). This is covered in **Chapter 3** but the table below gives a useful summary of some of the key points.

Whilst the latest science and research may not be able to pinpoint Ibsen's 'full identification and fulfilment of body and soul' exactly, cumulative evidence has shown the many specific benefits of spending time outdoors. We can see from the criteria for the Holistic Learning Principle (**Chapter 1**) that Forest School programmes aim to develop, where appropriate, the physical, social, cognitive, linguistic, emotional, and spiritual aspects of the learner.

Physical – health & fitness	Physical	Physical – Senses
Regular exercise has long been recognised as necessary to ensure we stay healthy and well throughout our lives. Although Forest School cannot replace regular sport, PE, or other focused physical activity in terms of increasing aerobic fitness, the fact that we are providing opportunities to walk, run, climb – to *move* – is important. That these opportunities are outside in woodlands or green spaces brings a whole range of associated positive benefits (Selhub & Logan, 2014).	'Motor skills matter because they are the medium through which children integrate sensory information and express knowledge and experience.' 'To fully develop their vestibular (movement) and proprioception (body position) senses children need access to opportunities to spin, climb, hang upside down, roll, balance, move up and down slopes, to throw and catch, to run and to jump...' (Goddard-Blythe, 2019).	Using our 'discovery' senses is one of the five pathways of connection to nature (Lumber et al. 2017). To see, hear, touch, smell, and taste the natural world around us not only aids our development but also helps foster a positive relationship with the natural world. 'Our senses are given to us not to be indulged, to be playthings or for decoration, but are mechanisms originally designed to help us survive and thrive in the natural world. Because life in the "developed" world is now so confined [...] our senses have little to do and consequently become either atrophied or over-sensitive, which in turn leads to many of the common ailments of today's existence, such as stress, anxiety and depression' (Sensory Trust, 2020).

Emotional	Finding and exploring death at Forest School	Spiritual
How we can support good emotional and mental health & well-being by spending time in the outdoors has really come into sharp focus in recent years (Mind, 2013).

Regularly being in green spaces can improve our sleep (Blume.,et al 2019) and lower our stress levels (Sunderland, 2013).

Research from Japan has shown time in forest environments 'reduce[s] the scores for anxiety, depression, anger, fatigue, and confusion, and increase[s] the score for vigour' (Qing, 2019). | Just as the sight of catkins, green shoots and frogspawn reveals the concept of renewal, the discovery of a dead animal at Forest School is equally relevant to the children's understanding of the circle of life. Remains such as pellets, feathers, and bones bring evidence of life cycles and predator-prey relationships to be explored. A pile of woodcock feathers discovered in our camp one morning not only led to an inquiry into the identity of the predator but also gave us an insight into a species we hadn't realised was sharing the woods with us. Such discoveries also inspire the children to create ceremony, such as during recapitulative play. | As we aim to offer self-directed, holistic learning opportunities, the role of death – in its inevitability and inextricable role in the constant cycling of the natural world – can provide moments where we can explore life's big questions and support spiritual development in our participants.

Enabling 'awe and wonder' or mindful moments can often happen in the outdoors too. An overarching aim of inspirational outdoor educator Steve van Matre and the Earthwalks programme is to cultivate 'feelings of kinship, reverence and love' using hands-on exploration of the natural world (Matre, 2019). |

'I recall the moving occasion when an eight-year-old girl sang a Chinese lullaby to a dead mole; another when a disparate group came together for the funeral of a mouse; and another when the group found a dead jay nestling and decided to leave it above ground so that it might feed another animal family. It was laid on green leaves around a circle of willow and offerings of pine-cones, seed heads, acorn cups and pieces of moss were arranged around the tiny corpse. The respectful response indicates a deep connection to the natural world brought by the Forest School experience.' – Kathy Grogan, Forest School leader, Learning Wild

Linguistic	Social	Cognitive
The issue of the increasing number of children not reaching the expected level of speech and language development has been widely recognised. The opportunity for increased interactions by spending time in the outdoors has – as well as the increases in self-esteem and autonomy – been found to correlate with improved speech & language development (Richardson, 2017).	The development of interpersonal (relating to others) and intrapersonal (self-awareness) skills is the foundation of creating a successful Forest School community of learning. Spending time outdoors, year-round, offers opportunities to light fires for sharing campfire cooked food and warm drinks, creating shared spaces of welcome and meaningful, chosen activity, claiming personal spaces for mindful time to be and everything else in between (Goodenough & Waite, 2020).	'One important interaction between individual and environment is the restoration of our attention, our energy, and ourselves by experiencing or viewing nature' (Ackerman, 2021).

The Kaplans' Attention Restoration Theory (ART) (Ackerman, 2021) attributes improved concentration and focus to spending time in a green space – particularly important for any Forest School that operates within an urban or semi-urban environment, where our participants may have arrived at school or setting already having had to exert large quantities of mental energy before starting their learning day. This deficit of restorative time and surroundings was captured as Nature Deficit Disorder by Richard Louv in *Last Child in the Woods*. Research has also begun on positive links between young children's cardiovascular health and their cognitive abilities (Keye et al, 2021), which joins up and rounds off our exploration into why getting out into green spaces is good for our children and young people, from an educational viewpoint.

Keeping in mind we want to support holistic development and provide these benefits through our Forest School programme delivery, what does this mean in the context of choosing or developing a site?

What might your Forest School site look like?

Each of the six principles has several criteria, provided by the Forest School community in 2012, that help define good practice. The Nature Principle quoted at the beginning of this chapter is no exception. The criteria help us to identify what a Forest School site needs to be effective:

- The woodland is ideally suited to match the needs of the programme and the learners, providing them with the space and environment in which to explore and discover.
- Whilst woodland is the ideal environment for Forest School, many other sites, some with only a few trees, are able to support good Forest School practice.

I once had someone express their doubts that they would be able to provide Forest School at their setting '*as we don't have any really large trees in our woodland or a stream*'. This common misconception amongst potential trainees – that you need the 'perfect' woodland to be able to deliver Forest School – can often become a barrier to establishing Forest School opportunities. It is worth mentioning here that every school, setting, or independent leader will be starting with a different blank canvas and that Forest School is not the space or site, it is the ethos!

Choosing a Forest School site

There are some basic elements that you need to consider as you decide whether your site can support a Forest School programme and provide the benefits mentioned above. Does it need developing in particular ways, and is that deliverable or would it be more suitable for offering other outdoor learning opportunities?

Do you have enough space?

Forest School requires a high adult:participant ratio (1:4) so will often have a maximum number of 15 participants to one Forest School leader plus other adult support (this is most often true with Early Years, SEND or nurture groups.) This smaller group size means smaller spaces can be utilised, although obviously it will also depend on the age and size of your participants! Bigger people need a bigger site, and what works for a nursery group may not work for teenagers. It is always worth remembering that people get *lost* in different size spaces. Equality of access is also a consideration here, as children and young people with mobility challenges may need larger spaces. Can we provide the right spaces for the cultural, gender, access, and lifestyle preferences and needs of our community of learners? As we want to support social and emotional development, does it have enough space to provide communal areas as well as more private spaces?

'We have stolen wild spaces and wild time from our children.' – Bob Hughes

---

Something I hear a lot from trainees and FS leaders delivering sessions to younger children is *'It's great, my site allows us to see the children all of the time'* and I often respond by asking why this is considered a clearly positive aspect of that space. This, for me, is an important point to consider: our social imperative to have our children always 'under surveillance' can inhibit play and natural interactions, particularly with older children and young people. It is unsupervised play that children and young people need developmentally, but this is often difficult to offer as it can seem to be in direct conflict with our duty of care as education and care professionals.

How do you access your site?

Is your potential Forest School site just outside the door, a short walk, or a minibus ride away? This affects the time, cost, and ease of delivering the sessions – the carrying out of site checks before and after sessions, maintenance, moving and storing kit and equipment. How far is the nearest toilet plus clean water for handwashing and drinking, and how do participants access this? How do you get around within the site? Is the site accessible to everyone who is going to be taking part? Very few issues are insurmountable, and within the Forest School community there is often a wealth of practical advice on adapting sites to meet the needs of our groups.

Site considerations to support equality, diversity and inclusion

I strongly believe Forest School and other outdoor education has a role to play in breaking down barriers, but I also acknowledge this isn't quick or easy work. We know that as a society we have on-going issues around inequality, bigotry, racism, and other non-inclusive views, and these are all too often the daily experience of many people in our Forest School community and groups.

We can all play our part by challenging views and behaviours that perpetuate inequalities, as well as embedding equality, diversity, and inclusion in our policies, procedures and working practices. Just as important is how we conduct ourselves at Forest School and beyond, and continuing to seek to make a difference.

As Forest School communities, we want to be welcoming, accessible, and inclusive; and assessing our site's contribution to this is an important step in recognising and removing barriers, where possible. Some of these points may seem contradictory but it's worth keeping flexibility in mind here – our Forest School delivery should adapt and change to meet the needs of each group we work with.

Some examples of **site** issues to consider:

- Wider access points, pathways, and turning points for wheelchair or mobility buggy users.
- The height of working stumps, tables, sawhorses, and benches to enable participation by wheelchair or mobility equipment users, or for those with other mobility issues or height or reach restrictions.
- The provision of the 'right' toilets and hand-washing spaces means you may sometimes need to provide at least two separate, self-contained single-sex toilets with hand- and other washing facilities; you may also need to work with participants to accommodate privacy or sensory issues around what they need to feel comfortable.
- For some people from certain communities or backgrounds, or with complex needs, we might need sites that are dog-free or that restrict access to dogs while sessions are running.
- Along with taking into account religious and lifestyle dietary preferences when providing and sharing food, we need to consider providing suitable food preparation areas and equipment (HSC Public Health Agency NI).
- Some noise sources could affect those with sensory processing differences, such as the sounds of traffic, humming wires, quarry workings, industrial sites, or planes overhead.
- Can we find sites that are easily accessible by bicycles and public transport, rather than by car?

Do you share your site?

Is it only you and your group that can access your site, or is it shared with others? This could be other classes or year groups, whole or other schools, the public, cyclists, dog walkers, and equestrians. How do you manage this?

Is your site robust enough?

Embedded in the Forest School ethos are regular sessions over long-term programmes. Is your site robust enough to cope with the number of participants and frequency of sessions you envisage? Our climate in the UK is changing – we can expect hotter, drier summers, periods of longer, heavier rainfall throughout the year, and wetter winters than we have been used to. How will this impact your site and its usage? How will you mitigate its effects?

The answers to the above questions will give you a clearer idea of whether that particular space or spaces will work for your Forest School delivery. If after reading the above section you feel that your site is suitable, you can continue to answer the next questions knowing that, in many cases, sites can be developed to become more complex, wild, risky, or safe, as required.

Is your site complex enough?

Forest School uses natural resources for inspiration, to enable ideas and to encourage intrinsic motivation. Does your potential site contain enough 'stuff' there to provide this for your group? In play terms we would be considering loose parts and affordances (how many different ways an item such as a fallen log could be used, manipulated, or played with); we also need to support the seven broad areas of holistic development where we can.

Landscape and learning

A useful allied consideration here is whether you have access to other or additional spaces, either within the boundaries of your current school or setting or close by. The ability to utilise a local park or gardens, beach or coastal area, or urban greenspaces such as cemeteries can enable you to manage the impacts of frequent use, especially seasonally. This wider use of and learning about a wider local area can really help create a sense of place, as well as help children and young people to understand concepts such as 'their' site being part of a larger nature recovery network – an idea we explore further on.

> *'Learning about your local area creates a Sense of Place. A feeling of belonging and being part of a community. Local knowledge builds communities.' – The Nature Premium Campaign*

Is your site safe enough?

Part of your Forest School leader role will be to carry out, review, and update site risk assessments, and this process will help to identify any hazards for which you may need to provide control measures. For instance, what forms the boundaries of your site – barbed wire fences, a stream, a road? This is another area where good ID knowledge and understanding of how the habitat functions as a whole is important – if you have a 'harmful' plant like Lords-and-Ladies (*Arum maculatum*) on site, for example, you need to be aware that it is poisonous, but also that it has value as a food plant for some birds and rodents, and a relationship with the small flies it captures to reproduce (Sussex Wildlife Trust). Providing a 'safe enough' space is what we are looking to achieve through site, leadership, and delivery mechanisms; and this leads me on to the next consideration.

Is your site risky enough?

The Risk Principle: Forest School offers learners the opportunity to take supported risks appropriate to the environment and to themselves.

What opportunities are there for supported risk taking and risky play? Can we run, climb, hang upside down, travel over uneven ground, and encounter plants and animals we might need to take care around? Can we light fires for warmth, to chat around, or to cook and share food? Can we learn some tool skills to help manage the woodland and, in turn, use some of its spare resources to make, craft, and build?

Does it feel natural, wild, special? This one can be intangible and may be considered the most non-essential consideration on this list, but I do believe it is worth keeping in mind when assessing or developing a site for Forest School. Of course, there are ways in which a space can be developed and made to feel more natural, wild, and special over the shorter- and longer-term. The key point this links to for me is access, particularly for sites within a school or setting. Do the members of your Forest School community have access to this space outside of your sessions – is it perhaps the 'wildest' corner of the playing field that the children can already use at break or lunch times? The success in delivering the benefits mentioned above are 'in part due to the way the [young people] experienced the setting as a significantly different space with a different set of expectations.' (Tiplady & Menter, 2021).

Is your site *too* wild and special? There are a whole host of international, national, and local level conservation designations that you will need to be aware of when deciding whether a site is suitable for hosting Forest School or other outdoor learning. If you discover your site has any of these designations, you will need to find out more details from the land manager, landowner, or relevant statutory body when seeking permission to use the site. If you can use the site, this information will enable you to put together a plan to sustainably manage the area. Rather than break up the flow of this chapter, these designations are provided in the online resource .

Case studies – from 'leave no trace' to permanent sites

All Forest School sites are very different but have common themes. In this next section we are going to explore some examples of active Forest School sites. To get an overall sense of each site I asked some members of our local Forest School community about the pros and cons of their current Forest School site set-up and landowner arrangements and agreements. In some interviews, they were asked to give three positives and negatives of their set-up, as well as some thoughts around practicalities such as sanitation, health & hygiene, storage space, access, and year-round sustainable use.

Case study – Swanwick Lakes Nature Reserve – managed by Hampshire & Isle of Wight Wildlife Trust

Forest School Leader and Trainer – Dawn O'Malley
Forest School Leader – Caroline Fox

Permissive access site used by schools, settings and groups booked through the Study Centre, as well as members of the public, including dog walkers. Bridleway along one boundary edge, so equestrians and cyclists with some access. The car park shuts between dusk and dawn, but the reserve is open all day and night, right through the year.

What are the positive aspects of delivering Forest School on a 'public access' site?

It is easy to tailor set-up to the cohort attending, allowing for needs and interests of the group, as all equipment is taken to and from site for each session. This also means the site looks 'fresh'.

We are also forced to be more mindful of the equipment and resources brought to site (as you have to carry it there in the first place), which can lead to clever rationalisation and innovation with your Forest School set-up and kit and more reliance on the natural loose parts and affordances of the environment; moving away from the reliance on 'educational toys' to support your group's play and learning.

With having to pack up site at the end of each session, this makes it easier to check for missing items before leaving site, as well as to check tools and equipment for breakages or wear and tear as they are being cleaned or packed away.

I have worked from a couple of public access sites as well as the beach, and I would say the positives of this way of working are that you are making a bold and clear 'leave no trace' statement through your delivery, and passing this message onto not only the children on the programme, but also to their families and the members of the public who may observe your sessions. It forces you to make more conscious and mindful efforts to minimise your impacts on the site and space every time you visit, whereas this impact mitigation can slip on a permanent site, where you could leave clearing up the debris from an activity until the next session, or end of the programme, or end of the year…!

What are the negative aspects of delivering Forest School on a 'public access' site?

As idyllic as working with a 'leave no trace' ethos sounds, in practice there are times when I wish there were permanent features that could be left in place, ready for the next session! It is time-consuming and sometimes exhausting carrying kit onto site, including water if there is no tap on site too, setting up shelters, setting up tippy tap handwashing stations, thoroughly checking for dog mess, litter, the state of the tree canopy, sharps on the beach, etc, before your group has even arrived on site. Sometimes it is unavoidable bringing lots of equipment onto site: for example, to do a simple cooking activity with a group, not having work surfaces that can be sanitised for preparing food is difficult; and so you may need a work-around solution, such as bringing a folding table to site, using cool bags and pre-prepared food, keeping cooking utensils and cutlery in sealed containers until use, etc. You then would need to plan for how to wash up and clear up leaving no trace, without the benefit of a building to pop into or a compost heap for veg scraps.

Not an issue for the way that we deliver and fund our programmes, but this extra staff time for getting equipment to and from site and setting up and packing away could lead to additional costs of sessions to participants.

The presence of the public themselves (and their dogs, horses, and bicycles) means we need to take steps to ensure site is not going to be 'invaded' by the public during sessions. At Swanwick, this involves regular on-site engagement of the public by staff and volunteers, plus use of daily signage if areas are being used for sessions. It also means we must be very mindful about what can be set up and left out in the woods whilst we come back to the Centre to pick up or drop off groups of participants, and what we need to bring with the group. We never leave tool bags or boxes or fire striking equipment unattended, for instance.

We have the landowner's permission to light fires as part of our Forest School delivery; however there is a difficult balance here between offering this activity for the learning and well-being benefit of your groups, whilst also setting a good example and leaving no trace – we don't want to encourage other members of the public to light unsafe, anti-social fires without permission, understanding or skill; so perhaps, depending on the site itself, it may be that even a temporary fire that leaves no trace is not appropriate if you are very visible.

This is also the case with cutting and using wood for woodworking projects, as well as simpler activities such as den building.

Below: The Forest School site – Swanwick Lakes Nature Reserve, Hampshire & Isle of Wight Wildlife Trust. ©Dawn Preston

Case Study – Four Marks Primary School – an average sized primary school near Alton, Hampshire

Foundation Stage leader and teacher, Forest School Leader – Esther Andrews
Class teacher and trainee Forest School Leader – Katharine Jackson

The school has a few different outdoor areas – a playground, a school field for play and sports, and a Year-R garden, as well as their Forest School area.

What are the positive aspects of delivering Forest School on a school site?

It's right there! We can head out of class and across to site quickly and easily, either for sessions themselves or for setting up and packing away equipment and resources. It also gives us the safety and security of being on site in an emergency – our procedures are the school ones, so everyone knows what to do and where to be if anything should happen.

It means that our kit and equipment is also right there, as well as being in secure storage. This allows us to be really flexible in responding to the children's interests and needs, as well as the weather, on any given day.

As we are a secure site, we also have no worries around anti-social behaviour, litter, or damage to the site; and this eliminates 'stranger danger' too, so the children can use the whole Forest School space without the need to be in sight.

What are the negative aspects of delivering Forest School on a school site?

As Forest School and the site is part of our school role, it does mean we as staff have the main responsibly to maintain it, which obviously takes extra time outside of school hours. We have even roped in family members to help with tasks during school holidays and weekends!

This is also true of all of the equipment and resources. We have had to gather kit together over time, using different sources of funding or asking for donated items. The equipment often needs drying – space for this in school is minimal – as well as the usual checking, counting, cleaning and maintaining, again meaning additional time for staff.

A big consideration is how the space is used across the school by other staff and classes. The children quickly become 'stewards' of their Forest School space, and other classes using the area without the same care and attention can cause upset. We have worked on making sure the space is 'booked' in the same way we use other shared spaces in the school, as well as asking for alternative spaces to be used for non-Forest School activity where possible. This helps with managing our sustainable, year-round use of the site too.

Over four years of hard work have gone into developing our school Forest School site so far, and we are very proud of it and what we have achieved!

Below: Four Marks Primary School gather around their permanent fire circle, Hampshire. ©Esther Andrews

©Esther Andrews

Case Study – My Little Explorers (MLE) – a forest kindergarten based in privately owned woodland at Farley Mount, near Winchester

Forest School Leader – Sam Victoria

MLE can also use the more open areas of nearby Farley Mount Country Park. MLE operates on weekdays, in term time only, and switches between two different fire circle areas through winter and summer. As the main part of the site is coniferous woodland, activity is deliberately kept away from more wildlife-rich areas of understorey, which helps with sustainable use of the site.

What are the positive aspects of delivering Forest School on a privately owned site?

© Sam Victoria

The site is private property so there is no public access! This lessens the risks from dogs (and their mess) and unknown adults, and makes the area more secure for our groups and our kit and equipment. We can have permanent storage on site, as well as infrastructure like our compost toilet, as well as benefitting from good access and car parking (that is locked when we are not on site).

My Little Explorers operating from the site is also beneficial for the landowner as it is good for their community profile, as well as in terms of finances, as they can claim tax relief due to our usage of the site. Having support from our landowner to deal with issues such as fly tipping and tree management is really a bonus, although this will depend on your contract or agreement.

The third positive for me is being able to share such an unspoiled and quieter area that is rich in wildlife with the children, and with our staff – we have even had little owls nesting in our compost toilet! This really helps embed messages around stewardship and taking care of the natural world around us, but also hugely promotes good mental health and well-being. There are always spaces to pause and stop and wonder.

What are the negative aspects of delivering Forest School on a privately owned site?

There was a huge amount of work to start and clear the site – including finding and removing lots of old barbed wire – which was all down to us. There are also infrastructure costs that the landowner is unlikely to pay for or provide. Our above ground ThunderBox composting toilet was expensive to purchase initially, for instance. We also don't have running water on site, so handwashing water is supplied by Aquaroll and is brought to site by car, we use bottled water for drinking, and we have a water butt that collects rainwater for play.

Being on a privately owned site can put limitations on what you can achieve – our Ofsted registration was tricky, for example, and we also have restricted days for activity. All our school holiday provision happens on a different site.

We are lucky that our landowner is nearby but not next door to where we operate, and we have a good working relationship. However, land ownership can change!

Above: Photograph of the My Little Explorers Forest Kindergarten setup, Winchester ©Sam Victoria.

Developing a Forest School site

A Forest School programme constantly monitors its ecological impact, and works within a sustainable site management plan agreed between the landowner or manager, the Forest School leader, and the learners.

At Level 1 you are asked to identify the impacts of Forest School activity on your site. If completing a Level 2 Forest School Award, you will receive training in completing and carrying out a simple site survey and ecological impact assessment. At Level 3 Forest School Leader you will need to evidence being able to carry out periodic site surveys and ecological impact assessments, and putting together a site/woodland management plan. This need, to be able to monitor impact on the flora and fauna on your site, is one of the reasons a Forest School leader needs a good level of wildlife identification skills.

The Forest School Leader training will also equip you to undertake your responsibility to carry out daily and other periodic site risk checks (see section on Tree Health below), as well as the tool and Personal Protective Equipment (PPE) choice and use required to manage your outdoor areas on a daily and seasonal basis.

Once you have worked through the considerations above and decided that your site can support the Forest School programme you are aiming to deliver, you will then need to work your way through the following steps, all of which could involve all of the participants of your groups.

Baseline survey

Carrying out an initial survey of a potential or existing site need not be a chore, or just down to the Forest School leader – it can be a fantastic learning opportunity for everyone! This important step enables you to know what is already there. Surveys will need to be carried out periodically to fully capture the wildlife on site through the seasons, but late spring/early summer is a great point in the year to schedule in your first baseline survey, as identifying trees and other flora can be a little easier at this point in the year. Much of our wildlife is nocturnal, so consider setting up simple light traps, torch lit walks, or some sessions out with a bat detector, which will help you to gain information on the moths, bats, and other invertebrates and mammals that may only be active at night on your patch.

Sacrifice areas and protection

Using the knowledge of your site gained through the survey(s), you can then identify the areas you want to use for gathering people, storage, or siting paths – these are sometimes called *sacrifice areas*. You can also identify those areas that may need protecting or are to be used sparingly or not at all. For example, it is good practice to make sure you don't site areas that suffer a large degree of trampling and compaction (like your fire circle and main gathering area) where your only patch of native bluebells grows! We use the concept of 'zoning' a lot on the 89 acres of nature reserve where I am based, and this concept can work equally well on smaller sites.

Tree health

When welcoming people to any woodland or wooded sites, we need to be actively monitoring the health of our trees. This may be your direct responsibility, or you may be providing information for others who manage your site, but at a minimum we should be carrying out a tree survey at least once every six months, as well as after any extreme weather events. Trees can become unstable, drop branches or fall during high winds; branches can be brought down by heavy snowfall; and prolonged extremely wet or extremely dry conditions can also lead to instability or conditions such as summer branch drop (Rushforth, 1989).

In reality, as Forest School leaders we will be checking our sites – including our trees – as part of our daily set-up routine, as well as dynamically risk assessing the changing conditions that may affect our trees throughout a session, such as increasing wind strength or thunderstorms with lightning.

It is important to remember here that standing deadwood is a valuable habitat for a wide range of wildlife and should be left in situ where possible (Back from the Brink, 2017). If you are concerned about a tree, then initially you need to cordon off and not use any area that might be directly affected if it did fail, and then have it thoroughly checked out and dealt with in accordance with your procedures and site management agreements.

What are we looking for when carrying out tree health checks? As a non-expert, some of the signs we are looking for that may indicate a tree is under stress and needs to be re-assessed for risk are:

- Movement of the tree – if the trunk develops splits or twists, or the roots have begun to lift from the ground

- Fallen branches – if larger branches are found on the floor, the likely tree(s) need a thorough check

- Attached but broken or deformed branches – dangling or snapped branches or broken branches resting on others

- Unusual or delayed leaf emergence – this could be a sign of a tree suffering from pests or disease, or dying back for natural reasons

- Shrivelling or other unseasonal changes to leaves – this could also be a sign of a tree suffering from pests or disease, or dying back for natural reasons

- Fungi – appearance of fruiting bodies (not necessarily a cause for concern but does need noting).

There are a number of tree pests and diseases that can affect tree health, such as Dutch elm disease, sudden oak death, and ash dieback. Another reason for getting to know what tree species you have on site is to learn and look for the signs and symptoms of these issues. There is a wealth of useful information – and a chance to get involved in actively monitoring tree health as citizen scientists – available through the Forest Research OBSERVATREE project (Observatree, 2018).

Fire and fire circles

On sites where you have the landowner's permission to light fires and enjoy all of the benefits this can offer, the siting of any fires and fire circle infrastructure does need to be carefully thought through with regard to nearby or overhanging trees (including their roots), prevailing wind direction, paths and tracks, and other site structures. You also need to know and account for your soil type – we cannot light fires directly on peaty soils due to the fire risk, for instance, or on shingle or pebbles due to the danger of the stones shattering.

All fires have an impact on the soil:

- Changing the structure by burning off the top layers of organic matter

- Changing the chemical composition, becoming more alkaline over time

- Impacting ground layer and soil invertebrates

- Reducing porosity (the ability to absorb rain), and leading to erosion and surface run-off into nearby water courses

- Regularly burned areas become less likely to regenerate and recover over time.

These factors – along with the nature of your site with regard to land ownership and management – will inform your choice of fire siting option. The following section outlines three common options for siting a fire.

Temporary fires but sited in the same place

On a permissive access site visited by members of the public, we must operate a 'leave no trace' policy when lighting and using campfires, mainly to reduce the likelihood of unwanted fires. We have permanent seating structures in our three main teaching areas and use two other temporary sites for shorter Introduction to Forest School programmes through the year. All traces of fires, including partially burnt wood and ashes, are removed and – due to the relatively low frequency of use – this is then scattered into the wider woodland. This approach reduces the impact to small areas of regular campfire use, and ensures we are showcasing good practice around using minimal resources and leaving our areas as we find them with our groups.

Right: Temporary cooking fire at Swanwick Lakes Nature Reserve, Hampshire & Isle of Wight Wildlife Trust. ©Dawn Preston

Temporary fires in different places

There are lots of ways fires can be lit with minimal impact by using portable equipment that will keep the fire off the ground, such as fire bowls or BBQ bases, or by building a mound fire using an old fire blanket and soil or sand. A deciding factor here will be how long your fire is to be alight and what you will be using it for. Quick 'five-minute' fires will have less impact than cooking fires, which by necessity must burn for a longer period of time.

©Tracy Standish

Above: A participant lights a temporary 'leave no trace' fire at Blashford Lakes Nature Reserve, Hampshire & Isle of Wight Wildlife Trust. ©Tracy Standish

Permanent or semi-permanent structure

If possible, building a structure is a great way to minimise your impact while concentrating it in one place. A built-up fire base minimises the effects on the soil by creating a physical barrier of other soil, clay or sand – retained with boards or logs – between the fire itself and the actual soil surface. If you are using fire daily, or very frequently, this also allows you to remove a build-up of burnt material and ashes periodically, again minimising impacts on the wider site. An additional benefit of a built-up structure is one of access – younger children often find working at a raised height easier when fire striking, as will individuals who are unable to reach the floor. The addition of a covered wood store is a bonus!

©Jodie Beasley

Above: A Permanent fire pit and wood store at Blashford Lakes Nature Reserve, Hampshire & Isle of Wight Wildlife Trust. ©Jim Day

Left: Permanent fire pit area at St. Anthony's Catholic Primary School, Fareham. ©Jodie Beasley

Below: Semi-permanent fire in a raised bowl on a school site. ©Jess Walton

Biosecurity

'Biosecurity means taking steps to make sure that good hygiene practices are in place to reduce and minimise the risk of spreading invasive non-native species. A good biosecurity routine is always essential, even if invasive non-native species are not always apparent.' – Non Native Species Secretariat

---

Invasive non-native species (INNS), as well as other terrestrial, aquatic and marine pests and diseases, pose a serious threat to biodiversity in and around the UK. Including biosecurity measures in our Forest School and other outdoor learning delivery (as well as everyday life) need not be onerous, and demonstrate good practice and a commitment to protecting our precious wildlife and habitats.

The simple steps outlined in the 'check, clean, dry' campaign are easy to remember and put in place, and are particularly important if you, your participants, your vehicles, or your equipment travel around multiple sites. Washing and drying things like boots and wellingtons, pond dipping nets, and wheelbarrow wheels, for example, will reduce the likelihood of spreading unwanted organisms. (Non Native Species Secretariat, 2021) (GOV.UK, 2018) (Environment Agency, 2010)

Water and Forest School

Water is the basis for all life on our 'blue planet' and is an endlessly fascinating and enriching substance for play, exploring, splashing in, and mixing with everything else!

Why do we need to consider water management at Forest School? Water is heavy and time consuming to transport, yet we need sources of fresh, clean water to provide robust health and hygiene procedures. We need to wash hands regularly to minimise many of the risks to our Forest School participants from hands on contact with the wild and wonderful natural world, as well as needing water for drinking and cooking. You may have access to a drinking-water outside tap, or you may need to carry water to the site in water barrels. Either way, you need to consider how to keep the water fresh and clean, as well as sterilising the containers you use for it.

Water is also a magical substance that can be used in endless ways in children's play and learning. Some settings may provide water for play in the same way as for drinking water, while others have systems in place to harvest rainwater for this, such as water butts with close fitting lids attached to shed or building gutters. Many diseases are water borne, so well-understood guidelines around the use of each type of water need to be embedded as part of your programme. We talk through providing water for wildlife a little further on.

Paths

Once you have zoned your site and decided where any major infrastructure items will be (fire circle/storage/hygiene areas), you then need to visualise, map, or actually physically walk through the site to figure out the likely 'desire lines' – which routes the Forest School community will want to take from point A to point B. Getting this right can really reduce unwanted impacts further down the line. Desire lines are often more of an issue during the wetter months of the year, as people seek to avoid walking through muddy or waterlogged areas. If not managed, widened or incidental paths can have a detrimental effect on not only underground, ground- and field layer flora and fauna, but also on tree roots. Managing desire lines – particularly on permissive or public access sites – can take time and effort, so should be well thought through at the planning stage. Consideration should also be given to what you use for your paths, as there may be unintended consequences with some path materials, such as crushed stone if it is very different chemically to the surrounding geology – an example would be a path

©Dawn Preston

base made of crushed chalk or limestone in an acidic coniferous woodland or heathland site, changing the pH of the soil and damaging the ecosystem by inhibiting flora designed to live on acidic soils.

What to do about natural 'hazards'

A question I get asked at least once a week through late spring and summer by visiting children is: 'why don't I deal with the stinging nettles?' (This invariably follows on from a member of the group experiencing a nettle sting!) I always appreciate this conversation starter, as we can then explore the concepts of food chains and webs and how we can have positive and negative impacts on the wildlife around us – those relationships that help connect us to nature.

'Many nettle patches hold overwintering insects which swarm around fresh spring nettles and provide early food for ladybirds. These same aphids are eaten by blue tits and other woodland birds that dart around the stems. In late summer the huge quantity of seeds produced are food for many seed-eating birds, such as house sparrows, chaffinches, and bullfinches. Nettles are also a magnet for other insect-eaters like hedgehogs, shrews, frogs and toads, at all times of year.' – RSPB

Each 'problem' plant or animal has a place in the workings of the ecosystem it lives in. Our role as Forest School leaders is to ensure our Forest School communities are aware of the risks from potentially-dangerous species – lords-and-ladies, giant hogweed, bees, wasps and hornets, cherry laurel leaves and berries, yew, stinging nettles, and more – that may be present on the sites we work in. Embedding easy to remember phrases such as 'no lick, no pick' can help to reinforce the message that good identification knowledge is required when exploring, picking, collecting, or foraging. We also need to provide the means to carry out a thorough hand-wash (as mentioned above). As Forest School is a long-term process, participants will become familiar with the seasonal ebb and flow of various flowering and fruiting plants and trees, as well as the cycle of activity of invertebrates and other animals. This cumulative experience will enable them to develop an awareness of the risks and how to keep themselves healthy and safe whilst out and about in our woodlands.

Is your site complex enough? Is your site risky enough? Does it feel natural, wild, special? If your answer to these questions was *no* or *not really*, then thinking through the next steps to expand the play, learning, and risk-taking opportunities will hopefully also lead to increasing the biodiversity on site – critical for helping us to reverse the ongoing decline of our wildlife.

Treading lightly on the earth

We need to take care when introducing living or non-living items to an area, for all of the reasons outlined in the section on biosecurity. However, this doesn't mean we can't build, create or plant, sow, transplant or cultivate certain species – we just need to have a good understanding of our site and be mindful of its unique ecosystem. Our default position must be 'do no harm' – to tread lightly and ensure our needs and wants work in concert with what is already there.

We also have a legal obligation to protect and not disturb several plant and animal species under current UK law (The Wildlife Trusts, 2021), including all bats and wild birds (as well as their nests and eggs), and iconic species such as great-crested newts, adders, stag beetles, dormice, purple emperor butterflies, bluebells, and red squirrels. There are lots more species we have a duty to protect and conserve, so best practice is to check against the protected species lists once you have undertaken your site surveys, as well as regarding information you may already have about the presence of certain wildlife in the wider area. You may also need to be aware of local Biodiversity Action Plans (BAPs), which are usually held by the Local Authority.

Habitat creation

Before we add anything to our sites, we must first know what is already there. It is tempting to leap in and enrich, but it is advisable to watch your site for at least a year before beginning management. Depending on the results of our baseline surveys, we may need to do little in the way of creating or enhancing habitats. However, if we are starting with a mainly man-made or planted space, such as the corner of a school field with a few non-native trees, we have both more scope for improvements and more hands-on work for our Forest School community to tackle!

There are many great initiatives we can get involved in around providing certain elements needed by our wildlife – you can 'bee kind' by sowing or planting species loved by our pollinators, or put-up bird or bat boxes, as common examples. However, a habitat doesn't just need to contain food or shelter, but *everything* that species needs throughout its life cycle. All these needs cannot or will not necessarily be provided by our Forest School sites, so connectivity to other natural spaces is an important consideration. Our sites can be critical parts of local 'nature recovery networks' – green and wilder spaces through which wildlife can travel and gain what they need to survive and thrive.

What other green space is your site bounded by or connected to? All 'wildlife corridors' – a hedged path, a non-mown buffer strip along the edge of parkland or playing fields, or neighbouring wildlife-friendly gardens – play a part in supporting wildlife, especially in very urban areas. Through our work with our Forest School communities, our sites can often be showcases of what can be achieved, and we can inspire others to make small changes to help our beleaguered wildlife.

Providing water for wildlife – separate to that we might need for drinking, cooking, and hand washing – is an easy way to provide one critical element needed by all living things. Keeping shallow dishes of clean water (with or without pebbles) or bowls of wet mud can provide drinking stations for bees, birds, and other insects, and double up as bathing stations for birds. Ponds can come in all shapes and sizes, and if you are lucky enough to have or be bordered by streams, ditches or lakes, then this is a real bonus! Ponds and water bodies are often a real cause for health and safety concern in education settings, but can be managed to ensure safe access by children and young people. If you can, do, as the wildlife – and learning – value is huge. However, if even a small pond isn't possible, creating or enhancing a marshy area for bog plants, a rain garden, or a mini drainpipe wetland can really increase the range of plant and invertebrate species on site. (Wildfowl and Wetlands Trust, 2018)

Keeping our native pollinators in mind, what do they need? Well, they need a good range of flowering plants available through their most active months – usually March through to October.

'These don't need to be showy garden plants but often humble wild plants that are sometimes viewed (and dealt with) as weeds such as dandelions, lesser celandine, white deadnettle, ivy and field speedwell, to name a few.' – Bumble Bee Conservation Trust

---

Below: A diagram showing the interconnections between different natural sites within a local environment.

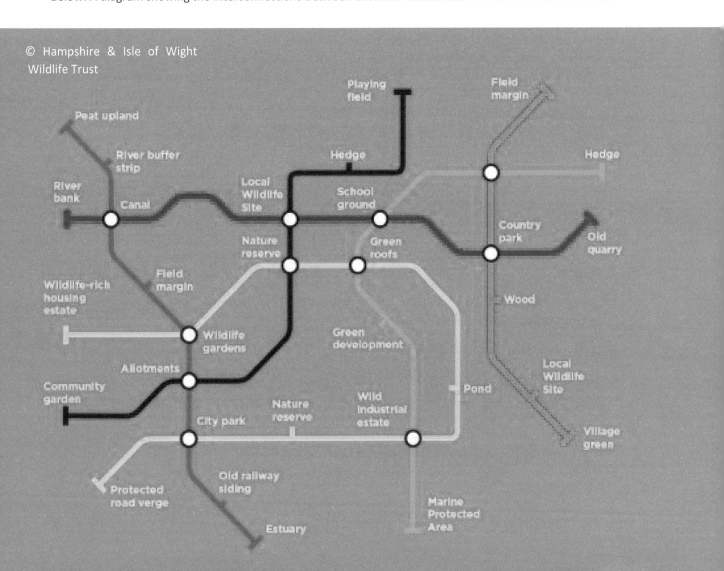

© Hampshire & Isle of Wight Wildlife Trust

Along with water (preferably rainwater) and food, they also need shelter – depending on species this can range from patches of long grasses, undisturbed areas under hedges, in holes in brick or stone walls, underground in the soil, or in hives. In less natural areas we can increase shelter sites by providing overwintering spaces, particularly for solitary bees, with 'bee hotels'. Make sure to factor in that these temporary structures do need maintenance and refreshing each year.

'As this is a temporary design, you'll need to move your bee hotel in the autumn and winter to protect the bee eggs inside. You can move it into a garden shed or similar. Basically, somewhere dry and unheated. Do this from October to February, and then put it outside again in March. Then, after the new generation of solitary bees has emerged (you'll see if they've made their way out of the hollow stems in the springtime as any mud covering the hollows will be opened up), you can replace the stems with fresh materials for a new year.' – Friends of the Earth

---

Lots of our wildlife needs different food or other requirements at different stages of their life cycles – all stages of this life cycle need to be provided for, either within your site or nearby. Finding out what wildlife we already have (or would like to encourage) and how to support all of its needs creates lots of learning opportunities for our children and young people, as well as a way to establish and reinforce those connections between our groups and the natural world.

The edges where habitats meet – when short grass changes to longer grass and wildflowers, or when this wilder strip meets the shrubby edge of a woodland, for instance – are where we can provide a really wide range of conditions to support lots of species, so actively planning these transitional spaces can be hugely beneficial.

Planting trees and hedges

The planting of trees has become a go-to activity for many people looking to improve spaces for wildlife, as well as a tool that can help mitigate climate change. It is also a really engaging and fun activity to carry out with children and young people! Planting either trees or hedges needs careful planning, not only in choosing the most suitable species and the most appropriate places but also in forward planning the ongoing care and maintenance as they establish themselves. If you are planting in and around buildings, you must also know where any underground services or drains are, and the required distance from these that you can plant your trees, particularly any canopy layer species such as oak, ash, beech, or willow.

If suitable for your site, broadening the range of species you have can be beneficial both for wildlife and for your Forest School community. We might plant hazel or willow to provide fast growing greenwood we can harvest in a sustainable way (see coppicing/pollarding); we might prune and manage elder to provide us with straight, slim branches we can hollow out and use for crafts; we might plant a mixed hedge including hawthorn, blackthorn, and holly to provide a wind break/shelter belt or increased security along an open boundary. We must also be aware of the human impact of planting certain species – for example, the risk of anaphylaxis from planting hazel, beech or other tree nuts in our sites.

It is good practice to source any saplings or whips as locally as you can. You could also collect a variety of tree and shrub seeds from around site and nearby and see how you get on with cultivating these! (Lipscombe & Stokes, 2008).

Managing for other natural resources

We can sustainably manage for other resources too, to provide opportunities to eat foraged food like blackberries, stinging nettles and wild garlic, or we can use the nettles and other plants to experiment with natural dyes. The seed heads of old man's beard, small amounts of paper-like honeysuckle bark, and strips of silver birch bark from dead trees or branches on the floor can all aid our fire-lighting; and bramble or nettles can be turned into useful cordage. Ensuring we harvest these resources sustainably and manage their continued presence for the benefit of wildlife takes planning and care. When collecting anything from the wild, I always use the mantra 'three for the wildlife, one for me' to help me be mindful of depleting sources of food or shelter.

Purposefully cultivated areas such as pots, planters, garden areas, orchards, or allotments can be a separate but still managed source of herbs, fruit, vegetables, and flowering plants.

Rewilding and wilding

A term and concept that has been growing in favour over the last few years is *rewilding* – the process of allowing green spaces to naturally regenerate, particularly from cultivated farmland. This is a longer-term way of re-naturalising an area, and if you have space to rewild an area then it could be a fascinating area for insight and study of the natural processes of succession.

Allowing areas to rewild can also be hugely valuable to animals. These areas are often disregarded because they appear untidy and worthless to us, yet they provide food and shelter for a wide variety of wildlife (Tree, 2018).

'Rewilding is the large-scale restoration of ecosystems to the point where nature is allowed to take care of itself. Rewilding seeks to reinstate natural processes and, where appropriate, missing species – allowing them to shape the landscape and the habitats within.' – Rewilding Britain

---

As Forest School leaders we are not managing our woodland and other green space sites at a landscape scale, so a better term for what we might achieve is *wilding* – identifying areas that we can leave alone as an active management choice. If there are areas you can set aside to do their own thing, it would be fascinating to watch and record the changes with your Forest School community over the years. Wilding would also cover other management choices we might make specifically with wildlife and biodiversity in mind.

Reflective Exercise 11 – Site design

Think for a moment about your current site (or if you don't have a site yet, think about a wood you know well). How would you design your Forest School set up? Where would your fire pit sit? What about a mud kitchen? Why not draw yourself a plan?

Now think about the repercussions of where you place your areas. Can you remember what grew there last week, last month or last year?

Can you reduce the impact you have on the site?

Maintaining your Forest School site

There is another criterion connected to the six principles that affects how we use our site:

Forest School aims to foster a relationship with nature through regular personal experiences in order to develop long-term, environmentally sustainable attitudes and practices in staff, learners, and the wider community.

Again, relationship is the key word here – not only between our Forest School community and the site, but also between the Forest School leader and others responsible for or impacted by our use and management of our sites. This may include a line manager, third party landowner, caretaker or land management team. We have already talked through this strand of the Forest School leader's role in **Chapter 10**, so I will keep to what needs to be done here, rather than who may be doing it!

Site management

Site management will follow its own seasonal pattern of busy and quieter times in terms of management tasks, and these won't always fall within term time! If you are delivering Forest School in a term-time-only school or setting, careful consideration needs to be given to areas that may need attention through the school holidays, such as mowing wilder grassy areas in late summer or watering new or established plants and trees.

Moving sites and site rotation

If you are lucky enough to have one large area of woodland or a number of smaller natural spaces, then you can consider using these in a rotation. This is usually of most benefit when considered seasonally, as we can often have a greater impact through the wetter, colder months of the year when ground conditions are muddy (and it is not always easy to remember where that patch of bluebells is). Consider mapping the area with your group and or moving or rotating your site. However, not every site or setting will have this as an option, so this is where we might consider fallow or rest periods for our sites or else rotating the use of 'base camp' with other spaces such as playing fields, nearby parks or gardens, or beaches.

Managing shrubs and trees

There are a few different techniques for sustainably managing shrubs and trees, including coppicing and pollarding, as well as pruning. Whenever we start dealing with the management and maintenance of trees, we have to adjust our sense of time, as we are often considering work taking place over decades, rather than seasonally or over an academic year!

Pruning: Cutting branches from a standing tree using the right, sharp tool for the thickness of the wood to be cut. This may be to keep branches clear from paths or seating areas, or to take away diseased or damaged wood to enable the tree to keep growing healthily. We always aim to prune branches as cleanly and as close to the main tree trunk as possible.

Coppicing: 'Coppicing, or cutting down a tree to produce new growth, has been a way of harvesting wood for thousands of years. Far from being destructive, coppicing has been the reason why many woodlands have survived, because the woodland had an economic value. Coppicing rejuvenates the tree, so some coppice stumps or "stools" are hundreds of years old and are an important genetic link back to the ancient woodlands.' (Agate, 2002).

Most of the native broadleaved trees we might have on our sites respond well to coppicing, such as ash, hazel, oak, sweet chestnut, field maple, and small-leaved lime, although some of these species would need careful consideration. We tend to use hazel as a source of greenwood for crafts, mainly because we can 'crop' this wonderful, fast-growing understorey tree in a safe manner with simple hand tools and techniques. With ash dieback becoming so prevalent, any material produced by coppicing ash and being used would ideally stay on site to prevent the disease from spreading. Field maple is a relatively uncommon native tree, so would need a local abundance to support managing and creating resources in this way.

Pollarding: Another sustainable form of tree management for our larger, broadleaved trees. This involves cutting the branches between 2-4 metres above ground level, and was historically undertaken to produce a crop of long, straight branches or poles. As this is done at height, few Forest School leaders will be qualified to manage their own trees in this way, but it may well form part of a management regime for sites with nearby power or phone lines, fences, car parks, or roads. It is an on-going form of management that needs to be undertaken anywhere between 5- and 20-year intervals, to ensure the safety of the pollarded crown.

Grassy areas

One of the simplest ways of beginning to make areas wilder and more complex is to ask for areas of grass that are mown to be left longer and a different mowing regime to be put in place. You will then need to survey these areas through spring and summer to get to know what species you have, and when they are mainly in flower – this will then determine the on-going mowing regime. It is easy to overlook grass species when doing this, but the long tussocks and seed heads provide important food plants and shelter for a number of invertebrates and small mammals.

Planted areas

As mentioned above, you may have other areas close to your Forest School site that are cultivated and used for garden plants, herbs, fruit, or vegetables. These areas can also be managed with wildlife in mind with careful planting, weeding, watering, and cropping. There are lots of places to find advice on 'wildlife gardening' – this series of guides is a good general starting point: https://www.wildlifetrusts.org/gardening [41]

So much of our connection to nature can be inspired by these 'gardened' spaces, so their value should not be overshadowed by our wilder and woollier areas – the more we notice nature daily by providing food for birds, or planting pollinator-friendly species and watching the resulting bees and butterflies, the greater our connection to nature and wildlife, fuelling a lifelong appreciation and respect for the natural world.

'Importantly, the relationship between pro-nature conservation behaviours and nature connectedness was mediated by the extent to which participants noticed nature. Or another way of putting it: the results suggest that certain nature conservation actions lead to people noticing more nature, and this increase in noticing nature leads to an increase in nature connectedness.' – Miles Richardson

---

Built infrastructure

It is not just the natural elements of our sites that need managing sensitively and sustainably. Depending on the type of site you are working on, you may need to repair or replace seating, storage, shelters, paths, fences, or water storage, as well as carrying out seasonally sensitive checks and maintenance of bird boxes or other animal homes. Using materials that are thoughtfully and sustainably produced or acquired is another way we can 'tread lightly' and model pro-environmental behaviours to our participants.

In conclusion

> ### Reflective Exercise 12 – Biodiversity
>
> Do you need to increase the biodiversity of your site?
>
> How can your Forest School have a more positive impact on your site and increase the biodiversity?
>
> Who will be responsible for maintaining the site, in the short, medium, and long term? What about during school holidays?

We opened this chapter by considering our role, as Forest School professionals, in nurturing a sense of place, stewardship, and connection to nature, fostered by long-term relationships with a woodland or other natural space. For many people training to become leaders or beginning to lead sessions, it is the natural history, the ecology, and the science of woodlands that is the least well-known and most daunting subject in which to start building knowledge.

Firstly, I would say that no-one ever stops learning about this huge and enriching topic – one of the joys of my job is that I learn something new about wildlife every single day, just by being on site! Perhaps most importantly, I also know that it can be one of the most rewarding, as this new appreciation for the complexities of the living world around us forges a stronger relationship between us as Forest School leaders and nature; that magical, mutually beneficial sense of 'kinship, reverence and love' we hope to inspire and instil in everyone who takes part in Forest School.

Appendix 1 - Resources

Nature activity ideas to encourage sensory learning and experiences:
https://www.sensorytrust.org.uk/resources/activities [42]

Wildlife identification resources:
https://www.wildlifewatch.org.uk/ [43]
https://www.field-studies-council.org/product-category/publications/ [44]
https://www.rspb.org.uk/birds-and-wildlife/ [45]
https://www.woodlandtrust.org.uk/trees-woods-and-wildlife/identify-wildlife/ [46]
https://www.buglife.org.uk/bugs/ [47]

https://www.plantlife.org.uk/uk/discover-wild-plants-nature **[48]**

MyForest for Education is an easy-to-use and free online application that enables any educator, or young person, to generate straightforward woodland management plans, maps, and ecological impact assessments for woodland sites and school grounds:

https://myforest.sylva.org.uk/education-promo **[49]**

https://www.forestschoolassociation.org/introduction-to-forest-school-and-the-woodland-environment/ **[50]**

The Conservation Volunteers (TCV) Handbooks:
https://www.conservationhandbooks.com/handbooks/ **[51]**

Wildlife & Countryside Act 1981 – protected fauna and flora in the UK:
https://www.legislation.gov.uk/ukpga/1981/69/schedule/5 **[52]**
https://www.legislation.gov.uk/ukpga/1981/69/schedule/8 **[53]**

Useful information and ideas on creating ponds and other wetland features:
https://www.wwt.org.uk/discover-wetlands/gardening-for-wetlands/ **[54]**

Managing grassy areas:
https://sussexwildlifetrust.org.uk/discover/in-your-garden/article/124 **[55]**

References

Ackerman, C.E.;. (2021, August 01). *What is Kaplan's Attention Restoration Theory (ART)?* Retrieved from Positive Psychology: https://positivepsychology.com/attention-restoration-theory/

Agate, E. (2002). *Woodlands: A Practical Handbook.* British Trust for Conservation Volunteers. 192.

Back from the Brink. (2017, 09 16). *ANCIENTS OF THE FUTURE.* Retrieved from Back from the Brink: https://naturebftb.co.uk/the-projects/ancients-of-the-future/

BBC. (2021). *Investigating ecosystems.* Retrieved from BBC Bitesize: https://www.bbc.co.uk/bitesize/guides/zmxbkqt/revision/1

Biology Dictionary. (2021). *Ecology.* Retrieved from Biology Dictionary: https://biologydictionary.net/category/ecology/

Blume, C., Garbazza, C., & Spitschan, M. (2019). Effects of light on human circadian rhythms, sleep and mood. *Somnologie*, 23(3), 147-156. doi:https://doi.org/10.1007/s11818-019-00215-x

Blythe, S. G. (2005). *The Well Balanced Child: Movement and Early Learning.* Hawthorn Press. 304.

Booy, O., Wade, M., & Roy, H. (2015). *Field Guide to Invasive Plants and Animals in Britain.* London: Bloomsbury.

British Ecological Society. (2021). *Glossary.* Retrieved from British Ecological Society: https://www.britishecologicalsociety.org/glossary/

Bumble Bee Conservation Trust. (2021). *Bumble Bee Conservation.* Retrieved from Bumble Bee Conservation Trust: https://www.bumblebeeconservation.org/

Cree, J., & McCree, M. (2012). A Brief History of the Roots of Forest School in the UK. *Horizons*, 60. 32-34.

Elgvin, D. T. (2009). *Henrik Ibsen's use of 'Friluftsliv'.* Retrieved from Norwegian Journal of Friluftsliv: http://norwegianjournaloffriluftsliv.com/doc/ibsens_use_of_friluftsliv_elgvin_2009.pdf

Environment Agency. (2010, April). *Managing invasive non native plants.* Retrieved from Mid Sussex District Council: https://www.midsussex.gov.uk/media/1725/managing-invasive-non-native-plants.pdf

Forest School Association. (2020). *Nature Premium.* Retrieved from Nature Premium Campaign: https://www.naturepremium.org/

Friends Of The Earth. (2020). *Build a bee hotel*. Retrieved from Friends of the Earth: https://friendsoftheearth.uk/bees/make-a-bee-house

Goddard-Blythe, S. (2019). Leaps Towards Learning. *Early Years educator*, 18-20. Retrieved from https://www.activematters.org/wp-content/uploads/2019/09/leaps_towards_learning.pdf

Goodenough, A., & Waite, S. (2020). *Wellbeing from Woodland: A Critical Exploration of Links Between Trees and Human Health.* Cham: Palgrave Macmillan.

GOV.UK. (2014, September 11). *Public rights of way: landowner responsibilities*. Retrieved from GOV.UK: https://www.gov.uk/guidance/public-rights-of-way-landowner-responsibilities

GOV.UK. (2014, March 6). *Tree Preservation Orders and trees in conservation areas*. Retrieved from GOV.UK: https://www.gov.uk/guidance/tree-preservation-orders-and-trees-in-conservation-areas

GOV.UK. (2018, September 26). *How biosecurity can prevent the introduction and spread of tree pests and diseases*. Retrieved from GOV.UK: https://www.gov.uk/guidance/prevent-the-introduction-and-spread-of-tree-pests-and-diseases

Hidden Disabilities Sunflower Scheme Limited. (2021). *Hidden Disabilities*. Retrieved from Hidden Disabilities: https://hiddendisabilitiesstore.com/what-is-a-hidden-disability

Historic England. (2021). *Conservation Areas*. Retrieved from Historic England: https://historicengland.org.uk/advice/hpg/has/conservation-areas/

Historic England. (2021). *Scheduled Monuments*. Retrieved from Historic England: https://historicengland.org.uk/listing/what-is-designation/scheduled-monuments/

Historic England. (2021). *The National Heritage List for England*. Retrieved from Historic England: https://historicengland.org.uk/listing/the-list

Hughes, B. (2015). *Play – The Challenges We Face.* Retrieved from Forest School Association: https://forestschoolassociation.org/national-conference-2015-condover-hall-shropshire/

Keye, S. A., Iwinski, S., McLoughlin, G. M., Steinberg, L. G., & Khan, N. A. (2021). Six-Minute Walking Test Performance Relates to Neurocognitive Abilities in Preschoolers. *Journal of Clinical Medicine*, 584. doi:http://dx.doi.org/10.3390/jcm10040584

Lexico. (2021). *Lexico : Sustainability*. Retrieved from Lexico: https://www.lexico.com/definition/sustainability

Lipscombe, M., & Stokes, J. (2008). *Trees and how to grow them.* Think Books.

Louv, R. (2005). *Last Child in the Woods.* Atlantic Books.

Lumber, R., Richardson, M., & Sheffield, D. (2017). Beyond knowing nature: Contact, emotion, compassion, meaning, and beauty are pathways to nature connection. *PLoS ONE, 12*(5). doi:https://doi.org/10.1371/journal.pone.0177186

Matre, S. V. (2019). *Earthwalks; an alternative nature experience.* Institute for Earth Education.

Mind. (2013, October 29). *Feel better outside, feel better inside: Ecotherapy for mental wellbeing, resilience and recovery.* Retrieved from BASW: https://www.basw.co.uk/system/files/resources/basw_112413-10_0.pdf

Muddy Puddle Club. (2020, June 10). *Writing an Equality, Diversity and Inclusion Policy and Action Plan for your Forest School.* Retrieved from Muddy Puddle Club: https://www.muddypuddleclub.co.uk/post/writing-an-equality-diversity-and-inclusion-policy-and-action-plan-for-your-forest-school?fbclid=IwAR1hipONJPEGAbnhSkriGdI-qfvbTZEuf0tPFaoODXTS2ntyfNITBmk0WVk

National Association for Areas of Outstanding Natural Beauty. (2021). *The UK's 46 AONBs*. Retrieved from Landscapes for life: https://landscapesforlife.org.uk/about-aonbs/aonbs/overview

National Parks UK. (2021). *Your National Parks*. Retrieved from National Parks UK: https://www.nationalparks.uk/parks/

Non Native Species Secretariat. (2021). *Biosecurity in the field*. Retrieved from Non Native Species Secretariat: http://www.nonnativespecies.org/index.cfm?pageid=174

Observatree. (2018). *Home*. Retrieved from Observatree: Monitoring Tree Health: https://www.observatree.org.uk/

Planning Aid England. (2019). *What are the types of nature conservation designations?* Retrieved from Planning Aid England: https://planningaid.zendesk.com/hc/en-us/articles/203220061-What-are-the-types-of-nature-conservation-designations-

Public Health Agengy (HSC) Northern Ireland. (2007). *Guidance on foods for religious faiths.* Retrieved from Public Health Agency: https://www.publichealth.hscni.net/sites/default/files/FaithsPosterA2.pdf

Qing, l. (2019). Effect of forest bathing (Shinrin-Yoku) on human health: A review of the literature. *Sante Publique*, 135-143. doi:https://doi: 10.3917/spub.190.0135

Rewilding Britain. (2021). *WHAT IS REWILDING?* Retrieved from Rewilding Britain: https://www.rewildingbritain.org.uk/explore XE "Exploration" -rewilding/what-is-rewilding/defining-rewilding

Richardson, M. (2021, March 5). *Actions for visible biodiversity help noticing nature and nature connectedness*. Retrieved from Finding Nature: https://findingnature.org.uk/2021/03/05/visible-biodiversity/

Richardson, T. (2017). *Speech and Language development in Forest School environment: an action reserach Project.* Sage. doi:https://dx.doi.org/10.4135/9781446273050145313666

RSPB. (2012). *Stinging nettles benefit garden wildlife*. Retrieved from RSPB: http://ww2.rspb.org.uk/our-work/rspb-news/news/315846-stinging-nettles-benefit-garden-wildlife

Rushforth, K. (1989). *SUMMER BRANCH DROP.* D O E Arboricultural Advisory & Information Service. Retrieved from https://www.trees.org.uk/Trees.org.uk/files/08/088789e7-c393-4661-9f2c-5b40d5eb7f6f.pdf

Selhub, E., & Logan, A. (2014). *Your brain on Nature.* Toronto: HarperCollins Publishers Ltd.

Sensory Trust. (2020, October 5). *How many senses do we have?* Retrieved from Sensory Trust: https://www.sensorytrust.org.uk/blog/how-many-senses-do-we-have

Sunderland, M. (2013). *Winning Hearts and Minds in Forest School : Handout from FSA National Conference Keynote Speech.* Retrieved from Forest School Association: https://forestschoolassociation.org/outputs-from-forest-school-association-national-conference-2013-derwent-hill-oec/

Sussex Wildlife Trust. (2020, May 21). *Species of the day: Lords-and-Ladies*. Retrieved from Sussex Wildlife Trust: https://sussexwildlifetrust.org.uk/news/species-of-the-day-lords-and-ladies

Sylva Foundation. (n.d.). *MyForest*. Retrieved from Sylva Foundation: https://myforest.sylva.org.uk/education-promo

The Wildlife Trusts. (2019, 10 15). *Nature Recovery Network*. Retrieved from The Wildlife Trusts: https://www.hiwwt.org.uk/nature-recovery-network

The Wildlife Trusts. (2020). *Equality, Diversity & Inclusion Strategy.* Retrieved from The Wildlife Trusts: https://www.wildlifetrusts.org/sites/default/files/2021-04/RSWT_%20EDI_Wild%20About%20Inclusion%20Strategy_2020-2025.pdf

The Wildlife Trusts. (2021). *PROTECTING WILDLIFE SITES : Different types of protected wildlife sites in the UK*. Retrieved August 10, 2021, from The Wildlife Trusts: https://www.wildlifetrusts.org/wildlife-and-wild-places/protecting-wildlife-sites/different-types-protected-wildlife-sites

The Wildlife Trusts. (2021). *UK Wildlife Law*. Retrieved from The Wildlife Trusts: https://www.wildlifetrusts.org/uk-wildlife-law

Tiplady, L., & Menter, H. (2021). Forest School for wellbeing: an environment in which young people can 'take what they need'. *Journal of Adventure Education and Outdoor Learning*, 99-114. doi:https://doi.org/10.1080/14729679.2020.1730206

Tree, I. (2018). *Wilding: The Return of Nature to a British Farm.* Pan Macmillan.

Wildfowl and Wetlands Trust. (2018). *Gardening for wetlands*. Retrieved from Wildfowl and Wetlands Trust: https://www.wwt.org.uk/discover-wetlands/gardening-for-wetlands

Woodland Trust. (2021, July). *Common non-native trees*. Retrieved from Woodland Trust: https://www.woodlandtrust.org.uk/trees-woods-and-wildlife/british-trees/common-non-native-trees

Bibliography

Introducing Sustainable Management of Natural Resources
https://cdn.naturalresources.wales/media/678317/introducing-smnr-booklet-english.pdf

The Woodland Trust (2011) *Sustainable management of forests, woods and trees in the UK – the Woodland Trust perspective.* https://www.woodlandtrust.org.uk/publications
https://www.woodlandtrust.org.uk/media/1831/sustainable-forest-management-policy-paper.pdf

Biodiversity intervention enhances immune regulation and health-associated commensal microbiota among daycare children (Roslund et al.)
Science Advances 14 Oct 2020: Vol. 6, no. 42, eaba2578
https://advances.sciencemag.org/content/6/42/eaba2578

The restorative benefits of nature: Toward an integrative framework by Stephen Kaplan (1995)
https://www.sciencedirect.com/science/article/abs/pii/0272494495900012

Mound fire: https://campfirekitchen.co.uk/mound-fires-leave-no-trace-fires/

Chapter 12 – Making *your* life easier with communication

Lily Horseman

To communicate clearly with all the different stakeholders involved in a Forest School programme, having a handbook or collection of working documents is vital. For those of us drawn to Forest School because of the freedom and the practical earthiness of it all, the paperwork side of it can feel like a burden. It can also be very empowering and will help you to advocate for the work you want to do. For people undertaking Forest School training, creating a handbook is part of the process. Think of your handbook as the 'power paper'. It gives you and others confidence in your work. Reframing it in this way might give you the motivation to sit down and do that paperwork. Let's look at each element and think about what you are trying to achieve with it and different ways to approach it. These might not be perfect in their first version and will keep changing over time.

We have seen in previous chapters (**6**) the first step is to think about who your **stakeholders** are. Who will be interested in your programme? Some people will be obvious, like the participants and their families; others less so. Within a school or setting, people are working to help facilitate your sessions at different levels, from senior management and administration to the staff involved with delivery. You might have volunteers and staff that you employ directly. There will also be the landowner and other users of the land, which might include dog walkers and neighbours. Make yourself a list of these stakeholders and how it will be best to communicate with each of them. Will this be through a website, a leaflet, a presentation, or a document? You will then need to work out how you will ensure that people get access to these and – bingo! You have yourself a communication strategy. Don't assume that just because you have created a document people will read and understand it. Think about the language you use, how you might meet to discuss it, and how to make the information more accessible for everyone.

The Principles

Once you have decided on the *who* and the *how* you can focus on the *what* and the *why*. Something that will be fairly universal to all Forest Schools is an explanation of the Forest School ethos. Of course, this is outlined by the six **Forest School principles** that were explored in detail in **Chapters 1** and **2** and which are available on the Forest School Association website. It is worth going a little further though, and exploring what this looks like for you and your programme through the eyes of your stakeholders. Put the principles into the language that your stakeholders will understand without losing the sense of what each one means. For example:

Forest School is a long-term process. In our programmes, this means that we regularly take small groups of learners into the woods (at least once a fortnight but we are aiming for weekly). This will be on a Wednesday afternoon all through term time.

You can work through this for each of the principles, and this will help you to start answering some of the bigger questions. This is a really valuable first step if you are interested in becoming an FSA Recognised Provider. The process of becoming a Recognised Provider aims to ensure your Forest School delivery meets the national minimum standards, following all six principles. This exploration of the ethos can be useful to make sure expectations are clearly laid out and agreed upon. This will create a foundation of understanding to help you advocate for your work if there are questions about the approach and delivery further down the line.

Stakeholders

There are a few key stakeholders – the participants and their support staff. The participants would be the children and their parents, if attending a family group. The support staff would be the staff or volunteers, who might or might not have Forest School qualifications. If you are running sessions with volunteers or with staff from partner organisations, having more information about the Forest School ethos and what *participant-centred* or *participant-led* means in practice is vital. This is especially true if those adults do not have Forest School qualifications. Think about how this principle of Forest School is translated into what you expect them to do practically.

I have had fantastic pre-programme meetings with staff from a school or setting, in which we have talked about what we want for the participants and how we will respond to them. It is worth having something written down as well, rather than relying on that meeting. Because of unavoidable changes, someone in borrowed wellington boots might be substituted at the last minute. Think about the key things that you need them to do in order for them to support you. This might be things like:

- Make sure everyone knows where the boundaries are and stays inside them
- If participants have their own ideas, think about how you can support or resource them without taking over
- Check in with the Forest School leader if you are unsure about safety or wellbeing.

Over time this may become more nuanced and complex, and could form part of your handbook that covers **the role of adults in Forest School**. At a session for families and childminders with young children, you could give out little 'strategy' cards (see below) from time to time, featuring ways to support exploration and development, explanations of things like schemas in play, or the benefits of certain types of intervention (and non-intervention). Letting people know beforehand **what to expect from the session** will help people to come prepared or to make an active choice to buy in or book in, and can be really helpful for neurodiverse participants to know what to expect. You might work with individuals to create short descriptions of particular situations, known as social stories, to help them feel able to take part.

Mini Stompers
Nature Play
support strategies

www.facebook.com/KendalMiniStompers

Balance

Why is it important?
The **vestibular** system controls children's balance, core muscles and spatial awareness. Giving children time and space for active exploration; spinning, rolling and balancing will build this system in a way that is appropriate for their level of development and is fully integrated with their brain. Strong core muscles help with fine motor grip and concentration.

Strategies

- Uneven places to walk, like woodlands help strengthen the core which is essential for balance. Slow down to their pace.
- Swinging and wobbling move in unexpected ways which forces trunk muscles to work harder.
- Follow stick lines and leaf roads to improve focus and attention
- Spinning and rolling allows the vestibular system to be stimulated in a very potent way.

Bookings, terms and conditions, and managing expectations

There are lots of different booking systems if you are working with multiple groups or are selling your services from outside an organisation. Making your terms and conditions clear from the outset is essential. Again, this is about managing expectations, and there isn't one right thing to put into these, as they are specific to your setting and situation. If you need to cancel a session because of high winds, will you refund or move the booking to another date? If they choose to cancel because of illness or another appointment will you refund them? Will you refund them if they find someone to take their place? If it is important to you to deliver Forest School and build the community of learners by having the same people at every session, every bit of your system has to reflect the approach you are trying to create. Having this clear from the outset avoids a breakdown in relationships and allows people to know where they stand.

Information gathering and sharing

At this point you should also consider what information you need from people to make sure you are ready to actively support them. Alongside the information about numbers of participants, their ages, and any medical needs that may impact on their experience, having an open question like *'Is there anything we need to know to best support you/your child/your class?'* can unearth some useful information that will help you to build connections with the participants as soon as they arrive.

What other information do people need before they come to the session? It can be useful to make it clear what **clothing and protective items** they should bring for different seasons and what you can provide. It is worth recognising that it can be colder in the woods than people anticipate, so remind them before they find that out the hard way. Using images and videos can help avoid assumptions, and will also help people who skim the information or have English as an additional language. You might think that everyone knows what 'boots or sturdy shoes' are, but showing an image and explaining that people need shoes or boots that cover the toes, support the ankle, and can cope with mud and damp ground ensures that no one is uncomfortable or excluded. I'm going to also mention here that it is worth spell-checking carefully if you ask people to bring *wellies*, as this can be autocorrected in such a way as to make you appear less than professional.

Another thing that you might consider adding into your communication is a bit about what the Forest School site is like and how to get there. Is it a public wood or private? Is there a toilet? Where are the best places to park? Will there be places to sit? Which entrance should people use? Will a map or pictures from Google Street View help? If your sessions are booked privately, can people bring dogs or babies or grandparents without checking with you first? Are there any safety or welfare issues you would like people to be prepared for?

Ratios, roles and responsibilities

The next thing to consider is the **roles and responsibilities** of different people at your Forest School. You might want to include yourself, any paid assistants and other members of staff, volunteers, parent helpers, and the participants.

If you are working with children without parents present, then you need to think about ratios. These will be set by the local authority but aren't necessarily appropriate in an environment that is higher risk and dynamic. Ratios must be tailored to the needs and experience of the group and site. You need to enable higher risk activities, allow for child-led play, and give capacity for supporting adults to undertake individual planning, observation, and reflection. It is good practice to always have another adult with you for safeguarding and to help you deal with emergencies.

The other thing to think about with ratios is the number of risky things that are taking place and the number of competent people you have to support the activity. For example, if you have tool work, tree climbing, and fires all happening, and only three competent people to keep an eye out, then what happens when there is an emergency? It will take too long to pack away a risky activity such that the facilitator can leave it and deal with something else. Consider using the plus one rule, and have someone who can float about and problem solve as issues come up.

Who is the designated first aider? Who administers First Aid to the First Aider? If there are a few of you in the session with a First Aid qualification, how do you communicate who does what? One technique is to have cards with a short explanation of the roles – the first aider, the person who gathers the group and keeps them away from the casualty, the person who contacts emergency services, etc. Sorting all of this out in advance can really take out the stress of working it out in the moment. This becomes part of your emergency plan and risk management strategy.

Communicating policies and procedures

The policies and procedures that you have are also part of your communication with others. Although they are often seen as a boring necessity, I love reframing them as part of the power paper pack. **Policies** are a way of stating what you believe or what you are aiming to do. They are your way of declaring to the world what you think is important on any given topic. A policy sets out the **what** and the **why**; the **procedure** covers the **who, where, when,** and **how**. Why is framing it as a policy important? For example, you have covered the role of play and participant-centred work in Forest School when you explored the principles. Why write a Play policy as well? This comes back to my point about power paper. When someone is questioning your approach, presenting them with a policy shows the importance and value you place on the subject. Other bits of power paper include the environmental impact assessment and the woodland management plan covered in **Chapter 11**.

Forest school: policies and procedures

Environmental Impact policy

Kindling Forest School will try and maintain a balance between the detrimental impact of our activities on the environment and the beneficial impact on the people taking part. Minimising the negative impact on the environment whilst encouraging people's understanding and connection to nature

"You only care for what you love, you only love what you have come to know."

All sites used for Forest School will be assessed from season to season to monitor positive or negative changes that sessions create in the environment. This assessment is intended to inform decision-making processes and ensure that the site can sustain use in this way,
A written site survey and impact assessment will support this process.

Kindling has adopted the Leave No Trace principles and follows the Country Code and the Foraging Code of Conduct.

www.kindlingplayandtraining.co.uk

Now let's get into those **procedures**. It is worth bearing in mind that our brains can only process so much information at once; by working out what you will do in various eventualities and thinking through your **Emergency Action Plan**, you are helping to take the stress off your future self. When something unexpected happens – a child getting lost, for example, or an accident or sudden illness, or an unplanned fire – your brain may start to go into panic mode. Having easily accessible information to hand will make sure you feel prepared.

Imagine trying to describe the parking places and directions of how to find you when you are also trying to deal with that emergency. Include the sorts of things you might forget in the moment, like grid reference, postcodes, and access directions from the nearest postcode. There are tools such as the What3words app that can pinpoint locations accurately. One option is to write this up and give it to parents who would need to collect their child in an emergency, and have it to hand as part of your welfare kit. Plan how you will communicate with others in that emergency. If you are on a school's grounds, can someone take a message back to other staff on your behalf? If you are the one who has the accident, are your emergency procedures clear and physically accessible for someone else to pick up and enact? One useful strategy is having cards on the outside of a welfare bag, that could be used by a helper or taken by a pupil into the office. Make clear what help you need. You will also need to think through all the things to have in place for every session, also known as your **Normal Operating Procedures**: toilets, timings, boundaries, travel plans, etc. Having this information together in one place, especially if you use multiple sites, can really help clear communication. This in turn helps your brain stop being overwhelmed so you can focus on the important stuff.

Forest school: policies and procedures

Emergency Action Plans:

In case of emergency Kindling Forest School practitioners, volunteers, parents and children will take the following steps:

Lost Child:
Step 1: Help children identify landmarks and where to go if they feel lost.
Step 2: Use call in procedures (1,2,3,come to me), reassure other children.
Step 3: Recall register or attendance list. Step 4: Some staff instigate a search of area, maintaining ratios for other children. Step 5: Contact School or setting. Establish when child was last seen, their emotional state, what clothes they were wearing etc, and make a written record. Step 6: Ask for local assisstance in search. Step 7: Contact Emergency services and follow advice Step 8: Once child has been located undertake review of N.O.P and investigate and report as appropriate.

Illness:
Scale 1 **Causes distress but no symptoms** : comfort child, maintain observation
Scale 2 **Some symptons:** Dealt with by Trained First Aider, make child comfortable,
          record in Accident / Occurance Book
Scale 3 **Severe Symptoms:** Dealt with by Trained First Aider, make the child
          comfortable contact parents, school and/or emergency services.
      Record in Accident / Occurance Book
www.kindlingplayandtraining.co.uk

Power paper and risk

Risk assessments are another brilliant part of your power paper pack. They are used to empower rather than to stop people from doing things. The point of the risk assessment or risk-benefit analysis is to have thought about the eventualities, how you can make it work and what the benefits are. When children and young people do something, you can feel comfortable if you know what the boundaries are: when you need to divert participants or support them to keep them safe from serious harm. The balance is that you also want them to continue to experience risk and challenge so they can gain the benefits. We do this process all the time in our everyday lives. The Risk Assessment is just a record that you have identified the risk and thought about what the boundaries are. Importantly, these are a tool so you can share what you have learnt or noticed with others.

You may have noticed that people talk about Risk Assessments (RA) and Risk-Benefit Analysis (RBA). These are similar but not interchangeable; they do slightly different jobs. The RA records the risks and the ways to manage those risks. The RBA does not just focus on the risks of the activity; it also includes the benefits of the activity, weighing up the potential harm with the possible positive outcomes if we carry on with the activity. A level of risk in our lives is acceptable to gain certain benefits, and the RBA process means analysing how the balance of risk and benefit can be held in place. There has been a move over the last few years for Forest School leaders to include the benefits, and their analysis of the risks/ benefit balance, as part of their communication about risk management. Risk Benefit Analysis is a really useful tool to show carers why we do various activities *and* how we minimise risk in one go!

Forest school risk benefit analysis

Climbing trees and rocks

Benefits of Activity Being off the ground provides children with the opportunity to challenge themselves whilst having fun and exercise. Climbing trees brings children into contact with nature and some children will find being in trees calms them and stimulates the senses. For some children they will have a sense of being allowed to do something new which is forbidden to them. Some children can excel at this activity because they are low in body weight, fearless, and have an unlimited abundance of energy. Tree climbing is a great way to build a child's self-confidence.
(play types: deep play, locomotor play)

Risk Benefit Analysis Climbing and being off the ground is one of the most memorable and rewarding for the children and young people who are taking part. The benefits outweigh the risks. With the control measures the chance of serious harm occurring is minimized. Longevity of experience suggests that the chances of a serious accident occurring are slight and children appreciate the trust being put in them to manage their own risk taking while tree climbing. "Climbing trees and falling out of them is all part of growing up and having small injuries helps children learn about risks. We take the view that it's a good thing to try to equip children and young people and help them make informed decisions about the risks that they take". ROSPA

www.kindlingplayandtraining.co.uk

The risk-benefit approach tries to balance the developmental needs of the child with the risks in the environment and the activity, and with the actions of the people in the session. The needs of each child are different. The best way to judge if the risks are proportional to the child's developmental needs is through observation. However, as the children are encouraged to test their own limits and challenge themselves, the activity may go beyond what is on the written risk assessments. A dynamic risk assessment is a useful tool to share with other adults: detail the thought process that is going on in your head as you are observing children managing their own risks. This is especially valuable as part of your pre-programme meeting, and helps the adult supporters who might not have experience of Forest School to see the internal process. This **Dynamic Risk Assessment** takes the form of a flow chart. This tries to put into place a structure of how to deal with risks that come up and manage the panicked un-thought of eventualities. You can find a Dynamic Risk Assessment Flow Chart modified for Forest School on the online resource:
https://forestschoolassociation.org/book-resources/ [1]

Forest school risk benefit analysis

<u>Climbing trees and rocks</u>

Highest risks

Dead branches

Slipping on wet branches

Child losing concentration or not using 3 points of physical contact with the tree or rock

<u>What you can do to help</u>

Flag or remove dead branches and highlight weak branches. Show climbers the strongest parts of the tree where trunk and branch meet.

Explain to climbers about using three points of contact with tree or rock.

Speak calmly and positively to children who are in trees. Don't give 'bunk u

Reduce numbers climbing to reduce peer pressure or if very wet.

www.kindlingplayandtraining.co.uk

Site checks

The Lead Forest School Leader will also undertake daily site checks, but it is the responsibility of all staff and volunteers (and children) to make sure the site is safe. There is acceptable risk and unacceptable risk. Acceptable risks are those a child can control. Unacceptable risks are those which the children are not developmentally able to deal with. This will be different for every group and site, and working through this in your own mind and sharing it is a really useful step in bringing everyone onto the same page. If hurt or harm should happen to someone in your Forest School session, the site check is one of the ways you demonstrate that you have not been neglecting your duties.

Recording outcomes and sharing observations

After the session, there is also an opportunity for **recording outcomes** and sharing these with stakeholders. If we are to truly understand learning and development, this cannot be reduced to a tick sheet. Humans are far more complex. There have been many forms and constructs devised for child observation. These can help us to try to hold on to our thoughts from one week to the next, but they can never truly reveal who a person is. With that in mind, there are many available systems for recording observations. Whichever one you use, or devise for yourself, consider what you are recording and why. What is there to see? How are you recording observations? Handwritten notes, photos, videos, drawings, written observations? Does your observation stray into judgment when put through the filter of your own experience? How can we best understand what we see? Asking a child questions, hearing their reflections, and giving children opportunities for further interpretation through drawing or writing about their experiences can all help give us insight into the meaning and motivations behind their observable actions. There is a danger here that in the rush to gain insight, we adulterate and diminish the learning that we are trying to promote. Interventions of this sort should be timely and not break the flow of learning.

Interpreting observations using theories of learning and child development can also help broaden our perspective on our observations. This effectively widens the lens we use to view observable behaviours. For example, you may be watching a child repeatedly stirring their boot through a pool of mud. By using the theory of Loose Parts (in which unfixed or loose resources offer multiple variables in play) you may notice that this is the only element in the environment that has this level of flexibility and open-ended opportunity. By looking at Play Types theory you understand the child's behaviour as mastery. If considering the Leuven scales of Wellbeing and Involvement, you may notice the contentment and engagement the child displays. These may all form part of your observations gathered after a session. This could be written, a discussion with colleagues, or spoken into the notes section of your phone. Finding ways to present this material as case studies showing individual progress will help others to understand and see the worth of the work you are doing. Using regularly updated scrapbooks, social media pages (if relevant permissions are in place), photo storybooks, and webpages to record the outcomes and tell the stories of growth and development gives you something to draw on when the worth of your work is being discussed.

The next chapter is a check list of equipment, paperwork and business-related items you should consider having in place before you start to deliver sessions.

Chapter 13 – Checklists – What do I need in place before I begin delivery?

Louise Ambrose and Nic Harding

This chapter is a list of things you should consider having in place before you begin delivery. Much of this is discussed as part of your Forest School leader training and may be present in other chapters within the book. Items prefixed with an asterisk (*) should be considered as essential; if they are not prefixed, they may still be important or desirable. Different groups require different equipment, so you will need to adapt your equipment list for each group. We begin with the business planning and management aspects of your Forest School.

Business planning

The business planning aspect of Forest School is critical for the success of your business. Further information on this can be found in **Chapter 6**.

Area	Items	CHECK
*Business plan or business case		
	Financial forecast	
	Stakeholder analysis	
	Business structure	
*Company/business registration		
	*Registration with Companies House (if applicable)	
	*Registration with HRMC	

Business management

The business management aspects should be considered as part of the day-to-day running of your business. More information on this can be found in **Chapter 7**.

Area	Items	CHECK
*Operations management		
	*Capacity plan	
*Financial management		
	*Accounts	
	*Cash flow forecast	
	*Income and expenditure record	
	*Invoicing system	
	*Advice on taxation	
*Human resource management process and procedure		
	*Completed personal information forms for any staff/volunteers	
	*Forest School Leader Training	
	*First Aid	
	*First Aid supplies	
	Pension information (if applicable)	
	Payment information	
	*DBS or alternative checks	
	Holiday procedure	
	Sickness	
	*Reporting procedure	

Area	Items	CHECK
	*Complaints/grievances	
	Petty cash procedure	
	Rotas	
	Expectations and behaviour	
*Knowledge management		
	*Policies and procedures for business	
	*Booking procedure and policy	
	*Complaints procedure	
	*Reporting procedure	
	*Evaluation procedure	
*Marketing management		
	*Market research	
	*Marketing strategy – general	
	*Marketing – targeted/segmented	

Paperwork

Chapter 12 has told us about the value of paperwork; if your paperwork is in order you will feel much more confident to deal with issues arising in your sessions.

Area	Items	CHECK
*Land use agreement, lease or licence (Chapter 10)		
	*Permissions	
	*Access rights	
	*Emergency protocol	
	*Risk management	
	*Site management	
	*Site based insurance	
Site specific risk assessment		
*Safety and risk assessment		
	*Activity risk-benefit analysis	
	*Pro forma for daily site checks	
	*Arrangements for any tree inspections	
	*Emergency procedures	
	*Accident and Incident forms and reporting procedures	
	*Near-miss form and protocol	

Area	Items	CHECK
*Permissions and consent		
	Permission form for each participant	
	Data gathered (medical needs, emergency contact, additional needs etc)	
	GDPR awareness & compliance	
*Safeguarding		
	Safeguarding policy and procedures	
	Disclosure form and reporting system	
	Current Enhanced DBS for all staff	
*Forest School handbook		
	With all necessary policies and procedures – this is created as part of your Forest School training	
Session planning and evaluation		
	*Session plans	
	*Session evaluations and reflections	

Area	Items	CHECK
Session planning - continued	*Participant observations	
	*Leader observations	
	Possibly methods of measuring participant development	
*Insurance		
	Public liability insurance appropriate to your site, group and activities	
	Employers' liability insurance	
*Evacuation plan		
	Responsibility check cards (**Chapter 12**)	
*Health and safety notices		
	Health and safety at work poster	
	Warning signs	
	Hazard tape	
	Laminated natural hazard ID sheets	

Communication

Communication is the key to successful relationships. If things break down, check your communication. Review it regularly and fix or change language to remain current and in line with your marketing and sales strategies.

Area	Items	CHECK
*Communication strategy (Chapters 6 and 12)		
	*Outlining all stakeholders and how you will communicate with them	
*Induction for staff/helpers (Chapter 5)		
	Training session with staff/helpers to ensure awareness of their roles and responsibilities	
	Formal Level 2 Forest School Assistant training for staff/helpers	
	Outline of expectations, roles and responsibilities	
	Systems for sharing reflections/observations after each session	
	Any other supporting documents for staff/helpers	
	Ongoing communication systems	

Area	Items	CHECK
*Communicating with managers (Chapters 8 and 9)		
	Establishing scope of programme	
	Understanding resources and logistics	
	Agreeing any ongoing reporting or evaluation	
*Communicating with parents/carers (Chapters 8, 9, and 11)		
	Providing opportunities to understand Forest School	
	Gaining required consents	
	Providing ongoing communications throughout programme	
*Communicating with landowner (Chapters 8, 9, and 10)		
	Providing opportunities to understand Forest School	
	Gaining required permissions	
	Exchanging various documentation – e.g. insurance, risk assessments, etc	
	Providing ongoing communications throughout programme	

Additional training and CPD

Training is critical for the continued success of your delivery. It prevents you from becoming stagnant, and increases your internal tool box and the opportunities you can offer to your participants. Consider setting aside a yearly CPD budget in your financial forecasts and planning. Conferences are often great value for money, giving you a mix of small CPD opportunities for a one-off cost.

Area	Items	CHECK
*First Aid training (see Chapter 5)		
	*Outdoor first aid course – minimum 16 hours; with paediatric if working with children	
*Safeguarding training		
	*For all adults working with children or vulnerable adults	
Food hygiene		
	Level 2 Food Hygiene and Safety for Catering – advisable if regularly cooking and/or handling food during sessions	
*Tree inspection		
	*Short courses can provide insight to some key visual indicators of damage and defects in trees	
	*Link with a qualified arboriculturist	

Area	Items	CHECK
Working with challenging behaviour		
	If working with learners with particular needs it is advisable to gain training or support	
*CPD plan		
	See **Chapter 14** for further skills and knowledge you may want to explore	
	Pick what areas of professional development you would like to focus on: in the next 12 months; in the next 3 years	
	List potential books, courses and online materials which may support this	

Kit and equipment

Your kit and equipment are a significant outlay for your Forest School. Do not be tempted to buy it all in one go, unless you have been given a grant to do so. Timing your purchases will help with your cash flow. Consider only buying tools you either have the skills to use and maintain or have the time to practice and master.

This is not an exhaustive list and your group may require specific equipment to reach the opportunities on offer. It is always worth remembering that knowledge weighs nothing, but kit weighs plenty. The most important piece of kit, other than your site, is *you*. With your imagination and enthusiasm, learners will thrive. Every Forest School session is different and each group of learners is unique, so a universal kit list is impossible. However, there is a useful reflection that will help you decide on what to kit out your classroom with. Before you spend your hard-earned cash, you can use the following reflective process to check if you really need that new piece of kit.

Do I need it because of a Health and Safety requirement?

This question will help you to create a ***must-have list*** to keep learners safe. You should include: shelter (from the weather); fire (the ability to make/provide a hot drink/food or warm a person); clothing (extra kit to keep unprepared learners warm/dry); First Aid; PPE; paperwork (including evacuation equipment and procedures); hygiene (water, tippy taps, soap, etc); mobile phone; walkie-talkies.

Do I need it to promote learning opportunities?

This question could help create an ever-changing list, dependent on the learners' needs. Some basic provisions will facilitate a lot of learning, e.g. rope, string, natural resources, tools, pots and pans, water, field guide sheets, magnifiers, tubes, etc. It is also helpful to think about: how often the object will be used; whether you can maintain it; whether you can transport or carry it to site; whether it needs specialist skills or training to use; and whether you have the right skills or knowledge to use it. Consider also: will it prevent a learning opportunity?

Do I need it to create a comfortable or usable space for learners?

This list will be dependent on your site or setting and may include toileting and privacy, seating, and hammocks or nets. It may also cover how equipment is transported or stored. Often items on this list will also appear in the other two lists – a comfortable kneeling mat may appear in Health and Safety in response to a risk assessment, for example.

If the answer to all three is *No*, do you really *need* the extra kit to carry and maintain?

Area	Items	CHECK
*Safety kit		
	*Emergency rucksack with First Aid kit and any other necessary emergency kit	
	*Means of communication – e.g. phone or radio	
	*Fire safety – fire blanket, plunge bucket, heat proof gloves	
	*Emergency plan	
	*Medical information	
*Welfare kit		
	Means of accessing drinking water – jerry cans etc	
	Handwashing facilities – e.g. tippy tap, bucket and soap etc	
	Toileting facilities – e.g. loo roll, trowel, sawdust (if compost loo)	

Area	Items	CHECK
	Appropriate outdoor clothing for all (learners and helpers)	
	Spare clothing to borrow	
*Site based resources and 'loose parts'		
	Seating – logs, benches, etc	
	*Appropriate access paths all year round – e.g. chipping in wet weather, bridges over streams, etc	
	*Fire area – clear of trip hazards and overhanging branches; with log surround	
	Resources for tool work – e.g. A frames, saw horses, benches, blocks, clamping jigs, etc	
	*A range of loose natural materials – e.g. poles and sticks of different lengths, logs, leaves, cones, seeds	
	A water source for play	
Construction and physical play kit		
	Ropes (if making swings/bridges ensure correct breaking strain)	
	Tarps	
	Paracord	
	Hammocks	
	Slackline	
	Pulley blocks	
	Buckets	

Area	Items	CHECK
	Pallets (can be a useful free source of timber for projects)	
Tools – appropriate to size, strength and ability of user		
	Carving – fixed blade knives, chisels, gouges, crook knives	
	Striking – mallets, hammers	
	Sawing – bow saws, folding pruning saws, hacksaws, Japanese handsaws, etc	
	Hole making – hand drill, bit and brace, eyed auger, gimlets, palm drill	
	Brashing – loppers, secateurs, billhook	
	Splitting – froe, axe, splitter	
	Digging – trowel, spade, digging stick	
Fire and campfire cooking kit (chapter 8)		
	Watering can	
	Fire-lighting box – with range of tinder and methods of lighting	
	Tripod or pothanger	
	Kettle	
	Billy can(s)	
	Grill	
	Tin foil	
	Skillet or pan	

Area	Items	CHECK
	Storm kettle	
	Dutch oven	
Crafting kit		
	String and/or wool	
	Scissors	
	Clay (or dig it out of the ground)	
	Mark-making kit – chalk, crayons, paints (non-toxic), brushes	
	Baskets	
Discovery kit		
	Magnifier pots and/or lens	
	Binoculars	
	Mirrors	
	Blindfolds	
Leaders' and helpers' kit		
	Camera	
	Notebooks and pencils	
	PPE – e.g. safety boots, hard hat, work gloves, etc	
Kit maintenance and storage		
	Safe and secure storage unit for kit and equipment	
	Robust and waterproof kit bags – especially for tools and ropes	
	Tool cleaning – oil, rags, brushes	
	Tool sharpening – waterstones	
	Washing lines and drying space – for drying tarps and/or waterproofs	
	Washing up facilities for cooking kit	
Area	Items	CHECK

Chapter 14 – Planting seeds for the future

Louise Ambrose and Nic Harding

In publishing this book, the FSA hopes to support the growth of quality practice and professionalism throughout our Forest School community. We want to promote and celebrate the ethos and principles we all hold dear. As you have reached this final chapter, you now have a greater understanding of the processes and requirements behind your delivery and are well equipped to follow your Forest School dreams.

It would be remiss of us to metaphorically shake your hand and wave goodbye without offering possibilities for you to continue your reflection. Our authors have all run Forest School for many years, and have slipped and tripped on their fair share of roots and brambles; it is only through overcoming these occasional setbacks that they have survived to deliver Forest School for more people and diversified their experience. They have been empowered by the rewards of delivering this amazing process. For many of us, starting a new business or project will be a somewhat tricky process of trial and error. We hope that by providing insight into our experiences, we have prevented some of problems we have had from affecting you and your businesses/practice.

In this final chapter, we will leave the unearthing of potential problems behind and concentrate on the positive influences that have raised the veil of ignorance and lit the lightbulb of epiphany. But before we meander through the lists of topics and training, we have to acknowledge that we live in a period of change: every day we are enriched by the diversity of people and nature that surrounds us. It is therefore impossible for us to give you a definitive list of things that will make you a perfect Forest School leader, and so we will not attempt to do so. In our attempt to keep the cost of this rapidly growing book affordable this chapter has been reduced in size; there is much more detailed and expanded document for **Chapter 14** on our online resource:

https://forestschoolassociation.org/book-resources/ [1]

Step outside… yourself!

A key aspect of being a Forest School leader is reflective practice. Considering our own strengths and weaknesses in a realistic way is crucial to furthering our skills as leaders. The quality of the Forest School experience hangs on you as a leader (so no pressure!). It is the leader who carefully weaves the threads of each element of the programme together, carefully crafting a unique picture for every programme. We affect everything. Developing our own self-awareness must therefore be a priority.

In modern society it is easy to judge ourselves harshly, critique our practice, and negatively compare ourselves to others. We would urge you to resist this temptation and instead go about it in a 'Forest School-y way': non judgementally and with compassion. How we treat ourselves is a mirror for how we are in the wider world.

One of the issues with self-development can be that we do not know what we do not know, so how can we develop it? This is explained eloquently in the learning model ('The four stages of learning any new skill') attributed to Noel Burch in the 1970s. It can be shown in a matrix consisting of two variables: consciousness (our self-awareness) and competence (our ability level).

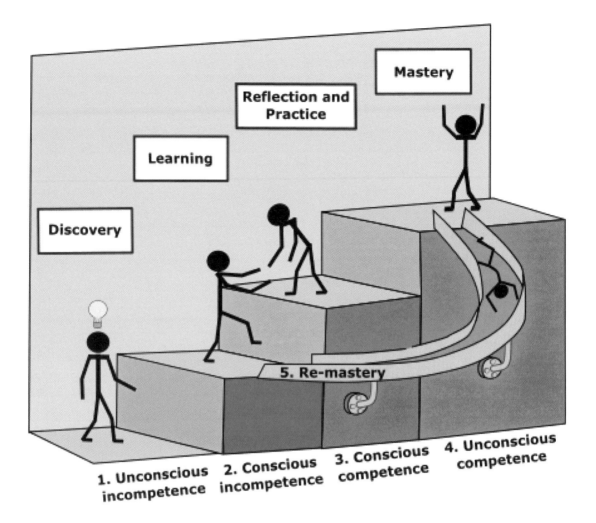

Above: Five steps to learning a new skill

- **Stage 1 – Unconsciously Incompetent**: We do not know what we do not know
- **Stage 2 – Consciously Incompetent**: We become aware of what we do not know
- **Stage 3 – Consciously Competent**: We know what to do but need to practice and apply it
- **Stage 4 – Unconsciously Competent**: We know it without thinking about it; mastery!
- **Stage 5 – Re-mastery**: We rediscover our skills through a new technology, environment or technique.

Using a Forest School example to illustrate the model:

- **Stage 1** – We may not have come across the idea of non-judgement in an educational paradigm before
- **Stage 2** – We notice that the majority of mainstream education uses sanctions and rewards, and judgemental language such as praise, and are looking for alternatives
- **Stage 3** – We discover and consciously apply non-judgemental practices, such as Non-Violent Communication and Restorative Justice approaches
- **Stage 4** – We communicate non-judgementally without thinking about it
- **Stage 5** – New research offers extra insight into previously-used phrasing and suggests better options, replacing previous techniques and catalysing a period of learning, practice and re-mastery.

'To know that we know what we know, and to know that we do not know what we do not know, that is true knowledge.' – Nicolaus Copernicus

---

Reflective Exercise 13 – CPD reflection

Hopefully the chapters within this book have helped uncover some aspects that may have previously been 'unknown unknowns' for you.

Take a moment to consider as many aspects of Forest School practice as you can. For example:

- Practical Skills – tool use, fire lighting, shelter building, rope structures, etc
- Woodland Ecology – species identification and wisdom, woodland management, nature connection, etc
- Learning and Development – learning theories, play, neuroscience, holistic development, etc
- Planning and Delivery – risk management, planning and observation, legal requirements, communication, etc.

Consider which of the four stages of learning you are currently working at for each of these elements.

Do you notice any patterns within your awareness? Perhaps you have mastered aspects of a particular theme? Perhaps there are gaps for you in some areas?

Pick some elements that are in the earlier stages for you. What steps might you take next in order to develop them?

Continuing the journey

The path to quality Forest School is often delightfully meandering, with many twists and turns and branching trails to explore. Each avenue offers a deepening of understanding and opens up new opportunities for practice. Forest School practice draws on a broad range of topics; from learning theories to fire-lighting, woodland ecology to neuroscience, legal requirements to making natural craft items, and much more besides. The Forest School training courses provide a strong foundation in these elements, but they are limited by time and assessment criteria. They can only serve as an initial marker for each area. The depths of each topic's pathways are waiting to be explored more fully.

To support your future trail-blazing we would like to offer here some signposting to paths you may like to wander down. We have used the different units of the Forest School qualification as a method to categorise the topics:

- Practical Skills
- Woodland Environment
- Learning and Development
- Planning and Delivery

Like it or not, your sessions are limited by your skills. The more skills you possess, the more responsive you or your Forest School leader can be to your participants' needs, and the richer the experience you may weave. This will mean that SLT or independent FS leaders will need to support and fund Continued Professional Development; whether that be training courses, research and reading, mentoring, or time for explorating and practicing skills.

'An Axe to Grind' – furthering your practical skills

Outdoor living skills

These are core practical skills often taught in Bushcraft courses, and are very useful to anyone spending extended periods of time outside, including Forest School leaders. These skills include:

- **Fire** – Different methods of fire-lighting; natural and man-made tinders; benefits and uses of different fire lays
- **Water** – Finding water sources; and making it safe to drink through filtering and purifying
- **Shelter** – Understanding the risk of cold and heat injuries; exploring properties of different materials in terms of clothing and shelter; shelter design; using tarps; using natural materials
- **Food** – Identification and harvesting of wild plants for food; understanding legal and safety limitations of foraging; preparing game.

Woodland crafts

Safe tool use is an assessed requirement for Forest School leaders undertaking their level 3 accreditation. Tool use and cooperative techniques can enrich your sessions if learners show interest in these skills. All sorts of useful natural items can be created: pegs, mallets, pot hangers, tripods, spoons and spreaders, spear throwers, beads and pendants, flag holders, fantasy creatures, fairy furniture, cars, candle holders, festive decorations, whistles, kazoos, xylophones, and anything else you fancy having a go at!

Other crafts may focus on natural fibres, such as making cordage from plant or bark fibres, spinning wool, using natural dyes, weaving, and knotwork.

Rope structures

Ropes and play structures can play a huge role in Forest School, from erecting shelters and swings to exciting games and activities. Working at height is one of the more high-risk experiences a Forest School may offer, and so it is essential to have a comprehensive working knowledge of knots, rope types, techniques, and maintenance.

You can find a good practice guide for installing rope swings in the booklet created by Monkey-do and London Play: http://www.monkey-do.net/content/tree-swings [56]

Food hygiene

If you are regularly offering snacks or cooking food at Forest School, it is recommended that you have a good understanding of food hygiene practices to keep your participants healthy and happy. You also may need to register as a food business with your local authority (existing Schools and Nurseries will usually be registered already if serving lunches).

Food safety and hygiene in the UK is overseen by the Food Standards Agency, who have detailed guidance of good practice on their website:
https://www.food.gov.uk/ [57]

Tool and equipment maintenance

Caring for your tools and equipment is an essential part of safe practice at Forest School. A blunt tool or over-stretched rope is an accident waiting to happen.

A basic understanding of tool design, bevel shape, and material may enhance practical skills. Edged tools will need regular sharpening. Get some instruction and you will find that everything you make will be easier and safer to do. You will also increase the life of your tools, thus reducing your equipment costs.

Personal Protective Equipment (safety boots, high visibility clothing, hard hats, work gloves, etc) needs to have systems in place for checking, cleaning, and replacing as necessary.

Expanding your understanding of rope materials and weaves, breaking strains, and loads will make your practice safer. Ropes and lines used for play structures (such as swings, bridges, ladders, etc) will need checking, cleaning, and periodically replacing.

Many books outline these practical skills, as well as online materials such as videos and websites. However, it is often easier to learn directly from others in person on a training course or skill share, if you have the opportunity.

'Into the Woods' – Deepening your connection to the natural world

Nature connection

Forest School provides a great opportunity for a deeper relationship with nature, other people, and ourselves, through what is often referred to now as 'nature connection'. Being nature connected is not a new thing; it is how our ancient ancestors existed, and is how many indigenous peoples today still live.

In our modern day society we have lost the cultural tools and mechanisms to support widespread nature connection. Many outdoor (and Forest School) programmes are great at getting people into contact with nature, and at providing nature knowledge; yet they do not necessarily provide connection modelling, which is a different skill set to nature education.

Since 1979, Jon Young has spent his life working with different Indigenous Elders exploring what makes a culture nature connected. To share this collected wisdom, Young and friends have arranged it into a map, known as the 8 Shields, using the eight compass points. They have observed various beneficial behaviours

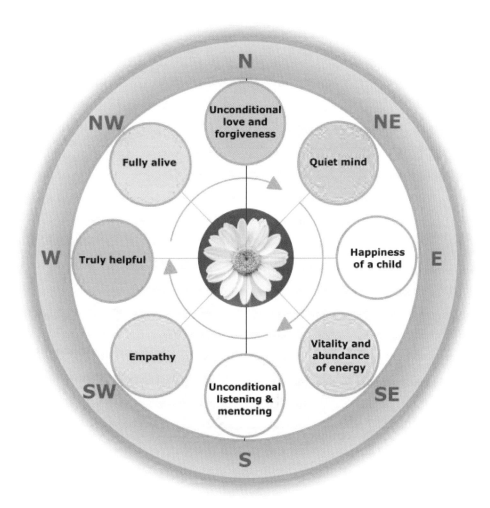

arising through being nature connected, which they call the 'attributes of connection'. It is through these attributes being displayed that you can tell whether someone is nature connected.

Young's book, *Coyote's Guide to Connecting with Nature*, is a fantastic resource for any leader wishing to use more connection modelling techniques in their programmes. It combines the theory and layers of the 8 Shields as well as being a resource bank of activity and games ideas.

Coyote's Guide to Connecting with Nature by Evan McGowan, Ellen Haas, and Jon Young (2010) ISBN-10: 1579940250

Jon Young's website is found at: https://www.jonyoung.online/ **[58]**

'If a child is to keep alive his inborn sense of wonder, he needs the companionship of at least one adult who can share it, rediscovering with him the joy, excitement, and mystery of the world we live in.' — Rachel Carson

---

Identifying woodland species

Recognising common species is a core skill for a Forest School leader, and is assessed to a basic level within the Level 3 accreditation. We would encourage you to get curious about as many species as possible – the diversity of nature is the foundation of Forest School. Getting to know the species around us in the woodland enables us to make judgements on safety, select natural materials sustainably, support the ecology of the site, and engage learners through exciting facts or folklore. Here are just a few of the many resources available that support species identification:

- The Field Studies Council produce a range of fold-out identification keys on all sorts of species: https://www.field-studies-council.org/shop/ **[59]**
- The Woodland Trust have an A-Z of British trees: https://www.woodlandtrust.org.uk/trees-woods-and-wildlife/british-trees/a-z-of-british-trees/ **[60]**
- The Mammal Society has a mammal species hub: https://www.mammal.org.uk/species-hub/full-species-hub/discover-mammals/ **[61]**
- The RSPB has a bird identifier:

  https://www.rspb.org.uk/birds-and-wildlife/wildlife-guides/identify-a-bird/ **[62]**

- Buglife UK have lots of information on invertebrates: https://www.buglife.org.uk/bugs/bug-identification-tips/ **[63]**

Ethnobotany

If you are enjoying discovering the wonderful world of plants, ethnobotany might be a logical next step for you. Ethnobotany is the study of the interrelationship between humans and plants, and explores how humans have used and interacted with plants culturally. From a Forest School perspective, playing with plants may open up new learning opportunities and skills in the following areas:

- **Food**: foraging, preparing plants, cooking recipes
- **Medicine**: making teas, tinctures, ointments; herbal First Aid
- **Barks and fibres**: making cordage or string, weaving work baskets and containers with bark
- **Fire lighting**: natural tinders, coal extenders, plant downs
- **Oils, tars, and resins**: collecting saps, processing, using adhesives
- **Dyes and inks**: collecting materials, fixing colours, making items
- **Stories and art**: folklore, songs, poetry, inspiration.

Track and sign

If animals are more your thing, you may prefer to investigate CyberTracker or Bird Language. **CyberTracker** is a system inspired by the indigenous trackers of the Kalahari and used to evaluate a tracker's skills. Learn more at:
https://www.cybertracker.org/ **[64]** or https://www.facebook.com/CyberTrackerUK **[65]**

Practical conservation

Volunteering with a practical conservation group is a great way to learn more about how to manage sites for wildlife, as well as getting plenty of tool use practice. Taking part in activities such as planting trees, laying hedges, digging ponds, removing invasive species, and sowing wild meadows can equip you with transferable skills to bring to your Forest School site. Many small landowners and local authorities rely on volunteers for conservation projects, and this is also common in not-for-profit organisations such as Wildlife Trusts, National Trust, etc.

The Conservation Volunteers (TCV) are a UK-based organisation connecting people with green spaces to undertake various projects:
www.tcv.org.uk/ **[66]**

TCV also have a range of comprehensive handbooks covering practical conservation, including woodlands and tool care:
www.conservationhandbooks.com/handbooks/ **[67]**

Woodland ecology and management

Understanding the ecology of different woodland systems is vital if you are going to make decisions about how to manage your Forest School site. Recognising the species present is a useful first step, but we would encourage you to discover more about how these plants and animals interact with each other and the other elements (such as soil, water, and air). Here are various organisations with resources that you may find useful:

- **The Woodland Trust**, a UK charity, have fact files on woodland species and habitats, and also information about biodiversity, climate change, and ancient trees; they record seasonal changes and produce various publications:

  https://www.woodlandtrust.org.uk **[68]**

- **The Forestry Commission** is the UK government department responsible for managing public forests. They are the department to contact to obtain felling licences or landowner grant support, and to report tree pests and diseases:

  https://www.gov.uk/government/organisations/forestry-commission **[69]**

- **The Small Woods Association** is a membership organisation and charity specialising in sustainable woodland management and social Forestry. They provide guidance, training and networking opportunities:

  https://www.smallwoods.org.uk/ **[70]**

- **Woodlands TV** is a YouTube channel (sponsored by woodlands.co.uk) that produces films and tutorials about woodland activities:

  https://www.youtube.com/user/WOODLANDSTV **[71]**

- **Sylva Foundation** is a charity managing a number of projects, including a variety of webtools to support woodland management. Their myForest for Education app can support Forest School leaders to create management plans. There is also a Woodland Wildlife Toolkit and a Deer Management tool: https://sylva.org.uk/ **[72]**

Tree hazard recognition and assessment

Inspecting the trees within your site will be part of any Forest School leader's risk management practices. Tree health is a complex subject, however, and you may not have enough experience or skills in this area to recognise problems developing in trees.

The responsibility for tree safety lies with the landowner and they may make arrangements with a professional arboriculturist to undertake annual inspections of trees in areas of high usage, such as your Forest School site.

There are training courses on basic tree survey and assessment available, which help participants to recognise key observable features on trees that may present safety concerns. This knowledge can be useful to Forest School leaders as an indication of when to call in a professional.

The National Tree Safety Group has also published some useful guidance on Common Sense Risk Management of Trees: www.ntsgroup.org.uk/ [73]

'The Long Road' – learning & development

As we discovered in **Chapter 2**, Forest School is a construct of many educational models and theories that value exploration, experience, and holistic growth. It should therefore be unsurprising to readers that acquiring a better understanding of underlying theories that align with the pedagogy may provide useful ideas when observing, planning, and facilitating sessions. The following is a brief overview of the types of learning and psychological theories we have found useful. There is a more in-depth explanation of the theories in the online resource https://forestschoolassociation.org/book-resources/ [1]

Behaviourism

Behaviourism, or behavioural psychology, dates back to the early 1900s. It is a theory of learning in which all behaviours are learned through interaction with the environment. Behaviourists believe humans are born as 'blank slates' and become conditioned to respond to environmental stimuli, as opposed to developing through conscious or free will factors or inheriting behaviours.

Constructivists

Constructivism is a philosophy of teaching and learning in which people actively construct or make their own knowledge and meaning. The learner creates their own reality through their experiences, and meaning is influenced by the interaction of prior knowledge and new events. You may also want to look at social constructivism, of which **Kathy Charmaz** is a key thinker. Kathy Charmaz discusses constructivist grounded theory in this *video:* https://www.doi.org/10.4135/9781473999350 [74]

'It's not how smart you are that matters, what really counts is how you are smart.' – Howard Gardner

---

Psychoanalysis and psychodynamics

Psychoanalysis is a set of psychological theories and therapeutic practices centred around the belief that all people possess unconscious thoughts, feelings, desires, and memories. This theory assumes much of our thought and behaviour is driven by the unconscious mind, where repressed emotions and trauma dwell. The aim of psychoanalytic therapy is to make the unconscious conscious, and often involves dreamwork, archetypes, and symbolism. The originator of psychoanalytic theory is Sigmund Freud; it was further developed into psychodynamics by his followers Carl Jung, Anna Freud, Erik Erikson, Melanie Klein, and Alfred Adler.

Humanists

Humanistic psychology is a perspective that expanded greatly in the 1970s and 80s as a reaction to the behaviourist and psychoanalytic theories. Humanists consider those approaches dehumanise us by suggesting that human behaviour is driven by external (behaviourism) or unconscious (psychoanalysis) forces. Two prominent Humanists you may come across during Forest School training are **Abraham Maslow**, whose familiar Hierarchy of Needs can be applied directly to Forest School, and **Carl Rogers**. Rogers revolutionised therapy in the 1950s by developing a person-centred approach.

'The curious paradox is that when I accept myself just as I am, then I can change.' – Carl Rogers

---

Ludic process and spaces

Understanding ludic space and ludic learning is a game changer for Forest School, especially when advocating for free play and freedom within the environment for experiential and participant-led learning.

'Ludic Pedagogy [is] a teaching philosophy that embraces the importance of fun, play, playfulness, and humor—without sacrificing academic or intellectual rigor. This philosophy integrates positive aspects and helps faculty create a learning environment that is less stressful—and (gasp!) enjoyable—for student and instructor alike, while increasing engagement, motivation, and learning outcomes.' – T. Keith Edmunds & Sharon Lauricella

---

The Colorado Paper – The Playground as Therapeutic Space: Playwork as Healing, by Gordon Sturrock and Perry Else:
https://ipaewni.files.wordpress.com/2016/05/colorado-paper.pdf **[75]**

Making Sense of Play: Supporting children in their play by Perry Else (2014). ISBN-10: 0335247105

Play types

Bob Hughes is a lifelong advocate of play work, and has produced many papers and books on the subject. In his 2006 book *A Playworker's Taxonomy of Play Types* (ISBN-13: 9780953566525) he identifies 16 types of play that children engage with in play development:

- Social
- Socio-dramatic
- Rough-and-tumble
- Exploratory
- Object
- Creative
- Communication
- Deep

- Recapitulative
- Symbolic
- Fantasy
- Dramatic
- Imaginative
- Locomotor
- Mastery
- Role play

As Forest School leaders we may observe some or all of these play types during sessions, and should consider how we can best support them in nature. Play Education is Bob's website: http://rphughes44.blogspot.com/ **[76]**

Risky Play

Within Forest School we are in a position to support risky play. Perhaps this is something that pushes our boundaries as leaders, but it is hugely beneficial for learners. Through risky play children learn to confront their fears, hone their skills, and master their own competencies to manage future risks. According to **Ellen Beate Hansen Sandseter**, there are six categories of risky play displayed on the next page. Forest School provides a natural context in which all six of these categories can be explored and supported.

Characteristics of risky play by E. B. H. Sandseter: *Children's Expressions of Exhilaration and Fear in Risky Play*.by E. B. H. Sandseter:
https://doi.org/10.2304/ciec.2009.10.2.92

Ellen Beate Hansen Sandseter's blog: https://ellenbeatehansensandseter.com/ **[77]**
https://doi.org/10.1080/14729670802702762 **[78]**

Great Heights

Climbing
Jumping from still or flexible surfaces
Balancing on high objects
Hanging or swinging at height

High Speed

Swinging at high speed
Sliding or sledging at high speed
Running uncontrollably at high speed

Dangerous Tools

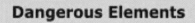

Cutting tools e.g. knives, saws, axes
Strangling tools e.g. ropes, string
Crushing tools e.g. hammers, batons

Dangerous Elements

Cliffs
Deep or icy water
Fire pits

Rough and Tumble

Wrestling
Fencing with sticks
Play fighting

Getting Lost

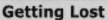

Going to play alone
Playing alone in unfamiliar
environments

Play motifs

David Sobel has observed children playing in natural spaces and interacting with nature throughout the world. From these observations he has identified seven 'play motifs' common to all children, regardless of socioeconomic status, ethnicity, or ecosystem, when they have safe free time in nature.

Sobel suggests that if we as adults understand these intrinsic play behaviours in nature, we can use them to design learning experiences which will engage learners naturally.

As a Forest School leader, recognising that these seven motifs are natural play behaviours may help us to plan our sessions.

Childhood and Nature: Design principles for educators by David Sobel (2008) ISBN-10: 157110741X
David Sobel's website: https://www.davidsobelauthor.com/ **[79]**

Working with behaviour

We live in a rewards-based society. Sanctions and rewards are hardwired into most mainstream schools, and the unconditional and non-judgemental environment of Forest School can be challenging for some educators to get their heads around.

Alfie Kohn is a compelling speaker and author on this subject, and has produced a number of publications discussing how external judgement (whether positive or negative) hinders the learning process and disempowers individuals. Understanding the language we use and the interpretation of the words of others is critical in Forest School, to create a community of free exploration and experience rather than judged activities. This is the knife edge between mainstream education and participant-led learning.

Alfie Kohn's website: https://www.alfiekohn.org/ **[80]**

'Punishments and rewards are two sides of the same coin and that coin doesn't buy you much.' – Alfie Kohn

---

Nonviolent communication (NVC)

This is a form of communication which is essentially non-judgemental. Developed by **Marshall Rosenberg**, it is a practical tool that can be used effectively at Forest School (and anywhere else!), to build relationships and to potentially de-escalate situations. There are two core parts to the NVC model: **empathic listening** to the needs behind the words or behaviour being expressed; and **honestly expressing** our own needs, emotions and requests.

As leaders, we have to be able to tune into our own feelings and needs, and also be willing to express them. It is this inherent vulnerability that makes the method so effective.

The **Centre** *for Nonviolent Communication* (*CNVC*) is a global organization that supports the learning and sharing of Nonviolent Communication:
https://www.cnvc.org/ **[81]**

Choice theory

Choice theory, created by **William Glasser**, is based on the simple premise that every individual only has the power to control themselves, and has limited power to control others. Individuals are empowered to take responsibility for their choices and to support others in taking ownership of *their* choices.

You can find out more by accessing our FSA Wednesday Webinar introducing choice theory at:
https://www.youtube.com/watch?v=erjJohicGr4 **[82]**
The William Glasser Institute:
https://wglasser.com/ **[83]**

Emotional Intelligence theory

Developed by **Peter Salovey** and **John Mayer**, emotional intelligence (otherwise known as EI or EQ) theory concerns the development of one's emotional skill and depth – a critical part of the holistic development that we witness at Forest School. The non-judgemental community and nature connection found at Forest School influence learners' behaviour and allow them to develop their EI naturally. Knowledge of EI theory and the beneficial effects of good provision may be useful when advocating on behalf of Forest School.
https://positivepsychology.com/emotional-intelligence-theories/ **[84]**

Emotional Intelligence: Why it Can Matter More Than IQ by Daniel Goleman (1996) ISBN-10: 0747526222

Understanding personal growth

Neuroscience

Having a basic understanding of the biology of human learning and development can be useful to tie all these theories together into a scientific construct. Studies of the human brain show just how interconnected our minds and bodies are, and how we learn in a holistic way.

Repeated sessions in a natural space are healthy for our brains as well as our bodies. Understanding the effects of stress chemicals and emotional hijacking in the brain provides us with additional insight when working with challenging behaviour and helping individuals to develop strategies.

This is of course just a snippet of a vast and fascinating subject, and we would encourage you to discover more about the brain and how being in nature can be beneficial.

Your Brain on Nature by Alan Logan and Eva Selhub is an interesting read:
http://www.yourbrainonnature.com/ **[85]**

Your Brain on Nature: The science of nature's influence on your health, happiness and vitality by Alan Logan and Eva Selhub (2014) ISBN-10: 1118106741

Molecules of Emotion: Why you feel the way you feel by Candace Pert (1999) ISBN-10: 0671033972

Reflective Exercise 14 – Ripple Effect Rings

Sometimes it is difficult to see the woods for the trees. There are so many topics we can learn and discover about that it can be easy to lose sight of why we are focusing on them. Knowing the 'why' of what we are choosing to spend our time on is vital if we wish to be able to effectively communicate to others (for example, to justify allocating time and resources towards it). This exercise, which we call the 'ripple effect rings', may help you to find your 'why' through exploring the benefits of different experiences.

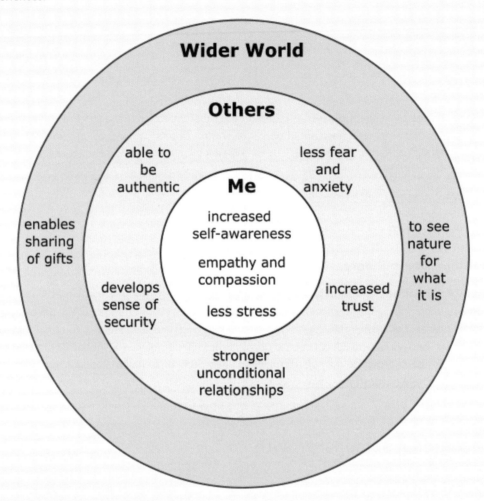

Draw out three concentric rings, as in the example above. Pick a particular skill, experience, or activity to focus on. In each ring write some reflections. In our example, we have chosen to focus on learning non-judgemental practices, such as using NVC and reading Alfie Kohn.

- The central circle represents you – how does the experience, activity or skill help you?
- The middle ring represents other people – how does this help you to help others?
- The outer ring represents the wider world – how does this help you to help the wider world (nature, environment, etc)?

This is an exercise that can be applied to any aspect of life, when you want to explore the potential effects of a decision.

Pack your bags – how the Forest School Association can support your journey

We started as a grassroots organisation – a group of leaders wanting an organisation to unite and represent us, and to support quality Forest School for all. Since 2012 our small charity has been serving the Forest School community across the UK and beyond. We offer practical support through:

- Weekly E-Newsletters – keep up to date about developments in the Forest School world
- Monthly Webinars – develop your skills and understanding on a range of relevant topics with guest speakers online
- National Conferences – gather with your 'tribe' to network and develop your skills and understanding
- Guidance Notes – gain advice on common Forest School issues
- Local Groups – join (or create) a local group to meet other leaders, share skills and support peers
- FSA Provider Scheme – celebrating Forest School practice which is in line with the six principles
- FSA Trainers Endorsement – supporting you to find quality training courses, with trainers who meet certain benchmarks
- Advocacy and Awareness Raising – we fly the 'Forest School flag' to raise awareness of its benefits
- Research and Evaluation – we signpost to relevant research, and have developed an app to collate Forest School evaluative data which can be used by leaders to support their projects.

We welcome anyone into our membership and hope you will consider joining us.
www.forestschoolassociation.org **[86]**

'This is the Way'– planning and delivery

The majority of this book has concerned itself with the various aspects of planning and delivering Forest School programmes. **Chapter 12** focused on communication and the 'power papers' to gather together for a successful programme; **Chapter 11** covered how to manage your site sustainably; and **Chapter 4** explored the role of a leader.

This section aims to mop up the last few topics that have not been mentioned elsewhere.

'Not everything that can be counted counts and not everything that counts can be counted.' – Albert Einstein

---

Evaluating your Forest School programme

Evaluation can be an area of contention within Forest School. On the one hand, we are working with the complex and unseen inner worlds of individuals' development, which seem difficult to record and measure; yet on the other, we find ourselves in a world in which everything must be monitored and evaluated or else be deemed without value (or worse, non-existent).

From our experience, Forest School programmes often have a foot in both camps. We may be required to do some sort of evaluation in order to justify the time and resources allocated to us; however, as Forest School leaders we also realise that these evaluations cannot adequately encapsulate the benefits.

At the time of writing this, the Forest School Association is developing an online app which will aim to collate first-hand data from Forest School leaders on a range of aspects from their programmes. We hope that this will give leaders a tool to use when evaluating their programme as well as a set of comparison data.

Embracing risk and challenge

In **Chapter 2** we learnt that appropriate risk is one of the principles of Forest School and so is actively encouraged. In **Chapters 5** and **12** we discussed how having various paperwork in place empowers us to roll with the child-led nature of Forest School in a way that effectively manages risk and benefits to learners.

As leaders we must consider our own attitudes and judgements around risk. We all have different backgrounds and life experiences which will affect how we see the world, including how we consider risk. What is risky for one person may be too easy for another; the value judgement is unique to the individual. These personal value judgements around risk will ultimately shape the programmes we facilitate, in terms of both the types of activities we offer and the features of the site we explore.

There are also hidden dangers in shying away from risk. Tim Gill, author and Patron of the FSA, writes about the risk-averse society we are living in and explores the possible harms and losses of opportunity children face when we wrap them up in cotton wool. Perhaps Forest School can be part of the solution to this.
No Fear: Growing up in a risk averse society by Tim Gill (2007) ISBN-10: 1903080088
Tim's blog: https://rethinkingchildhood.com/ **[87]**

Monitoring species on your site

In **Chapter 11** we discussed the importance of managing your Forest School site in a sustainable way and undertaking an Ecological Impact Assessment. These are also important aspects of Forest School leadership training.

In order to effectively manage your space, you will need to have a baseline of plant and animal species present, and you will need to undertake ongoing monitoring to see how this baseline changes over the duration of your programme. There are various different surveying methods you could adopt, and you can find a list of these in the extended chapter on the Online

The Field Studies Council offers training and publications on a variety of species: https://www.field-studies-council.org/ **[88]**

> ### Reflective Exercise 15 – Looking back
>
> Take another look at the results of our first reflective exercise, where we considered what we needed and wanted from creating a Forest School.
>
> How have you met your aims?
>
> Are there any areas which have not been fulfilled?
>
> Are there any new areas of discovery?
>
> Are there any new client groups that your training or knowledge has opened up to you since you read the Introduction and Chapter 1?

Step forth - your adventure awaits!

Thank you for choosing to read this book – we are honoured to have been your guide for this part of your Forest School journey. Now is the time for us to part ways and for you to step forth into uncharted territory.

Every Forest School programme is different; a wonderful weaving of the individual learners, the natural space, and the style of the leader. Even the same Forest School programme will change over time, evolving through the seasons as relationships grow, connections strengthen, and skills develop: this is the value of the Long-Term Principle. The six principles of Forest School provide the roots, and it is up to us to nurture the unique shoots, leaves, flowers and fruit of each programme.

There are no fixed instructions for running Forest School sessions, and that's what makes it so exciting – who knows what you'll discover together! As Forest School leaders we gently feel our way, trying things out and seeing what works with different individuals. We are all unique and as leaders our different gifts will shine through. Nature will continue to teach us lessons we never knew we needed to know.

There may be bumps (or even mountains) in the road along the way, but we remain observant, flexible, and resilient. We know the importance and potential transformative power of Forest School, and so we keep going, one muddy step at a time.

We can all help spread the healing power of Forest School by being the change we want to see in the world, as Gandhi suggested. The sentiment is sound: we can all be Forest School advocates through the quality of our practice, by embracing the six principles. We can evaluate our projects, mapping how learners benefit and grow through our programmes. We can network and support peers, so we can share ideas and feel connected. We can spend time connecting with nature for our own well-being, and practicing skills to develop our repertoire. We can talk passionately about our work to whoever will listen, for we never know what far shores the ripples of our stories may reach. We may not change the world, but we can change ourselves; the world will follow.

'We but mirror the world. All the tendencies present in the outer world are to be found in the world of our body. If we could change ourselves, the tendencies in the world would also change. As a man changes his own nature, so does the attitude of the world change towards him. This is the divine mystery supreme. A wonderful thing it is and the source of our happiness. We need not wait to see what others do.' – Mohandas Karamchand Gandhi

---

A final point to remember

When delivering Forest School, it is easy to forget that to connect others to nature we must first be connected ourselves. Connection takes all of our thought, feeling and senses. There are times when we are opposed by others or dragged about by the whims of politics or finances, and life can become a challenge. At these times it is easy to lose oneself in graft and conflict.

Breathe, and remember what we do. Take a moment, find a spot near your favourite tree, and feel the calming power of nature. Reconnect with your reason for starting down the Forest School path. Connecting to nature is not a luxury but a fundamental need; being reflective is not spending time but investing it in a better life. Nature connection is not just critical for our professional capability – it is also an important part of our health and wellbeing.

References

AZ Quotes. (n.d.). *Carl Jung Quotes About Nature*. Retrieved 08 05, 2021, from AZ Quotes: https://www.azquotes.com/author/7659-Carl_Jung/tag/nature

Edmunds, K., & Lauricella, S. (2021, April 23). *Ludic Pedagogy: Schooling Our Students in Fun*. Retrieved from Faculyt Focus: https://www.facultyfocus.com/articles/philosophy-of-teaching/ludic-pedagogy-schooling-our-students-in-fun/

Freud Museum London. (2018). *Anna Freud and Child Psychoanalysis*. Retrieved from Freud Museum London: https://www.freud.org.uk/education/resources/anna-freud-life-and-work/child-psychoanalysis/

McLeod, S. (2018, October 8). *Pavlov's Dogs*. Retrieved from Simply Psychology: https://simplypsychology.org/pavlov.html

Round, J. (2013, January 14). *Play Theorist and Activist*. Retrieved from Playful Minds: https://playfulminds.co.uk/2013/01/14/bob-hughes-play-theorist-and-activist/

Index

£5 OFF **Your First Year's Forest School Association Membership***

Discount Code: rootsup

*Discount available on online registrations with a credit or debit card only

F

G

H

I

S